CHURCH LEADERS ARE SAYING —

Everything you need to know about hands-together and about hands-on for Christ's kingdom. Some people look at our world and ask "why?" Phill Butler looks at the way our world could be and asks "why not?" If the apostle Paul were ministering today, he would recommend this book.

LEITH ANDERSON
Pastor, Wooddale Church, Minneapolis, Minnesota

Networks, partnering, and strategic alliances are hard to build but create incredible leverage. I saw Phill's work in collaboration in partnerships firsthand traveling through the Middle East; and it was amazing. Using his principles, we have been able to build partnerships in the inner city, are creating a learning center and a youth center, and are partnering with the city, a Catholic church, the Hispanic community, and the Korean Cambodian refugee community. We have created partnerships with other churches and organizations globally. Phill Butler's book is a practical "how to" with exciting, real-life examples and the "why" behind it all. If you are serious about partnerships, this book is for you.

KENTON BESHORE
Senior Pastor, Mariners Church, Newport Beach, California

This is a book that many of us have been awaiting for a long time. I know of no one who the Lord has used more effectively in launching ministry partnerships than Phill Butler. Phill writes from a deep reservoir of experience as he has been used of God to launch literally scores of significant ministry partnerships around the world. No one is better equipped than Phill to provide this significant book for all of us to not only read, but to be led of the Holy Spirit to put the principles into practice wherever we minister.

PAUL CEDAR
Chairman, Mission America Coalition

CHRISTIAN EDUCATORS ARE SAYING —

Building partnerships in mission is difficult. But it is one of the most practical ways to fulfill our Lord's Prayer; that his disciples be one so that the world might believe.

Phill Butler is the best person I know to show us how to do it. This work, based on years of experience, breaks new ground and gives us invaluable orientation for the future. Everyone involved in mission should read and reflect on it.

PAUL PIERSON
Dean Emeritus, School of Intercultural Studies, Fuller Seminary

What a timely book! If you weren't convinced that collaboration and partnerships are powerful, you will be now. If you didn't know how to make partnerships work well, you will now. This relevant book based on real experience will help all of us be better stewards of the resources God allows us to use in serving humanity in his name.

ROBERT C. ANDRINGA, PH.D.
President, Council for Christian Colleges & Universities

I remember when an older Christian leader challenged me to rethink mission. He asked me to remove the "my" in my mission vision and make it an "our" vision for mission. From there we developed the standard for the Billy Graham Center— "we will do nothing alone if we can do it together." I rely heavily on Phill Butler's thinking about partnership and collaboration to carry out this kingdom mindset. I'm so glad his book is completed. Now, I won't have to spend thousands of dollars to fly all over the world to hear him!

LON ALLISON
Director, Billy Graham Center, Wheaton College

Phill Butler was the first trailblazer for genuine partnership in the evangelical church, and in this book he has drawn a map all of us can follow. From his influence on my campus working with faculty and staff, to teaming with him in the Lausanne movement, I have seen up close his ideas lived out in ways which make us all more effective in ministry through partnership. Phill's expertise and insights help bring together the broad mix of God's people, and he has taught us to stand on each other's shoulders so that we can see over the horizon.

DR. ROGER PARROTT
President, Belhaven College

MISSION LEADERS ARE SAYING —

No one person in the modern history of missions has worked with greater creativity and relentless purpose or with greater or more strategic fruit for his labors. Phill Butler here collects and distills years of hard-earned insight into the all-important concept of totally autonomous entities joining forces in the most crucial of all human endeavors. This is one of those very rare books which became an essential classic the day it was born.

RALPH D. WINTER
General Director, Frontier Mission Fellowship

This book by Phill Butler is destined to make a significant impact on the work of contemporary Christian organizations. Mission groups and churches are discovering that God blesses cooperative efforts when those involved cease to be concerned about who is in control and who gets credit. Phill has extensive experience in facilitating collaboration among partners with a common objective without requiring a compromise of doctrinal convictions and relinquishment of resources. The kingdom of God throughout the world will not be established by "Lone Rangers" but by the people of God working together. Phill Butler is to be commended for putting this useful guide into print; it is not theory but grows out of a lifetime of servant leadership.

DR. JERRY RANKIN
President, International Mission Board, Southern Baptist Convention

The 1990s was one of the most remarkable periods in the history of the spread of Christianity. It was a decade of gathering the greatest harvest of any since Pentecost. It was a decade also that for the first time gave us a full list of the world's peoples to be discipled. It was a decade of amazing cooperative effort to bring the Gospel to them. At the heart of this effort was the ministry of Interdev under the leadership of Phill Butler which helped catalyze many regional, national, and people cluster partnerships that so contributed to this harvest. It is from this worldwide strategic ministry that Phill has drawn to give us distilled wisdom that is so applicable to the ministry challenges of the 21st Century.

PATRICK JOHNSTONE
Editor, Operation World

KINGDOM INVESTORS ARE SAYING —

For years I have believed in and supported kingdom partnerships. Partnerships that clearly define roles and outcomes increase effectiveness and reduce duplication. The stories and recommendations in *Well Connected* offer practical ideas and suggestions of how people and ministries can work together and have greater impact than if they worked alone.

HUGH MACLELLAN JR.
President, Maclellan Foundation

Phill Butler has actually gotten organizations to work together in teams overseas, each organization using its different talents and gifts to cooperate in planting the Church in a part of the world, and doing the work of ministry, in a manner truly worthy of 1 Corinthians 12 and 14. You will be relieved and rejoice to hear that competition has become cooperation in some of the toughest mission fields of the world! Don't miss *Well Connected*, by Phill Butler.

HOWARD AHMANSON
President, Fieldstead and Company

Collaboration is the form of the future as networks replace command and control hierarchies everywhere. Increasing its one world—one body of Christ. Phill Butler, who I have known for years, is the reigning expert. *Well Connected* is the how-to and the why-to book for this global revolution. It's a must read.

BOB BUFORD
Founder and Chairman, Leadership Network
Author, *Halftime* and *Finishing Well*

INTERNATIONAL MINISTRY LEADERS ARE SAYING —

I have been impressed in my interactions with Phill regarding the concepts of kingdom collaboration with partnerships in which we have both participated. Phill has a practical approach when it comes to turning dreams into reality. . . .

He is someone I trust in doing thorough research and development on these challenging topics.

STEVE DOUGLASS
President, Campus Crusade For Christ

Phill Butler brings a passionate, realistic, and hopeful perspective to Christian partnerships. He understands the challenges partnerships face and brings a wealth of experience and insight to understanding how they succeed. *Well Connected* does not try to present a nifty superficial solution but instead communicates vision, wisdom, and hope. For Phill, partnerships are about people, processes, and prayer. As he states, we're made for partnerships, and God moves when we work together. I pray this book will inspire and aid many.

DEAN HIRSCH
President, World Vision International

It has been said, "The reason so few good books are written is that so few people who can write know anything!" That's not the case with Phill Butler. For years he's not only talked about the importance of partnering and collaborating for the kingdom, he's done it while showing others the way with extraordinary results. Now this master communicator, and broadcast journalist turned missiologist, shows the rest of us how to multiply our individual loaves and fishes through working together here and abroad. This is a must read.

DICK STAUB
Center For Faith & Culture, Broadcaster, and Author

Phill Butler and partnership are almost synonymous. For years, he explored, tested, and successfully implemented the biblical concept of partnership to advance the church's ministry. Follow Butler's law of kingdom collaboration and experience joy, unity, and release of power. This book is long overdue.

TETSUNAO YAMAMORI
Author, Director Emeritus, Food For The Hungry,
International Director, LCWE

well
connected

RELEASING POWER, RESTORING HOPE THROUGH KINGDOM PARTNERSHIPS

Phill Butler

Authentic

Authentic Publishing
We welcome your questions and comments.

USA   1820 Jet Stream Drive, Colorado Springs, CO 80921 www.authenticbooks.com
UK   9 Holdom Avenue, Bletchley, Milton Keynes, Bucks, MK1 1QR www.authenticmedia.co.uk
India   Logos Bhavan, Medchal Road, Jeedimetla Village, Secunderabad 500 055, A.P.

Well Connected
ISBN-10: 1-932805-54-0
ISBN-13: 978-1-932805-54-3

Published in partnership with World Vision
34834 Weyerhaeuser Way South, P.O. Box 9716, Federal Way, WA 98063 USA
www.worldvision.org

Library of Congress Cataloging-in-Publication Data

Butler, Phillip, 1936-
  Well connected : releasing power and restoring hope through kingdom partnerships / Phillip Butler.
    p. cm.
Includes bibliographical references.
  ISBN-13: 978-1-932805-54-3 (pbk.)
  1. Interdenominational cooperation. I. Title.

BV625.B88 2006
267'.13--dc22
                          2005034221

Cover design: Paul Lewis
Fractal Art image "Dendrite" by Dale A. Clark ©2002 — http://www.koolpages.com/tiedyeman/new.html
Interior design: Angela Duerksen
Editorial team: Megan Kassebaum, KJ Larson, Betsy Weinrich

Printed in the United States of America

TO SYBIL

WHO HAS WALKED

THE WHOLE JOURNEY

WITH ME

For centuries, Christians have dreamed that the world might really be changed if believers worked together rather than doing their own thing.

Now, in hundreds of places in dozens of countries people from all kinds of ministries are working together in strategic partnerships. They are seeing that this Kingdom dream can come true. As you might expect, the results are amazing!

AFFIRMATION

Working together is God's idea. He lives in community, in relationship, outside of time, in eternity. Our individual potential is only realized, our wholeness only experienced, in relationship with others. God created us to trust and to work with others. Believers throughout history have sought to respond to God's call to unity—with him and with each other. The Bible is full of stories of God's people working in partnership, in some cases, just in twos and threes. In other cases, hundreds joined hands to do what individuals could never have done alone.

But Satan's strategy is to destroy God's design. Satan's success, at least at some level, means that darkness is always present.

Over the last 200–300 years, the intense individualism of Western societies has made the journey toward wholeness, relationship, and cooperation much harder.

That individualism has infected our lives, our theology, our churches, our educational paradigms, and the fruits of the missionary movement. This book seeks to identify some of the key issues as we journey back to what God designed us to be and do. And, on the way, it documents and shares stories from believers' experiences in working together around the world. Through those stories, I've sought to provide biblical and practical principles that will undergird and empower our practical, day-to-day action.

KEEP IN MIND

International security and persecution of the church are constant concerns in many areas of the world. Because of these factors, and for consistency, in most cases the names of individuals and the locations of events, case histories, and other references cited in this book have been changed or omitted. In other stories or case histories I have combined the experience of different partnerships or networks to highlight strengths, weaknesses, or to illustrate important elements of the point being made.

Dear Reader,

World Vision invites you to share your response to the message of this book by writing to World Vision Press at worldvisionpress@worldvision.org or by calling 800-777-7752.

For information about other World Vision Press publications, visit us at www.worldvision.org/worldvisionpress.

CONTENTS

Everybody wants quick results. Most folks want to invest in Christian work that yields clearly visible spiritual fruit—the "reaping" that Jesus talked about. Partnerships address the whole process of the spiritual journey and empower everyone to be a strategic part—and know it!

All of life's important decisions are a process, some acknowledged in a specific moment, but they are the result of dozens if not hundreds of influences. This is a critical realization if we want to encourage friends and neighbors to consider Jesus! This chapter unpacks how working together can change everything—for the good!

PART THREE: BEHIND THE SCENES

If we're on a journey, how do we know when we've arrived? The destination is the vision that drives us on. Big ideas, even in small communities, can have huge consequences. The chances of realizing the big vision are immeasurably greater when we join hands and work together.

The real eternal game is not one of guns and money. Ultimately, all real change is empowered by the Holy Spirit. But how do we connect the power of prayer to the daily reality of trying to help God's people work together? Here's the story.

History proves the quickest way to kill a potential partnership or strategic network is to call a meeting! Get an idea, call a few people together, hope/expect that they'll understand and "buy" your idea? Unlikely! Here are the most basic keys to success.

PART FOUR: ON THE WAY

Someone's got to know the big picture and most of the key players. Partnership takes time, is driven by vision, and is sustained by commitment. These pages guide you through this "R&D" stage step by step, show you how to avoid putting your foot in the wrong place, and explain how to get the outcomes you pray for.

PART SIX: SPECIAL CASES, SPECIAL OPPORTUNITIES

We live in an increasingly global, interconnected world. Communication is being revolutionized and teams from around the world connect to complete a single task. These developments coincide with the globalization of the church. Linking Christians who are spread over vast distances but bound by a common vision is not only possible, but also essential. What are the trends, special opportunities, and unique challenges of this new world order?

The modern city may be the greatest challenge the church faces today. Complex, fragmented, full of special interests, and competitive in spirit—it's not easy to work together here. It's often lonely, sometimes brutal. Get insights on how to analyze your city, define specific objectives, gather others around a common vision, and move forward, together.

All truth is God's truth. The central, lasting values of effective partnerships and networks are relevant everywhere: in business, service clubs, law enforcement, social work, science, education, or the arts. See how the Kingdom values and partnership principles in this book are relevant, no matter where God has placed you.

The future is in collaboration. Going it alone won't work any more. Those in God's company must undergo profound changes in order to experience his blessing. The journey will be marked by wonder, faith, and probably tears, but, most certainly, by great new experiences of power and hope!

Internet Based Resources
Our Ministry: Are We Good Partnership/Network Material?
Partnership/Network Diagnostic/Evaluation Tool
Being Well Connected: 15 Critical Principles
Selected Bibliography: Partnerships and Networks

HOW TO READ THIS BOOK

This is not an ordinary book. It addresses and suggests action steps regarding the most critical problem facing God's people today—divisions in the body of Christ. It shows how to bring God's people together in practical, working partnerships and networks for his glory. And it leads us toward new models of ministry that strengthen our credibility with the world and bring believers immense joy and fulfillment.

The book contains:

- Stories of Great Victory and Disappointing Failure
- Case Histories
- Principles for Success
- Critical, Practical "How To" Information
- Principles Vital to Any Effective Evangelism and Ministry Strategy
- Evaluation Tools
- Directions to Other Resources

Just Curious?

Part one and the introduction will give you a great overview of the challenge, how the book works, and what's to come.

Want a Fresh Look at Evangelism and How God's Message Works?

Part two, the section on the essential God Design, unpacks the ideas related to God's remarkable plan for his creation to work together for his glory. It demonstrates how all the pieces and the whole process are vital, and, because of that, the tremendous motivation for and power of partnership.

Want to Know the Keys to Partnership Success?

Part three, Behind the Scenes, takes a look at fundamentals present in every successful Kingdom-minded collaborative effort. You may be surprised at the driving force, the real power, and what comes first!

What about the Nuts and Bolts—the "How To"?

Part four, On the Way, walks you through the process of exploring, launching, and sustaining an effective Kingdom partnership or network. You will get a detailed look at the process, be presented with action guidelines, and develop progress checkpoints along the way.

More than the Mechanics of Collaboration!

Part five, Working It Out, provides ideas on what it takes to be an effective partnership or network facilitator. Sharing credit is always a challenge, but here you will learn about the special challenges of partnerships. You will learn the elements essential to effective meetings, plus you will get a look at structures for effective collaboration—and how to pay for them!

Wondering about Other Options?

Part six, Special Cases, Special Opportunities, looks at special opportunities and challenges, like the growing number of regional, international, and specialized networks. There's a chapter on partnerships for cities, large and small, and a section on how these principles apply to business and other areas of professional life. Plus, take a brief look at the implications for future partnership if we are serious about real breakthroughs for God's glory.

ACKNOWLEDGMENTS

My deepest thanks to those people who have given so generously of their lives and resources—making this journey of exploration and realization of a dream possible. My experience has truly been one of partnership. It's been an extraordinary privilege to get to know, love, appreciate, and work with so many of God's people.

First, my family who have always provided unstinting support despite seeing both the inside and the outside—the agony and ecstasy—of the journey day after day, week after week, month after month, year after year. It's the long-term commitment that gets the job done.

Then friends on every continent who have provided encouragement and who have unselfishly shared their knowledge, hospitality, good will, counsel, and other resources. Your diversity and love are shining illustrations of the truth and power of his Kingdom.

Colleagues in early days of broadcasting, Intercristo, the various "lives" of Interdev, and, now, visionSynergy. These colleagues are the ones who have explored the vision and turned dreams into reality, hundreds of times—often against the greatest spiritual odds. In the far corners of the globe, they continue to be shining lights of generosity, hope, vision, and life-changing action. Along with them, the hundreds of partner ministry friends and colleagues who have made the commitment to "a better way," taken the risks, and , through steady resolve, have transformed the way ministry is being done. By exploring what it means to work together for Christ's glory, these folks have produced and continue to produce spiritual fruit far beyond the capacity of any single person or ministry. This book is really their story.

There are those individuals who have supported me and the vision and ministry in prayer every single day for years. You and God know who you are. Without you I would not be alive and there would be little to show for the journey. There have been those who banded together on special occasions to address powerful Satanic opposition to God's people working together. Your prayers have been the stuff of which spiritual breakthroughs have been made.

The Kingdom investors—crucially important partners who have provided the prayer and financial resources which have made the realization of this dream possible. Often in the face of seemingly impossible odds, they have joined us in the risk of obedience to the call and the "better way." They have encouraged, challenged, and served as lasting friends. These investors, large and small, and their faithfulness have shaped my own faith and sense of responsibility, and been an indescribable blessing.

Those who served on Boards of Trustees and who have provided governance over the various ministries with which I've been associated. Their counsel, generosity, accountability, and friendship provided both sustenance and surprise over the journey.

Editors David Sanford and Amanda Bird with their experienced eyes and steady hands provided input which helped shape the finished product. And publisher, Tim Beals, of World Vision, who believed in the book and its potential value for God's community worldwide.

And, with thanks for God's grace, so often filled with questions and, yes, fears and doubts. But, on the journey of understanding and implementing Kingdom partnerships, what a privilege it's been to explore the reality of his character. In that, to experience at least some more complete understanding of his desire to bless his people and their lives as they live and work *together*. His design for us all.

INTRODUCTION

There's cause for tremendous hope!

Despite centuries of division, disappointment, and even despair, hundreds of individuals around the world are now proving every day that God's people can work together. And, working together, they are accomplishing miraculous things—things that would never happen if they were working independently. In short, in many places, the dream is turning into reality. Jesus' prayer of John 17:21 is coming true: "I pray that they may all be one. Father! May they be in us, just as you are in me and I am in you. May they be one, *so that the world will believe that you sent me*" (italics added, GNT).

When Dr. Christian Barnard of South Africa did the world's first heart transplant, it produced a wide range of reactions—wonder, outrage, and in some cases professional jealousy. Open-heart surgery in those days was a "black box," in which predicting outcomes was difficult and success inconsistent. Today around the world thousands of open-heart surgeries take place every day. Selection of patients, critical success factors, advanced technology and training, plus years of practical experience have dramatically increased the chances of success.

Based on the experiences of the last twenty years, I'm convinced that, despite all appearances and centuries of conflict and division, followers of Jesus from extremely varied backgrounds really can work together. In doing so, they can make an extraordinary, enduring impact. In the early days they had little experience to go on. But my colleagues and I have now seen it happen well over a hundred times. It's not a fluke or one-time, exceptional experience. All the key components necessary for effective Kingdom collaboration are known. The primary issues that need to be addressed, the vision needed to make the difference, and the skills required to launch and sustain effective, durable partnerships and networks in the church are known, tested, and replicable!

I want you, your friends, and your colleagues to have that hope. You and your friends can do this! You can help God's people come together to accomplish things never possible when individuals work only on their own. You can make a huge difference. Following the God design, you can turn ministry dreams into reality.

PARTNERSHIP:
Two or more people or ministries who agree to work together to accomplish a common vision.[1]

But let me start with the dark side.

EARLY DAYS—JOURNALISM AND COMMUNICATIONS

It's been a long road. I grew up in a Western society that is the ultimate model of individualism. "If you can dream it, you can do it," the saying goes. My professional background was journalism and the communications industry.

I remember the heady stuff of writing to fifty-minute deadlines and delivering the hourly newscasts on radio; the countless interviews with the famous and the newsmakers; the trips, long before I was really qualified, to cover NATO and key European stories such as the Berlin airlift; working in a newsroom where colleagues had lined the walls with every award the industry could bestow; the adrenaline rush to frantically complete the research, write the story, find a phone in some obscure overseas city, and then call the story in to New York to meet the 4:00 a.m. East Coast deadline before the newscasts started pouring out across the U.S.

THE GOD DESIGN:
The way things were to be and work before man's sin. The vision of how things can be as God renews our minds, hearts, and ways of doing Kingdom work.

As I made the transition from reporting to the business side of the industry, I was plunged into the world of marketing, advertising, audience ratings, and demographics, intense media competition, and the agony or ecstasy of the successful or failed sales presentation. It was proud, high-velocity, and frequently highly individualistic work.

Along the way I did consulting and training with increasing frequency for Christian communications agencies. That experience, much of it once again international, exposed me to many good people doing good Kingdom things but generally not actively coordinating their efforts.

Communications Industry to Christian Organization

After many years, I stepped out of my career in broadcasting. It was one of those steps of faith so many others have taken, one where God's voice seemed to overwhelm reason. Sell the sports car. Don't be too concerned about what you don't have in the bank account. Just trust him. So, in 1970, with encouragement from my first wife, Jeanne,[2] and many friends, I launched a ministry called Intercristo. Intercristo was an effort to connect my communications background and management experience to the world of Christian service I had begun to encounter.

The problem was clear. Internationally, thousands of critical missionary positions were unfilled because information about them wasn't available. Meanwhile, in the resource countries, thousands of well-intentioned Christians wanted information about where their vision, experience, and devotion could be used in God's service. Opportunity and resources weren't connecting very well.

But solving the problem was not easy! Intercristo was designed to be a clearinghouse for Christian service opportunities around the world. We needed media to tell Western Christians about the opportunities, a small team of people to correspond with hundreds of Christian organizations who needed staff, and computers to handle the huge volume of information needed to link interested people with opportunities worldwide.

People like Paul Little of InterVarsity, Sarah Jepson of Seattle's Bank & Office Interiors, and Jack Frizen of the Interdenominational Foreign Mission Association all played key roles in making an impossible dream come true. Intercristo became, I believe, the largest ongoing, cooperative effort in the history of the church. While many other Christian job centers now exist, thousands of Christian ministries, large and small, domestic and international, continue, to this day, to fill their personnel needs through Intercristo. Tens of thousands of believers, in response to radio messages, posters on college campuses and in churches, or a website visit, inquire about where God might use them in some kind of service. All of this is possible because God's people worked together.

Growing Questions:
The Connection of Scripture to Life

Exposed to a growing range of Christian ministry, I saw increasing conflict between my day-to-day experience and what Scripture seemed to teach about God's people working together. Simply put, my own study and conversations with friends seemed to reveal a huge gap between the ideal and the real of the Christian world.

In his John 17:21 prayer, Jesus stated his desire—the ideal for the church worldwide: that they should be one as he and the Father were one. But what about reality? As I looked around and talked with others I found that:

- Division and mistrust were everywhere. Churches and Christian organizations weren't talking, much less consistently working together.

- Many before me had debated, worked, and tried to bring God's people together, with little lasting success.

- From the Old Testament to Paul's epistles, Scripture, based in a traditional, community-based culture, consistently appeared to address itself to both individuals and the wider community they belong to. However, it seemed that in the West the gospel message was relevant primarily to individuals.[3]

- As a byproduct, inside the church there was typically no working, functional community—small groups, accountability groups, maybe, but real community?

- In contrast, from my international experience, I knew that the major unreached people to which the church had been sending missionaries for the last 200–300 years were all community-based, relationally intensive cultures. How could our Western, individualist brand of Christianity have any credibility or power in the community-based Islamic, Hindu, Buddhist, and animist cultures?

- The church's essential lack of credibility and seeming irrelevance at home was obvious. When input is wanted on public issues, media representatives almost always call on a wide variety of special interest groups before contacting the church.

- With occasional exceptions, talks with church leaders reflected frustration with trying to "connect" their ministries and their people to the evident, crying needs in their communities.

Outside the church, on the other hand, symphony orchestras, sports teams, contractors working on major buildings, and complex businesses dealing with the "value chain" all understood that very different people and skills have to work together to produce outstanding results.

From Genesis to Revelation, God's design seemed clear: Made in his image and based on Christ's transforming work in us, we're to live our lives in restored, open, trusting relationships that allow us to live and work *together.* So what was wrong? What *is* wrong?

Communications Consulting to Kingdom Collaboration

The year 1985 was a watershed in my life. I had stepped down as head of Intercristo six years before. I now led a small team of Christians who had similar interests in effective communication. We had formed a small agency called The International Development Organization, Interdev for short. Our Interdev team provided consulting, training, and research for Kingdom communications projects in Asia, Africa, and Latin America. We did virtually nothing in the West—Europe or North America.

In 1985, with our board, my Interdev colleagues and I were doing long-range planning. We had no buildings, no endowment, no large patrons or on-going funding constituency. Our only "assets" were our network of relationships, our experience, a specialized but positive professional reputation, and the Lord! We asked ourselves, "Based on our experience and the resources we do have, what priorities over the next five to ten years will enable us to be the most responsible stewards and have the greatest Kingdom impact?" After much prayer and reflection, the answer came down to one thing: around the world, duplication of effort, division, and lack of coordination seemed to be the greatest single roadblock to Kingdom advance. Shouldn't we at least try to help God's people do something about this critically important, seemingly pervasive problem?

SMALL BEGINNINGS, HUGE IMPLICATIONS

With modest funding from three trusted sources, many questions about how to proceed, plenty of naysayers, and no good "models" to copy, we stepped out. We rewrote Interdev's charter to focus on this new vision and began talking with agencies we had already worked with, from Hong Kong in the East to North Africa in the West.

In June of 1986, the first meeting of fourteen individuals from eight ministries gathered for three nights and four days in an old hotel to answer one question: "If we want to see real spiritual breakthroughs in our region, is there anything of importance we can only do together rather than continuing to work individually?" The group came up with a list of twenty critical items that they could only accomplish together! But, of course, when you haven't done one thing together, you can't start with twenty. Through much prayer and discussion, they narrowed the list to one priority for cooperative action for the next twelve months. The first strategic partnership in my experience was born.

STRATEGIC PARTNERSHIPS: Looking at the whole challenge; identifying all the needed resources; then engaging those varied elements in a single lasting collaboration. Realizing a challenging goal that may be simple to state but complex to achieve.

What I didn't realize at the time was as the world around us changed radically, God was about to surprise us—overtaking us from behind with what would become a global partnership movement.

Today, hundreds of ministries are engaged in dozens of strategic partnerships around the world. In many countries, language groups, and cities, training programs are helping concerned individuals replicate and sustain the partnership vision in their own areas of ministry.

Keep in mind: throughout this book I will affirm that there are many forms of partnership. The stories, principles, and ideas in this book will, I believe, help almost any partnership be more effective. However, I will consistently encourage readers to think strategically, to look at the whole challenge, the whole problem. Whether it is your own neighborhood, your town, a particular slice of society you want to reach or serve, or an entire language group, think through what resources will be needed to address the whole challenge. Then find ways, through partnership, to link all these resources in a creative response.

THE CHURCH'S GREATEST CHALLENGE

So, based on all this experience, what is my sense of the church's greatest challenge today? Lack of money, prayer, or people? What?

Looking back over forty years around Christian ministry in the West and internationally, I'm convinced of one thing: The brokenness in the church, the divisions that abound, and our consistent resistance to the God design of restored relationships and practical unity is our (the church's) truly great sin. It is the world's roadblock of all roadblocks to belief. On the outside, it is the greatest single roadblock to power and credibility in our engagement of the world. Inside the church, it is the greatest impediment to the joy, refreshment, and fulfillment God intends for us. And it is the greatest impediment to the great, undying hope that the person and power of Jesus can bring to every believer and to his church.

Little did I realize in 1985 that God was taking me from a world of intense individualism and competition into another world. My new world was one in which, personally and professionally, I had little experience. This world focused primarily on the common good rather than on myself or my own organization. This journey, even to the present, has been marked by intense resistance and, at times, great discouragement. At the same time, I have had a growing awareness of God's blessing and the powerful things that can happen when his people join hands to work together.

WHY THIS BOOK?

Seeing how partnerships, based on sound scriptural and operational principles, can totally transform Kingdom initiatives, I have written with four primary readers and five primary objectives in mind.

The readers:

- The thinking layperson who knows in your heart of hearts that the gospel has more power to change lives and communities than you are experiencing. This book will show you how ordinary people, joining hands and hearts in sustainable partnerships, can see extraordinary Kingdom results.

- The church or Christian agency executive or staff member who has a bigger dream but who lacks "how to" models and tools. This book will help fire your vision and show you ways to accomplish Kingdom outcomes that your organization alone can never realize.

- The church or Christian agency executive or staff member who is captured by the natural, powerful forces of ego, turf protection, fear of loss of identity, or desire for control. This book will show how you and your organization can be set free to do more than you ever dreamed.

- The Kingdom leaders of tomorrow. It is time to break the stranglehold that Satan has had on the church for centuries—dividing believers, destroying the church's credibility, and undermining her power in Christ. This book provides you, tomorrow's leadership, with a completely new way forward: scriptural, theoretical, and practical tools, plus many case histories of how partnerships can transform ministry.

The objectives:

- First, to bring hope—to you and other members of Christ's church. When we work together, we really can make a difference in the world. I believe this kind of hope, coupled with courage, vision, and scripturally based, proven partnership skills, will help us turn dreams into reality. We can demonstrate that Jesus' life and message are truly powerful when released in the way God intended.

- Second, to provide a reasonably thorough case for why God's people working together are far more powerful and effective than individual initiatives. The God design is deeply rooted in Scripture and demonstrated in both secular and religious partnerships. Truth is always God's truth, wherever it appears! This is why non-Christians can put people on the moon and bring them back! Like the principles of rocketry and celestial mechanics, partnership principles work for believers and non-believers alike. It's another of the thousands of examples of God's grace!

- Third, to provide a tool kit of awareness, skills, and "how to" processes that you and others can actually use to develop and sustain effective, working partnerships. The tool kit has been assembled and proven effective over twenty-five years of "hands on" work in a wide range of partnerships at home and around the world.

- Fourth, to be a tool for "selling" the vision to others, if you already believe in the ideal of God's people working together. They may be skeptical, they may need to be presented with a more substantial case, or they may be fearful or openly resistant.

- Fifth, to encourage and empower you and others in the church to take the life-changing message of Jesus' love to those on the "outside"—the unreached of the world. They may be secular friends in your neighborhood, immigrants in your city, or an unreached people group of several million in a country thousands of miles away.

My Scriptural "North Stars"

On this journey I've been guided by two Scripture passages that have been like twin North Stars for my life.

The Apostle Paul's only commentary on how he prioritized his geographical destinations is found in Romans 15:20–21:

> My ambition has always been to proclaim the Good News in
> places where Christ has not been heard of, so as not to build
> on a foundation laid by someone else. As the scripture says,
> "Those who were not told about him will see, and those who
> have not heard will understand." (GNT)

Over the last thirty years, this passage, again and again, has helped define the bull's eye of God's call on my life. While there were constantly calls and opportunities in the West, the compelling need of those who had never even had a chance to hear about Jesus just kept calling my heart, filling my mind, and directing my feet. The passage became the *where* of my life.

The only basis for evaluation of the church that Jesus gave the pagans or those on the "outside," are these familiar words from John 17:21–23:

> I pray that they may all be one. Father! May they be in us, just
> as you are in me and I am in you. May they be one, so that
> the world will believe that you sent me. I gave them the same
> glory you gave me, so that they may be one, just as you and
> I are one: I in them and you in me, so that they may be com-
> pletely one, in order that the world may know that you sent me
> and that you love them as you love me. (GNT)

If Jesus gives the world this basis for judging the church and his credibility, what must be the world's reasonable conclusion? Right! Jesus was a fake and the story about God's love is just about as believable. Tough words? Yes. But look at the world around us and the billions who have either never heard of him or who, having heard, have rejected the message.

Jesus' compelling words in John 17 became the *what* of my life.[4]

Granted, millions of God's people are the salt and light in countless visible and invisible places in society. Granted, those people have, on many occasions, joined hands with others to do wonderful things in the name of Christ.

I'm not saying that divisions in the body of Christ are the only reason people don't follow Jesus. Many reasons can be cited why our family members, friends, neighbors, or those in distant lands have not or are unwilling to accept the good news. Satan mounts a constellation of roadblocks to belief.

The Joy, Hope, and Power of Working in Partnership

In this book I identify some of the more and less obvious reasons for divisions in the church. But my focus is not on the negative. There is too much good news—in Scripture and in the growing illustrations of a new vision gripping the church around the world.

I tell stories of places where new vision is being raised and hope restored—where God's people are really coming together, and where, in many cases, real breakthroughs are occurring. Possibly more important, the book provides both scripturally rooted and practical means for taking real, positive action!

> May God, the source of hope, fill you with all joy and peace
> . . . so that your hope will continue. (Romans 15:13 GNT)

PARTNERSHIP IN PRACTICE: For a couple of days, about thirty Christian workers in a tough culture had been meeting in a workshop on the principles and practice of partnership. I had been facilitating a morning session when, at the back of the room, I saw a man was weeping. It was clear. I could see him wiping his eyes and, eventually, take out a handkerchief. "What," I thought, "could I have said that would have caused this response? Is it possible that some tragedy from his past has crossed his mind in the last few minutes?"

You can imagine that during the coffee break I felt compelled to speak quietly to the man. "Are you all right?" I asked. "I noticed during the last session that you seemed to be pretty emotionally upset at one point."

I couldn't have been more surprised when he responded, "Upset? No, I wasn't upset. Those were tears of joy! In the workshop this morning at last I've finally seen how my life fits into the whole picture of God's work here in the country. For the first time in my life, I see that I have a real role along with others in God's plan. I see where I really fit into a whole evangelism strategy so these wonderful people can come to know Jesus!"

In lonely and difficult places, in countless working meetings over the years, I have seen hope ignited in individuals' hearts. When they see they don't have to work alone but can really join hands with others, it touches their hearts and shows on their faces. Working with others in partnership can completely change your perspective on ministry and the potential God has for you. The lonely place may be in a culture thousands of miles away or a neighborhood close to home. But working alone, no matter what the circumstances, is usually a lonely business.

We all need hope to live. The Viennese psychiatrist, Victor Frankl, in his book *Man's Search for Meaning* states that, even in the most horrific circumstances, hope keeps us alive. Frankl's years in a Nazi concentration camp gave him a unique perspective on the power of hope!

The "unreached" are unreached for very real reasons. They're often at a great distance from sources of the gospel message—physically, culturally, or in their worldview. Whether in the lonely streets of great cities, the squalor of squatter villages, or the remote vastness of a jungle or desert, anyone trying to reach and serve people in such places takes risks. Personal encouragement and support are often rare. Satan is especially active through his dark, powerful agents attacking those who venture to share Jesus' life-changing, eternity-changing love. When we go it alone, God's design indicates, we're extremely vulnerable. When we go together, we go in strength.

Effective, lasting partnerships can:

- Save critical resources, reducing duplication and waste of money, people, and other assets (efficiency).

- Produce greater results in a shorter period of time (effectiveness).

- Engage the whole range of spiritual gifts distributed within the church (inclusiveness).

- Share risk, allowing us to consider ideas and dreams that, going it alone, would seem unthinkable.

- Help reduce grand and complex visions into understandable, achievable steps.

- Empower believers to celebrate diversity while working together in unity.

- Bring credibility to God's message as we demonstrate the power of restored relationships.

- Release the power of the Holy Spirit in ways rarely seen when we work independently.

- Bring hope as participants realize they are not facing the challenge alone.

- Provide fulfillment and refreshment for participants as they progress toward realizing the impossible dream—whatever the dream may be.

Scripture makes clear that moving back to the God design yields huge benefits. Trusting, open relationships, and the asset of synergy when all of the pieces of God's design are working together can transform ministry. This book is born out of years of seeing the extraordinary power released when God's people work in effective, durable partnerships. In this book we'll explore those benefits, deal with the roadblocks, provide practical "how to" action strategies you can employ, and share case histories along the way.

What dream do you have that the God-design of partnership can release? He wants you to have the joy of realizing that dream. So read on!

 Share your ideas and response to this chapter, tell your own story, or get connected with more partnership resources at the book's website
www.connectedbook.net

PART ONE
The Big Picture

1

QUICKSTART

AN OVERVIEW OF PARTNERSHIP PRINCIPLES & BENEFITS

Core Idea

Each partnership's purpose, people, and place are unique. But all effective, durable partnerships share common experiences—no need to reinvent the wheel. Acknowledging the principles enables success. Ignoring them can spell disappointment, even disaster. Though their appearance, cost, and mission are radically different, a single-engine private airplane and a 747 jet carrying hundreds of people and tons of cargo both fly because of the same aerodynamic principles. Each design produces unique benefits, yet both planes fly according to the same laws of physics. Distilled from twenty years of field experience, this brief chapter gives an overview of the principles that power effective Kingdom partnerships and the benefits they produce. Around the world, every day, acknowledging these principles helps turn dreams into reality.

Working in neighborhoods, cities, specialized communities, or international settings, success in collaboration is often elusive. Over twenty years of field experience has revealed certain core principles that power virtually all effective, lasting strategic partnerships. Build your ministry partnership with these principles and the likelihood of success is high. Ignore them and failure is very likely! While the rest of the book unpacks these ideas in more depth, here's a quick start overview: a look at the key success factors and the benefits that employing them can produce.

PARTNERSHIP PRINCIPLES

1.   All effective strategic partnerships are driven by an energizing, challenging vision. This vision must be beyond the capacity of any single person or agency to achieve alone. Only the vision will keep you going. Partnership for partnership's sake is a sure recipe for failure. Warm fellowship isn't enough.

2.   Trust, openness, and mutual concern are vital ingredients. Partnerships are more than coordination, planning, strategies, and tactics. The heart of the gospel is restored relationships. God longs for Jesus' finished work to be demonstrated in our relationships. Investing time in getting to know, understand, and genuinely appreciate each other isn't optional.

3.   Effective, lasting partnerships need a committed facilitator. Bringing the partnership to life and keeping the fires burning, the facilitator must demonstrate patience, tenacity, vision, and the spirit of a servant. This prophet, servant, and resource person needs training, nurturing, and encouragement.

4.   Effective, durable partnerships are a process, not an event. Every lasting partnership has exploration, formation, and operation stages. Forming them usually takes much more time than you expect. The quickest way to kill a partnership is to call a meeting. Build personal relationships; get to know the potential partners, the priority issues, and the perceived roadblocks. Doing this will produce huge dividends later.

5.   Effective, durable partnerships have limited, achievable objectives—in the beginning. As the group experiences success and confidence increases, objectives can broaden. Don't attempt too much too soon. Early objectives need:

A. Kingdom significance that captures the vision and motivation of the group.

B. Relevance to each partner's vision and objective.

C. Achievable, tangible outcomes that are vital for fulfillment and encouragement.

6. Effective partnerships require substantial, ongoing prayer. Good ideas, strategy, and breaking through the traditional paradigm of isolation and independent action aren't enough. Satan wants to fragment the church, destroy relationships, and neutralize God's power in the world. Working together requires actively enlisting a prayer support network. It's essential.

7. High participation and ownership is vital. Effective partnerships are never top-down or hierarchical in character. Enlist the widest possible participation in objectives, plans, decisions, and ongoing communications. Actively engage people in the process, not just the dream.

8. Start by identifying priority felt needs among the people being served. Don't start by trying to write a common theological statement or a constitution. Start with the felt needs of the audience you want to reach or serve. Kingdom priorities, barriers to spiritual breakthroughs, resources needed, and realistic priorities for action must be distilled and agreed on in light of those. Lasting partnerships focus primarily on what (objectives) rather than how (structure).

9. Partnerships composed of churches, ministries, or other organizations need a partnership champion in each of those groups. These people see how their group can benefit from such practical cooperation. The champions sell the vision to their colleagues, provide ongoing, two-way communication, and help keep the partnership focused on the expected outcomes.

10. As effective partnerships become more complex, they serve at least four constituencies: the people we're trying to reach or serve; the partner agencies/ministries; the funding and praying constituencies behind each of these ministries; and, eventually, the partnership itself. Each constituency needs information, a sense of participation, and a feeling of fulfillment or success.

11. Partners with clear identity and vision are the best. Individuals, churches, and other ministries involved need to have and live by their own clear sense of mission or calling. Otherwise, they will never understand how they fit in, contribute to the overall picture, or recognize how they benefit from the joint effort.

12. Acknowledging, even celebrating, differences is important. Effective partnerships concentrate on what they have in common, like vision, values, and ministry objectives. But it is important to value and demonstrate respect for each partner's history, vision, and current activity.

13. Effective partnerships don't come free. Just participating in the exploration, planning, launch, and ongoing coordination takes time and money. Deeper commitment may require still greater investment.

14. Effective partnerships are even more challenging to maintain than to start. Keeping the vision alive, the focus clear, communication active, and outcomes fulfilling takes awareness, concentration, and long-term commitment by the facilitator or facilitation team.

15. Expect problems and proactively deal with them. Make sure the partnership has a means for dealing with changes, exceptions, disappointments, unfulfilled commitments, and simply the unexpected. Small problems must be addressed immediately. A wise man knows one thing—the only predictable thing is the unpredictable.

PARTNERSHIP IN PRACTICE: Resistance to the gospel had been intense in this part of the world. Most missionaries working in the region agreed that a strategic element of witness was sharing the good news through television. TV could effectively leapfrog closed doors and many barriers erected by hostile governments. However, differing programming philosophies had kept broadcasters from any real cooperation. Efforts had been made to encourage partnership. Meetings had been held, but discussions seemed to always evolve into a focus on differences and why cooperation couldn't happen.

Facilitators committed to the broadcasters and to effective witness in the region didn't give up. Finally, a different approach was proposed. A decision was made to candidly acknowledge participants' differences, but to focus on issues essential to all broadcasters—things like technical facilities, negotiation of air time costs, etc. By beginning with issues they had in common rather than the areas of sharp difference, cooperation began. It was slow going and involved certain "costs" for all parties—time invested, certain compromises on technical points, and willingness to acknowledge each other's roles. But trust was formed in the process of sorting through the less controversial issues, opening the door to wider issues of Kingdom stewardship and greater credibility because of the broadcasters' functional unity.

PARTNERSHIP BENEFITS

As you work your way through the book, you'll recognize a wide range of powerful benefits that flow out of effective partnerships. In the following chapters

I deal with these and many more benefits in detail—what they really mean and how to recognize and achieve them. But, for the moment, here's an abbreviated quick start overview. I trust it will encourage you to keep reading!

1.   Potential and options for action expand. Working alone, no matter how sophisticated or substantial your resources, limits what one person or ministry can accomplish. Working with others who complement your strengths expands your potential and your horizons of ministry and impact.

2.   Achievement of goals accelerates, costs decrease, and waste is eliminated. An effective partnership produces efficiency and reduces the gaps and overlap that result when we all do our own thing. Return on Kingdom investment increases.

3.   Individuals and ministries are able to capitalize on their strengths. Effective partnerships allow people or organizations to do what they do best, to maximize their contribution rather than spreading themselves too thin by doing many different things—often poorly.

4.   The bigger picture comes into focus. Effective partnerships let you see what's needed to accomplish the bigger vision, identify the missing pieces, and connect with resources to accomplish the vision. Getting all the pieces together, focused on a common objective, is a sure recipe for better outcomes.

5.   Flexibility increases. Partnerships encourage individuals or ministries to play their unique roles. When they don't have to do everything, they have more options in timing, more available resources, and the ability to concentrate on what they do best.

6.   Risk diminishes. The larger or more complex the vision or project, naturally, the greater the resources needed. Working in effective partnerships, we can share the load and reduce risk while increasing the speed of progress or the quality of the outcomes.

All of these principles and benefits are outlined in both Old and New Testaments. But four benefits are so explicitly featured in Scripture I want to highlight them here.

7.   Resources and roles fit together more naturally. When we join hands with others, we discover different, often complementary, strengths. Effective partnerships frequently allow us to identify what additional resources are needed and, together, engage the agencies or ministries with those resources. *(Romans 12, 1 Corinthians 12, Ephesians 4)*

8. God's power is released in a special way. Working alone on challenging projects, particularly in our own strength without God's presence and power, can be scary! He's promised that the Holy Spirit's power will be present and released in a special way when we join with his people in partnership. *(Psalms 133)*

9. Our work gains significant credibility. God's people working together demonstrate the core scriptural truth: Jesus' work restores relationships. God promises that this has a powerful effect on our credibility—whether the audience believes *our message* or not! *(John 17: 20–23)*

10. We receive refreshment and new hope. In challenging circumstances, hope keeps us alive. Whatever our vision, in our community or elsewhere in the world, the knowledge that others share our vision refreshes our spirits and sustains our hope. *(Matt. 5:9, Psalms 133)*

These principles and benefits, along with dozens of case histories and examples, are unpacked in the chapters ahead. Read on—with hope!

Share your ideas and response to this chapter, tell your own story, or get connected with more partnership resources at the book's website

www.connectedbook.net

2

WHY PARTNERSHIP?

WHAT'S THE MOTIVATION?

Core Idea

The question is in the back of all of our minds: Isn't it really easier and quicker to just do it yourself? Why spend the time and energy trying to work with others—particularly people or ministries with such different ideas? The fact is, in powerful new ways partnerships are demonstrating that your vision or that of your ministry is more likely to be realized if you work with others rather than doing your own thing. Motivation is everything. Here we explore why linking hands with others can really make a difference.

IT'S NOT A NEW IDEA: SCRIPTURE POINTS THE WAY

The idea of people working together to achieve something they can't do alone is goes back as far as there are historical records. God designed us to live as he does, in unity—working together. (This theme is developed more fully in chapter 4, The God Design—Relationships: Wholeness, Unity, and Diversity.) Throughout the Scripture, the message keeps coming through.

Let *us* make man in *our* image. (Genesis 1:26, *italics* added)

Then the Lord God said, "It is not good for the man to live alone. I will make a suitable companion to help him." (Genesis 2:18)

The Lord said, "I am going to make you like God to the King, and your brother Aaron will speak to him as your prophet." (Exodus 7:1)

. . . half my men worked and half stood guard, wearing coats of armor and armed with spears, shields, and bows. And our leaders gave their full support to the people who were rebuilding the wall. (Nehemiah 4:16)

Two men can resist an attack that would defeat one man alone. A rope made of three cords is hard to break. (Ecclesiastes 4:12)

He called the twelve disciples together and sent them out two by two. (Mark 6:6b)

Under his control all the different parts of the body fit together, (so) the whole body grows and builds itself up through love. (Ephesians 4:16)

. . . we are partners working together for God, and you are God's field. You are also God's building. Using the gift that God gave me, I did the work of an expert builder and laid the foundation and another man is building on it. (1 Corinthians 3:9-10)

So, the first motivation is that God designed his creation, his people, to work together. All outcomes will be stronger, more effective as we do so. The few passages mentioned here give us just a hint of God's intention and the associated power and blessing when we follow his design.

THE BUSINESS, EDUCATION, AND SCIENTIFIC COMMUNITIES KNOW THE POWER OF PARTNERSHIP

As I will say again and again throughout the book, all truth is God's truth. So, we should not be surprised that business, education, and science agree that a partnership approach is essential.

Strategic alliances provide access to far more resources than any single firm owns or could buy. This can greatly expand its ability to create new products, reduce costs, bring in new technologies, penetrate other markets, preempt competitors, reach the scale needed to survive in world markets, and generate more cash to invest in core skills.[1] (Jordan D. Lewis, Business Management Strategist)

Making those improvements is more and more the product of partnerships—but as we move toward reaching every child, there is a need to ensure that every partnership is working effectively.[2] (Dr. Carol Bellamy, Executive Director of UNICEF)

THE KINGDOM—MANY MOTIVATIONS, MANY PARTNERSHIP OPTIONS

Partnership means many things to many people. Whether it's two individuals joining forces on behalf of some local cause or a complex, multi-agency, international collaborative initiative—a conscious commitment to partnership can be powerfully motivating and full of practical benefits. Some examples:

- Two individuals committed to launching a ministry to the poor through their church decide to pray together about the vision. People like this may meet face to face, via telephone, or coordinate their efforts through correspondence on the Internet. These prayer partners are following the scriptural models that promise blessing when people join hands and hearts.

- A few missionaries were scattered over hundreds of square miles. It was lonely, communications were terrible, and the closest believer was usually another missionary 8–10 hours away over roads that were impassible four months of the year. Plus, response from the highly resistant animistic people group was, at best, discouraging. Twenty-four missionaries and a small group of national believers met, talked, prayed, and, while from very different backgrounds, agreed that the only way to see real change was to join hands in an ongoing, working partnership.

- Five Christian families on a street in a single neighborhood were concerned about a way to serve their neighbors and be a witness at the same time. They committed to having a monthly informal dinner for their street—all five sharing in the cooking and rotating the dinner among their five houses. They committed to doing it for one year with invitations to all around the street. A simple opportunity is given each time for neighbors to share their concerns—whether they are believers or not. And, each time, a member of two or three of the Christian families just briefly prays for the needs. Their short-term partnership to witness and serve had long-term potential implications.

- Three student ministries at a midwestern university began meeting to plan and pray about how, working together, they could more effectively reach the thousands on the growing campus. Four years later, on a retreat, leaders of the three ministries acknowledged that the hundreds of lives that had been touched and changed could never have been realized without their ministry partnership.

- Leaders of a local church in Arizona met leaders of a growing church in Latin America at a conference ten years ago. On the way home, the Americans said, "You know, we could really get involved with those folks. They could help fire our vision, and we could provide them helping hands of all kinds." After several false starts, a lasting partnership was born between the two churches. Today, lay and pastoral leaders from both churches say, "It's changed our lives and our ministries in the communities around us."

- Turf wars and egos were plentiful. For years there had been talk about greater cooperation by Christian ministries in the city. Everyone knew there were serious gaps and overlap. Finally, following a pastor's prayer retreat and significant relational breakthroughs, inner-city leaders, churches, specialized ministries, city-wide Christian media, and urban churches began meeting, talking, and listening—together. It took six months, but they finally established clear, near-term goals that had great Kingdom value and represented real needs in the city. Long-term survival and lasting success had yet to be tested, but a real ministry partnership had been born.

Beyond these examples, you can probably imagine a dozen more.

So, Why a Book?

Ask your friends or professional colleagues, "On challenging projects that involve multiple skills over a period of time, do you think it's more effective if people just all do their own thing with no coordination? Or, do you think it would be helpful for them to find some way to partner together to achieve the task?" Generally people will smile and say, "Why do you even ask? It seems like a rhetorical question! Of course, people should work together." However, the same people will usually quickly add, "Partnership's a great idea—but it's so hard to get a real cooperation, keep it going, and see any real, practical outcomes."

But, before we talk about the up side, let's hear from the loyal opposition.

Why Not Partnership?

My colleagues and I, who have worked actively in the partnership movement, have heard just about every reason imaginable as to why an individual or their ministry should *not* work with others. Often it is hard to get people to be honest. But, if you press a bit you find there is hardly ever an original reason. They've all been stated before—thousands of times. Here are the fifteen that most frequently emerge, often stated in less candid or clear terms but with the same meaning, nonetheless.

1. Theological purity is important to us. (In short, exclusivity is more important than inclusiveness.)

2. I'm not sure how I/we'd fit in. (In other words, I/we don't really know who we are.)

3. Frankly we think we should, and probably can, do it alone. (The omniscient fable.)

4. I think sharing on a project like this would be difficult. (In short, partnership with others may intrude on my/our pride/ego.)

5. In partnerships, relationships and goals can get confused. (In other words, we're not sure of ourselves.)

6. We just don't see any need to change the way we've been working. (It's the ruts leading to oblivion syndrome!)

7. Who actually came up with this idea? (The *not invented here* syndrome.)

8. Honestly, we have a very specialized funding base that is concerned about what we're doing. (Meaning, don't let our donors know we can't do this whole thing alone.)

9. Frankly, we think partnership is a waste of time—we see no potential added value. (The old individualistic ways are good enough; why try anything new?)

10. We don't have the people, time, or other resources to invest in trying to work with others. (Meaning, we're not sure what our potential is and don't want to find out.)

11. Working with others isn't our style. (It's the institutional inertia, lack of flexibility, living in the past syndrome.)

12. Fear of success—how would we possibly share credit with others? (Think of the confusion!)

13. I/we are responsible to our board or constituency. (Meaning, how could we explain our need to work with others to achieve success?)

14. We've been doing quite well on our own, thank you. (Read: fear of exposure of our organization's weaknesses or idiosyncrasies.)

15. Our work is so unique that cooperation would have little/no value. (Meaning, they don't have a clue as to the problem or the potential.)

There is an answer to each of these issues. And in this book I address all of these issues in one way or another. Just keep in mind that an aspect of Jesus' ministry that most consistently got him in trouble was that he was too *inclusive*. Sinners, outcasts, people on the fringe of society—they were his stock in trade. In Mark's gospel, chapter 9, even Jesus' disciples needed help to understand that "he that is not against us is for us." We need to keep in mind that "different" is not the same as "bad." The truth of the gospel is that, in Christ, we can live without fear, have a secure identity, celebrate our different gifts and callings, and work together for his glory. It's the community of Open Arms!

It is often helpful for a ministry to do an assessment of how well they might do in a real, working partnership. So, in the Appendix, you will find a simple "Partnership Readiness" checklist that will help you examine your corporate culture and determine how suited you are to connect with and work alongside others.

Motivation: Socio/Economic Conditions

In the past it may have been possible to "go it alone." The smartest rarely did. But, today, world conditions are forcing business, social initiatives, and Kingdom strategies to acknowledge the same truth: if you want to work smart, you work together.

Here are some of the global realities that make partnership an imperative, not an option:

- Enhanced communications/increased awareness. There is simply too much data available to too many people for anyone to blithely claim ignorance. With the data available today, if you try it alone, you will be ill-equipped, have serious blind spots, and be less effective.

- Widely distributed, accessible economic, technical, and human resources. While there certainly are "pockets" of isolated resources, today's communications and transportation options make it possible to link resources globally in a common vision.

- Increased specialization/proliferation of organizations. It is an age of specialization. No single agency can reach a city or an unreached people group. No company can develop and bring a new product to a large market without alliances and partnerships.

- New demands for performance and accountability. Increasingly business investors as well as Kingdom donors know that going it alone frequently means duplication of effort, waste, and inefficiency.

- High risk/cost of new ventures. Trying to reach/serve all the kids in your neighborhood, dealing with unemployment in a city, taking the good news to people who have never heard, or developing a new technology are all costly initiatives where partnerships and strategic alliances can spread the risk.

- Rapid growth of non-Western resources. In both the church and general society, non-Western countries now offer world-class human, technical, and other resources. Frequently they are closer, physically and culturally, to the focus of the ministry we have in mind.

PRIMARY MOTIVATIONS/BENEFITS

So, if you have this book in your hands, what has motivated you to pick it up and even get this far? Desire to excel or be more effective? How about a desire to attempt something too big to attempt alone? It could be you have a sense that God's design for his people is to work together. Just maybe you're thinking if you could forge some kind of partnership with others, things might go better. Any or all of those ideas are great places to start.

Let's look at the question, "Why partnership?" in more detail.

Truth is always God's truth. There is no other source. Whether it's the sciences of mathematics, biology, physics, chemistry, or astronomy, his indelible footprint is everywhere. But his truth is equally evident in the arts, history, and human relationships. The extraordinary thing about God's grace is that it is not selective. As the Scripture notes, "The rain falls on the just and the unjust." Unbelievers can send men to the moon *and* bring them back safely. In my home state, unbelieving farmers can successfully plant, tend, and harvest crops. So, in the practice of partnerships, it should not be surprising that businesses and ministries often find *parallel* motivations or benefits. Here are some examples of where general business or social initiatives find common motivation for turning to a partnership, network, or strategic alliance approach.

1. Efficiency: Processes can be accelerated, costs can be reduced, waste eliminated, and the frequent gaps and overlap of everyone doing their own thing can be minimized.

2. Focus on strengths: Partnerships allow organizations to do what they do best: maximize their contribution by doing what they do well—rather than having to do many things, often poorly.

3. Effectiveness: Partnerships usually force us to look at the bigger picture, see what is needed to accomplish the vision, and then identify the missing pieces. Getting all the pieces together and focusing on a common objective is a sure recipe for better outcomes.

4. Greater flexibility: Roles, timing, availability of resources, and ability to concentrate or focus on more than one project, if necessary, are increased when working in partnership.

5. Expanded resources: When we join hands with others, different, often complimentary, strengths are discovered. The mere fact that we have come to-gether frequently allows us to identify what additional resources are needed and, together, identify those resources and encourage their participation.

6. Risk is reduced: The larger or more complex a project, naturally, the greater resources needed. Working in partnership, we can share the load, reducing risk while often increasing speed or quality of the outcomes.

7. Expanded options for action: Working alone, no matter how sophisticated or substantial your resources, there is a limit to what you can accomplish. By working with others who complement your strengths, your potential and your horizons are expanded. This may mean consideration of new products, services, or geographical areas you can enter.

WEAK MOTIVES

1. Save money. Wrong. While it's true you may be able to do something you could never dream of doing alone, your action should be driven by a vision.

2. Everybody's talking partnership. Wrong. Partnership has to clearly be a good move for you, your ministry/agency, and the Kingdom. Doing something because "everyone else is doing it" is a dead end.

3. We're weak and need help. Wrong. The best partners, individuals or minis-tries, are those who know who they are, know what they can contribute, and have a vision driving them on. Only get involved in a partnership if you have a vision and know you can contribute something toward its realization.

PARTNERSHIP IN PRACTICE: When the various leaders came into the room, honestly, they really couldn't imagine what kind of real, practical benefit could possibly come from these meetings. Explore partnership? What's the point?

The truth was, everybody was already working as hard as they could. And they all knew what was going on in the region. So why waste time? Previous efforts like this had always failed to produce anything of value.

During the first few hours, time was taken to have each ministry share their vision, whom they were working with (audience they were trying to reach), services or products they provided, something about their history, and the make up of their team.

You can imagine the surprise when, by the end of the first day, of the thirteen ministries present, five acknowledged they translated and published the same evangelistic booklet—without knowing others had done the same! All admitted, honestly, it was embarrassing. You can also imagine why, three days later, coordination of communication/media efforts was established as a high priority as they had decided that, yes, there really were things they could do more effectively together than continuing to work independently.

Biblical Motivation

As I mentioned earlier, the Scripture is full of models, principles, and admonition for us to pay attention to the God design and work together in partnership. For centuries, Christians have felt they could probably be more effective, touch the people of their community, and change the world if somehow they could work together. As we work our way through this book, I explore why we don't work together and what it takes to break the pattern of independence. We also examine a wide range of case histories that demonstrate the powerful benefits and motivation for partnership. Here are just a few of the more significant biblical promises.

Working Together:

1. We demonstrate the power of the gospel to change lives, producing open, trusting relationships (Philippians 2:1–11).

2. The Holy Spirit's power is released in ways only possible when we dwell in unity and work together (Psalms 133, Galatians 5:16–26).

3. We demonstrate good stewardship. Working together we maximize our use of the resources God has given us as costs are reduced and effectiveness is increased (Matthew 25:14–30).

4. The credibility of our message is strengthened. Jesus says that those watching our lives and work are more likely to believe that he is who he says he is when they observe us working together. This is particularly true in the traditional, community-based cultures of Asia, Africa, and Latin America. (John 5:31–47, 10:38, 17:23)

5. The Body of Christ becomes a powerful, unified community, demonstrating real love, committed to each other, to growing in Christ, and to witnessing to the world around us (Ephesians 4:1–16)

6. We encourage use of the full range of gifts and abilities distributed by the Holy Spirit among God's people (Romans 12, 1 Corinthians 12).

7. Encouragement, refreshment, and hope replace loneliness and despair when God's people work together rather than working independently (Psalms 133).

Summing Up

In working together, powerful motivations and benefits lure us on. When we follow the God design of open, restored relationships, we will be more effective and efficient, we are more likely to be working in our area of strength, our message will be more credible, hope will be strengthened, we will see more spiritual results sooner, and our mutual and individual dreams will become reality. What more could we ask?

 Share your ideas and response to this chapter, tell your own story, or get connected with more partnership resources at the book's website
www.connectedbook.net

3
PARTNERSHIPS, NETWORKS, STRATEGIC ALLIANCES

SO MANY IDEAS—SO MANY DEFINITIONS!

Core Idea

 Every time two or more people agree to work together on something, temporarily or long term, you have a partnership. Much is being said about "networking" and "partnership" these days; what do we really mean? Knowing what kind of partnership is most appropriate for the challenge we want to address can be critical. Knowing the strengths and weaknesses of the different kinds of partnerships can save us time, energy, and frustration.

So many of the good things we take for granted are the result of partnerships—a conscious decision on the part of two or more people or agencies to work together to realize an objective none of them could achieve alone. Think about it: a healthy family, a congenial neighborhood, a good local school, a great symphony orchestra, a championship football team, a quality hospital, a great scientific or medical advance, a victorious army, the local emergency telephone service ("911" if you live in the U.S.), or putting a man on the moon and safely bringing him back—each of these requires a complex combination of skills, relationships, vision, planning, organization, and common commitment to bring all the elements together *and keep them together* to realize the dream.

PARTNERSHIP IN PRACTICE: Jack thought he had a pretty good piece of property for the dream house he and his wife wanted to build. One day he assembled electricians, his banker, some carpenters, plumbers, and a bulldozing company all on the property at the same time. For about fifteen minutes Jack tried to describe the house he and his wife wanted. As Jack went on, the professionals looked at each other and Jack with increasing disbelief. When Jack finally came out with his concluding statement, they still were hardly prepared: "I know you've all got good professional reputations, so I'd like you guys to get together and get this job done for my wife and me."

And you're saying to yourself, "How could this guy be so dumb?"

Imagine trying to build a house without:

- Defining your motivation—why you want to build the house?
- Defining "success"—how will you know if you have the house you hoped for?
- Defining how many will occupy it and what layout or floor plan will serve your lifestyle.
- Determining the costs—all the costs.
- Deciding how to determine your plans: Buy someone else's design? Hire an architect?
- Making sure you know the building codes for the neighborhood.
- Identifying a contractor who will actually build the house to specification, on schedule, and at the agreed price.

These and dozens of other questions, large and small, are familiar to anyone who has built a home.

Building a satisfying house involves dreams, extremely diverse, highly developed skills, knowledge of materials, good planning, financial resources, and constant oversight. It's a complex partnership in which human, technical, legal, and financial resources must intersect.

We may laugh at Jack and his approach to trying to get his house built. But in dozens of locations around the world, well-intentioned people like Jack call meetings of diverse people, hoping to get them to work together to achieve some objective. In most of those cases, the objectives will never be met, frustration will be high, and the dreams will not be realized.

This book is all about helping you move your dream to reality by effectively engaging others in the vision. It will give you principles, examples, and practical tools so you can effectively connect the needed resources and realize the vision. And when the project is complete, everyone involved will say it was a good experience!

Every ministry partnership exists for a purpose. *If there isn't a dream, there's no need for a partnership!* Defining that purpose, the process you'll follow, who will be involved, and the distribution of responsibilies greatly increases your chances for success.

Partnerships are like a journey or a project; the longer or more complex the vision, the more you need to think and plan—and pray! You can't foresee all the problems you'll encounter. And waiting to start until you have *everything* in place is usually a recipe for achieving nothing. But knowing more about partnerships before you start can be a huge help, increasing your confidence and your likelihood of success.

This chapter is a brief look at what partnerships are—and aren't. Later we will take a closer look at how to explore, launch, and sustain an effective partnership. But for now, let's get one step closer to understanding the terms we're using.

NETWORKS VS. PARTNERSHIPS

Networking—it's a huge buzzword. At the same time, everyone seems to be talking about partnership. What in the world do they mean? Are partnerships and networks really the same, and if they're different, so what? The answer is no, they are not the same. And yes, understanding their differences can have a real impact on what you do and how you do it. In the real world, both networks and partnerships are needed to release Kingdom power and restore hope to your friends and colleagues along the way.

Networks

The study and understanding of human networks has actually become a specialty in the fields of sociology and communications. Networks can be simple or complex, weak or strong. For example:

- Weak or informal networks are less active or intense in their relationships, often only sharing information or interests. They are frequently "on demand," or fellowship-oriented.

- Strong or more structured networks are often task-, project-, or issue-oriented, have well-defined structure, responsibilities, and objectives, and require substantial time commitments.

For the sake of simplicity, here is a working *definition of networks*: Any group of individuals or organizations sharing a common interest, who regularly communicate with each other to enhance *their individual purposes*.

Note the key phrases:

- common interest
- regularly communicate
- individual purposes

Networks generally are designed to facilitate ongoing communication and information sharing, helping members of the network do their *own individual work* more effectively. The only real points of connection may be a common area of concern and regular communication.

The network may be composed of pastors, building contractors, doctors, mission agencies, or neighbors. It may be structured, with membership, regular meetings, a newsletter, website, etc. Or it may be informal—just an agreement to meet on certain occasions to share information and, maybe, encouragement.

Partnerships

When individuals or organizations move beyond just communication and fellowship and into coordinated action around a common concern, partnerships frequently begin to emerge.

The examples we have cited so far in the book show that partnerships can take many forms for many purposes. They can range from simple to complex, informal to highly structured, short-term partnerships to those that last for years.

Here is a *definition of partnerships* that will get us started: Any group of individuals or organizations, sharing a common interest, who regularly communicate, plan, and work together *to achieve a common vision beyond the capacity of any one of the individual partners.*

Here the key phrases are:

- common interest
- regularly communicate
- work together
- common vision
- beyond the capacity of any one of the individual partners

Partnerships don't exist *just* to share information or encourage fellowship. Information and encouragement *are* part of the partnership process. But they are *means* to an end, not the partnership's purpose. While networks may bring people or organizations together through a common interest, partnerships galvanize linkages around a common vision or outcome. By working together on that common vision or outcome, they can achieve ends far beyond the capacity of any of the individual members of the partnership.

Here are a couple of examples:

NETWORKS IN PRACTICE: Four Christian camps in the region faced similar challenges. Their leaders decided to start meeting once a quarter. As the group met regularly, its members began to see the significant "value added" for each of their camps. The group shared information on camping regulations; other developments in their region; case histories of "best practices" in programming, recruitment, personnel, etc. Camping ministry specialists were brought in for inspiration and ideas on innovation. And the group set up a "hot line" among themselves so they could call on one another if they had sudden technical or personnel problems.

The four camps were operating a classic network that provided:

- encouragement
- information/education

- access to each other's strengths
- potential help in times of emergency

The network, by sharing these points, made it possible for *each camp to carry out its own ministry* more effectively.

PARTNERSHIP IN PRACTICE: The leaders of six Christian camps serving a large, multi-city metropolitan area met occasionally as part of an informal network. In one of these meetings, a camp director said, "I have the feeling that the actual percentage of both kids and adults from churches in our area who are involved in a camping experience every year has been steadily declining. I'd like to see us do some research to see how big our 'market' is and what percentage of that market we are actually serving."

Another director spoke up. "I'm sure that's true. But I'm also concerned that 95% of the camping participants we serve are already in local churches. How could we really break out and begin to touch the lives of those on the 'outside'—those who aren't getting access to the good news?" A year later the camps had forged a partnership that had completed the research and set objectives on how they wanted to "grow" the numbers involved in camping. They had also put together a joint information/recruitment plan with all the churches of the metro area. Finally, they had established a common fund to provide scholarships to give disadvantaged kids, single parents, and others on the "outside" the opportunity to have a camping experience—and hear of Jesus.

The six camps had developed a classic partnership that provided all the elements of network mentioned above—shared information, encouragement, and education—but went beyond the network because they:

- Looked at the "big picture" and dreamed dreams beyond the capacity of any of the individual camps.
- Provided, through several working groups within the partnership, action plans that turned specific initiatives from dreams to reality.
- Were able to have a greater Kingdom impact in the region while returning real, tangible benefits to each of the participating camps.

- Were built on the best of each camp's capabilities but accomplished something bigger—the impossible dream none could have realized alone.

NETWORKS AND PARTNERSHIPS: MUTUALLY EXCLUSIVE OR COMPLEMENTARY?

Frequently:

- Common efforts start as a network and morph into a partnership.
- Networks are often critical elements of the operational plans of partnerships.

In a later chapter we will look at how partnerships and networks often work side by side. But for now, let's make clear: networks and partnerships are not mutually exclusive. More often than not, they can and should play complementary roles.

What is your vision?

- Maybe it's geographically defined—your neighborhood or the city.
- Possibly you want to share the love of Jesus with an ethnic or language group—in your city or in some country overseas.
- You may have a desire to reach or serve a special segment of society—refugees, the homeless, single parents, handicapped, or those who are institutionalized in prisons or mental health care facilities.

PARTNERSHIP IN PRACTICE: In the old movies, we saw the leather helmet-and-goggle-adorned pilot leaning out of the open cockpit of the airplane, desperately trying to see the ground through the fog. Later, when radio connected the pilot with the ground, the people on the ground became the pilot's "eyes"—for at least part of the journey. Still later, an intricate network of technological innovations interfaced with human beings to give the pilot electronic reference points to the landing site: a radar image of the terrain ahead, radio beacons on the ground, a GPS-based assessment of exactly where he was, and, ultimately auto flight controls that could see through virtually blind weather conditions and put the plane on the designated runway—safely.

Whatever the vision, being able to imagine or understand what kind of partnership might work best puts you a big step ahead. Today you don't have to "fly blind!" In almost every case, someone has had your experience—been there, done that—and, most likely, would be delighted to share with you what they have learned on the journey.[1]

ELEMENTS IN DEFINING YOUR PARTNERSHIP

Here are four elements that help define every partnership.

- The diversity of the partners
- The duration of the partnership
- The structure of the partnership
- The location/context of the partnership

Think about your dream or your current collaborative efforts.

DIVERSITY OF PARTNERS

They may be individuals who just share a common concern, specialists, organizations—private or public—or institutions. How many need to be involved to realize the dream? The diversity of your partners is a key part of defining your partnership.

Your partnership may be:

- Bi-lateral: Two people or two organizations working together.
- Multi-lateral (small): Three to ten people or organizations.
- Multi-lateral (large): Ten or more people or organizations.
- A partnership or network composed of people or ministries with the same or very different backgrounds.

It may not just be a question of *how many* are or should be involved. You may need to think about *what kind* of people, experience, or special skills are needed. Obviously, the more complex the vision, the more people may be needed—and the greater the potential achievement!

A KEY PARTNERSHIP PRINCIPLE:

Don't wait to start until you have "everybody" you want or need! That's a recipe for frustration and inaction. Keep in mind:

- You need a few people who are trusted and capable—individuals who have a vision for and some knowledge about the challenge you want to address and who are committed to at least trying to work together.

- The diversity and competence of your initial partners brings credibility to the partnership you are developing.

- As this core group begins to work, other partnership needs will surface, as will the additional people the partnership requires.

- Momentum and simple but tangible progress early on will have a big impact on your ability to recruit others into the partnership.

- While the vision may be big, be ready to start relatively small with limited, achievable goals. These "doable" objectives are vital to early success and a sense of fulfillment and momentum—even if your long-range vision is still in the distance!

DURATION OF THE PARTNERSHIP

How *long* do you think it will take for your partnership to realize the vision? How much staying power will the group need to see the initiative through? How will the length of time required affect how you plan and implement your partnership?

If your partnership comes together, what kind of partnership will it take to realize the dream?

- Short-term partnership: One to three months
- Medium-term partnership: Three months to two years
- Long-term partnership: Two or more years

A short, intensive burst of vision-driven energy often is catalytic in helping people or organizations come together. It may be a crisis, a brief "window of opportunity" that emerges, or some kind of high-priority event that galvanizes people and ministries into effective partnerships.

A KEY PARTNERSHIP PRINCIPLE:

The longer-range the vision, the more challenging it probably will be to form and sustain the partnership. Increasing the number and diversity of partners adds still greater complexity.

PARTNERSHIP IN PRACTICE: International relief and development agencies have found cooperation easier (not simple!) in short-duration crises like sudden, short-lived famine (Africa), post-earthquake food, medical, and housing shortages (Turkey and Nicaragua), or the post-tsunami havoc of December 2004. The long-term challenge of providing sustainable food and other critical services for a country or region has been much more difficult to meet. Following devastating natural disasters, helping communities rebuild their lives, commerce, schools, health care, and other critical elements of the infrastructure has called for partnerships with real "staying power." That has occurred, but rarely.

Think about circumstances in your own city or community that parallel the example given above about relief and development agencies. What types of issues or problems could be addressed with short-term, intensive partnerships? What types of challenges in the community would require a more sustained, long-term partnership? Why the difference?

Part 4 of this book, "On the Way," deals in more detail with the principles and challenges involved in keeping partnerships working effectively.

Structure of the Partnership

A principle in architecture says, "form follows function." Simply, this means that the structure of your partnership should be *as simple as possible* and still meet your objectives. Any talk about organizational structure should *always* be preceded by:

- Agreement on at least an initial clear, compelling vision or reason for the partnership.

- Thorough thinking, prayer, and planning about what main activities will be required for the partnership to realize the vision.

- Definition of near- to medium-term action steps the partnership must take to achieve its initial objectives.

- Agreement on who can/will do what, how communications and accountability will occur, and what the funding options are for your action plan

- Agreement on what sort of timetable combines the urgency of the need or opportunity with a realistic assessment of how long it will take to achieve key, early action priorities.

I have never seen an effective, durable partnership that started first by talking about structure. This is almost always a dead end and frequently raises issues that are either irrelevant in the beginning (you don't really know what the partnership needs yet!) or, worse, are divisive and discouraging.

In part 3, "Behind the Scenes," a whole chapter is devoted to the critical nature of vision.

A Key Partnership Principle:

 Always remember that what attracts and keeps people committed to a partnership are: 1) a great vision—something they or their organization could never accomplish alone, and 2) seeing results—real, practical progress toward outcomes that provide fulfillment and encouragement. Talking about organization never excites people or sustains vision!

Still, adequate structure and organization are necessary for a partnership to realize its vision. It is probably as bad to *avoid* discussions and decisions about structure as it is to start with them!

Partnership in Practice: One of the great illustrations of commitment to practical, working unity in the Body of Christ has been Billy Graham. Beginning early in his ministry, Dr. Graham insisted that the churches had to work together in the cities where he was called to hold evangelistic crusades. He was convinced that this approach was biblical and that God would bless it. In his earlier years, he was heavily criticized for this, as the crusades brought together churches with such wide-ranging theological and traditional convictions. For Dr. Graham and his team to even consider going to a city, the churches had to come together to issue the invitation. This hurdle of functional unity even at the invitation stage was not always easily reached. Far from it! Often team members worked months with interested lay and church leaders just to get to this level of cooperation. In some cities the churches never got this far. They simply couldn't agree to work together at this level.

But for those that did issue a joint invitation, from this stage forward, broad, growing church and community cooperation and support characterized the crusades—right up through the follow-up stage. For years I have been convinced that one of the key reasons Dr. Graham's ministry has seen such extraordinary blessing is his quiet but relentless commitment to this principle.

Having said that, I will point out that the vast majority of these crusades have drawn Christians in those communities together for a limited period of time to achieve a specific, limited objective. In many cities, churches and other ministries have sought to capture the spirit of cooperation found leading up to and during these crusades. But, few cities have experienced lasting, strategic Kingdom collaboration flowing out of these crusades—partnerships that specifically sought spiritual transformation of the community over a significant period of time.

As in the case of relief and development ministries cited above, moving from a great vision of limited time and scope to a long-term vision of even greater scale is an extreme challenge. Reasons for this are addressed at many points in the book.

As you might expect, partnerships can operate very effectively with widely varying structures. Structures for collaboration range from very informal to very formal.

Some examples:

- Awareness: Individuals or agencies are simply aware of each other (to varying degrees) and communicate or connect on an occasional, ad hoc basis.

- Networks: Multiple individuals or ministries make a conscious effort to develop a means of sharing information (meetings, website, newsletter, etc.) on some topic of common interest and value to each participant.

- Covenant: Individuals or agencies form a simple, verbal agreement to work together toward a common vision. May be linked to a document in which they state their common vision (what they want to do) and values (how they want to accomplish the vision).

- Consensus-Based Partnership: Groups work together with no formal membership, voting rights, financial dues or many similar things often associated with cooperation. To operate this way the partnership has to be a vision-driven group with trust and clear, tangible outcomes outweighing the need for a highly structured organization. They may simply come to consensus on the main points and circulate their agreement in a written summary of the meeting.

- Strategic Alliance: Partners may simply agree on a memo of understanding that deals with issues such as vision and values, the need for a facilitator or facilitation team, how to handle reporting and money, and, possibly, how the group will measure its success or effectiveness.

- Constitution: Ministries, churches, or individuals forge a formal, contractual relationship. Each party obligates itself to certain terms or conditions—placing itself under the authority of the partnership, at least for selected parts of its work.

For more details on the elements in these types of partnerships, see chapter 16, "Effective Partnership Structures—Form Follows Function."

Here is another way to look at the continuum of collaboration:

Who is Involved?	How Are They Organized?	What is the Focus?	Level of Complexity
	Informal Commitment	City	Low
	Network	Local Community	
1. Five Local Churches		Complex Project	
	Consensus Partnership	Country or Language Group	
2. Two Friends	Strategic Alliance	Short Term Project	
3. Multiple Ministries	Constitutional Agreement	Local Neighborhood	High

Case #1: Five local churches are concerned about the young people in their community. They form a consensus-based partnership which requires a moderate level of organization, facilitation, and ongoing attention to see effective outcomes.

Case # 2: Two friends find they are both concerned about the single mothers in their neighborhood. They decide to pray and work together to try to do something. Their organization is very simple—even though the challenge they face may be daunting!

Case #3: More than twenty Christian agencies, all focused on a major unreached people group, form a consensus-based, strategic evangelism partnership. The number of individuals and distinct ministries involved is large. The challenge of forming and sustaining an effective working partnership among so many is complex.

But, particularly in the early stages, *don't think first about structure.* Think and pray about vision. *What* you and others are thinking of doing is critical. An effective structure for *how* you will do it is much more likely to result if you and others share a compelling vision.

Later in the book I discuss in much greater detail ideas and models for structuring your partnership.

Wrapping up the discussion about definitions, *keep in mind:*

I said that throughout the book I affirm that there are many valid forms of Kingdom collaboration. However, I will consistently encourage readers to think *strategically;* to look at the whole challenge, the whole problem, and to think through what resources will be needed to address this challenge. Then find ways, through some kind of collaboration with others, to link all these resources to address the whole challenge. Throughout the book I'll continue to encourage you to look at the whole picture and develop a response that will engage all the available resources. It's that strategic approach that almost always produces the best outcomes and the most satisfying experience.

Note: For the sake of simplicity, throughout the book I will use the generic term "partnership" for all forms of Kingdom collaboration, except where more specific definition or "unpacking" of the particular type of collaboration is vital to understanding or learning more about the "how tos."

But enough about the rather dry topic of definitions, let's move on to far more interesting material, like how God designed us to work—together.

 Share your ideas and response to this chapter, tell your own story, or get connected with more partnership resources at the book's website
www.connectedbook.net

PART TWO
The God Design

4

THE GOD DESIGN—
RELATIONSHIPS

WHOLENESS, UNITY, AND DIVERSITY

Core Idea

God designed men and women to live in harmony, in open, healthy relationships—whether in families or communities. God's design is based on his own nature. Adam and Eve's tragic decision in Genesis destroyed the transparency, trust, unity, and beauty we were designed to share. Their sin produced the roots of fear, division, and darkness that divide people and institutions today—within the church and outside it. Ministry partnerships are only effective and durable as they build trust, work actively at restoring relationships, and celebrate diversity within unity. In doing that, partnerships begin to again reflect the beauty, joy, power, and fulfillment God designed for us.

"Let us make man in our image."

In the early chapters of Genesis, God states his design for us.[1] While each individual was to be distinct, God's design for all of humanity was openness, transparency, and unity in this diverse creation. Adam and Eve, each unique, were to be "one flesh." This oneness reflected the magnificent unity Jesus speaks of when he says, "I and the Father are one."[2]

PARTNERSHIP IN PRACTICE: Franklin had already visited over a dozen ministry leaders working in the city. Some were pastors of churches. Others were leaders of local specialized ministries dealing with youth, the media, and urban issues. While working on other inter-church projects, he had gotten to know many of these leaders personally. A number of pastors in the city had been meeting and praying together for more than two years. But, now they felt an urgency to put feet to their prayers. Their dream was for God's people in the churches to demonstrate the love and power of Christ by really connecting with each other and the needs of the city through some kind of partnership initiative.

The problem was that no one was quite sure where to begin. So Franklin was asked to visit the majority of pastors, one on one, to get their initial thoughts on next steps.

At first he thought it would be an exciting assignment. But a few weeks into the role, Franklin was surprised, disappointed, and unsure of what to do. In talking privately with the pastors and ministry leaders, he found that ministry pride and desire to protect ministry "turf" were widespread. Further, he had uncovered long-standing, unresolved relational problems among several of the Christian leaders that seemed to be real, practical roadblocks to authentically working together.

In short, no sense of unity or common vision existed on which to build. Over coffee, Franklin confided to a friend, "I'm not sure what to do. Honestly, going forward in these circumstances seems unrealistic to me. We'd have to start so far back to deal with so many relational issues before we could ever dream of moving forward. Trying to do anything together in this situation would mean papering over these real problems. That can't be God's way."

Are we surprised at what Franklin found? Probably not. It's a scenario we've all personally encountered or sensed, as we have seen brokenness—in families, in the world around us, and, yes, inside the church.

Restored open relationships are critical to lasting, effective partnerships. So, let's take a brief look at what really happened in the early chapters of Genesis.

God's creation, man, woman, and the natural world, were made in his image. All the elements of creation naturally, beautifully fit together—functioned in harmony. There was trust, freedom, beauty, responsibility, joy, and a positive sense of the value of each part of creation.

Each element in creation had a useful role and received respect because it had been created by God and given to Adam and Eve, the stewards. Adam and Eve were absolutely unique but essentially complementary. Each one's individual wholeness and identity were, ultimately, made complete *in relationship with the other*.

But following Adam and Eve's fateful decision in Genesis 3, *relationships* were destroyed. Consider these five levels.

- God and man, who had previously met and talked openly and freely in the garden, were now alienated. Aware he had broken his trust with God, Adam went into hiding. Man's open relationship with God was destroyed. The haunting words, "Where are you?" (3:9) tell the story.

- Adam, who previously had known no fear, much less shame, now admitted to God that he knew he was naked. Having had his eyes opened to good and evil, Adam had lost the sense of his wholeness, beauty, and value. He looked at his internal "mirror" and decided for the first time that he didn't like what he saw. Man's relationship with himself had been destroyed. "I heard you in the garden, and I was afraid" (3:10) is a telling line.

- In shifting the blame for his own sin to Eve, Adam denied responsibility. Trust between the two was never the same. The pattern established, shortly afterward Cain refused to accept responsibility for Abel's whereabouts and lied to God. Man's relationship with others had been destroyed. The words, "Am I my brother's keeper?" (4:9) have echoed down through history.

- In the created order, Adam and Eve had great responsibility, freedom, and joy. Work, given before the fall, was to be creative and fulfilling. Human reproduction was to be a joy-filled experience. Now, the soil would resist and would yield only at the "sweat of Adam's brow." Childbirth would now be accompanied by cries of pain. Relationship with the created order was destroyed. "You will have to work hard and sweat to make the soil produce" (3:19 GNT) was a far cry from Eden's initial abundance.

- In the garden were two trees. One tree gave eternal life. The other was the source of the knowledge of good and evil. Having broken God's design and eaten of the second tree, man was denied access to the first. In an act of love, God drove Adam and Eve from the garden insuring they would never eat of the Tree of Life and live forever in darkness.[3] Relationship with eternal life in the intimate presence of God had been destroyed. "You were made from soil, and you will become soil again," (3:19b GNT) God said. Then he added the angel with the flaming sword at the edge of the garden ". . . to keep anyone from coming near the tree that gives life." (3:24 GNT)

The results of Adam and Eve's decisions and actions were devastating. The need for restoration was tragically evident. Enter "the Lamb that was slain from the creation of the world" (Revelation 13:8).

You may ask, "What do God's design and the Genesis story of its destruction have to do with ministry partnerships?"

Let's take a closer look.

A Key Partnership Principle:

All durable, effective partnerships are built on trust and whole relationships.

- Trust in the members—starting with the leadership (facilitator or facilitation team). Ultimately, trust must exist among all the participants.

- Trust in the process. The way the partnership is formed and operated sends strong positive or negative signals with far-reaching implications.

- Trust in the partnership's vision, specific objectives, and plans for implementing the objectives.

Note: Chapter 11, "On the Way—Part Two: Formation," suggests key elements of trust and how it cannot only be developed but also maintained at all three of these levels. A helpful diagram on the process of trust building is included there.

With that principle in mind, here is more background that anchors our partnership in the God design.

Jesus suggests that the status of my relationships with others is a key marker of my own heart—of having a right relationship with God. In Luke 10 we read about the lawyer who challenged Jesus regarding how he could be assured of eternal life. Jesus challenged him back, asking what he thought the Scriptures said. The lawyer, in his now famous response, said: "'Love the Lord your God with all your heart, with all your soul, with all your strength, and with all your mind'; and, 'Love your neighbor as you love yourself'" (Luke 10:27 GNT).

Jesus' response was stunningly simple: "You are right . . . do this and you will live" (Luke 10:28 GNT).[4]

When forced into a relational situation, particularly when stress is involved, our true character emerges with remarkable clarity. A dozen people unexpectedly forced into a lifeboat for thirty days find out very soon about each other's real character. The same dozen taken as hostages and held in a tense life-or-death environment for a week face the same reality. Simply put, there's nowhere to hide your "real self."

Working independently in ministry frequently allows us to mask our deepest feelings, qualities, and ambitions. Working in partnership, particularly over months or years, has a way of revealing what we otherwise might want to hide about ourselves *and about our view of others!*

People and ministries simply cannot work together effectively over any length of time without dealing with the relational brokenness. It continues to haunt us from the earliest events in the Garden of Eden.

In quoting the Old Testament's commandments, the lawyer in Luke 10 touched on the heart of the issue: In partnerships we must have open relationships with each other. Faking it, employing trite or pious phrases (often shortcuts to avoid thinking about or discussing the real issues), or dodging the issues some other way ultimately leads to failure. It just won't work. In the end, it all comes out anyway. So, we might as well face up to the issues and deal with them squarely. The God design is always best.

A fascinating factor of the lawyer's response and the Old Testament commandment is that evaluation of our love for our neighbor should be based on knowing and understanding our love for ourselves! In these days of excessive self-absorption, it may seem awkward to suggest, but consider this: In Genesis, it was Adam's relationship with God and his own internal sense of brokenness and nakedness, that sent him into hiding, filled with shame and fear. Adam knew who he was and who he had been, and he had an overwhelming sense that a terrible change had occurred.

The church's emphasis in salvation has often been on getting right with God, never addressing that God wants to restore our sense of internal wholeness. Yes, according to Scripture, we are to love ourselves. Not in a humanistic, narcissistic way, but in a way that understands who we are in Christ, that we've been made in God's image, that we have infinite value, and that we can make a difference in the world.

There are three parts to the love in the God design:

- Wholeness with God
- Wholeness within ourselves
- Wholeness with others

Over the years I've observed hundreds of believers in a wide range of roles. It's my assessment that those who have come to a healthy understanding of *who they are and their own value in Christ* are almost always the most effective in relating to others.

Durable, effective partnerships are always built on authentic approaches that build trusting, open, and restored relationships.

PARTNERSHIP IN PRACTICE: In my role at Interdev, I was asked to lead the Exploration phase of a possible strategic evangelism partnership for a country just emerging from years of Marxism. In the Exploration phase we sought to identify possible participants, their history of ministry in the country, their vision for the future, and the type of work they normally did. (See chapters 10–12 for a full discussion of the typical phases in the life of a durable partnership.)

For decades, the country had been considered essentially impenetrable—except by the power of prayer! Over the preceding ninety years, only a handful of expatriates had lived in the country. Complicating matters, lying just below the surface of Marxism, was the influence of hundreds of years of a powerful, dark, traditional religion.

During the eighteen-month Exploration phase, I traveled to multiple countries and talked with the CEOs of more than a dozen ministries. In many cases the work required multiple visits to each of these agencies. Private, confidential conversations with these leaders revealed a troubling history of brokenness between Christian workers who had any interest in this country. The brokenness was so great that several indicated, "If that individual shows up for any of these discussions, I won't participate." Remember, these were Christians committed to preaching Jesus' power of reconciliation and restoration!

After months of these private discussions, it was finally time to gather the potential ministry leaders. Would God's Spirit point the group to some type of real, functional partnership? Or were the divisions so great that real Kingdom partnership was a hopeless dream?

Round-the-clock prayer teams were established. Seasoned, godly counselors were recruited, briefed, introduced, and made a core part of the meeting's facilitation team. In the daytime, participants explored the potential for working together in the country. Discussions dealt with a host of complex problems and possibilities. In the evenings, despite extraordinary demonic opposition, the counseling/reconciliation teams toiled in sessions of prayer and restoration with ministry leaders—in some cases all night long.

In the end, God brought the group to a breakthrough of consensus on the way forward in partnership. Satan had received a huge setback. But having held the people of this country in his darkness for so long, he wasn't about to give up easily. He continued to haunt the partnership—the facilitators, over subsequent years, constantly having to monitor and address relational issues critical to the partnership's health.

However, had the issue of broken relationships not been faced squarely with sensitivity, love, and firmness, the partnership never would have been launched. Most certainly it would not have been a key part of the extraordinary spiritual power God let loose in this country after 2,000 years of darkness.

This is challenging stuff! Unfortunately, reconciliation is a process far too often avoided by the church. We don't want to deal with the tough, often ugly issues of sin—particularly inside the body of Christ. But, if we're ever to see real breakthroughs, in our own neighborhood, city, or in some distant unreached people group, there is no alternative. The process calls for great intent, courage, and sensitivity.

This story has been repeated over and over, from partnership to partnership. Only the personalities and the intensity of the relational issues vary. Count on it—Satan's trademark of broken relationships is one he vigorously defends.

Now, what are we to make of this? Let me suggest a few things.

- The God design of whole relationships is actually central to any Christian life or any type of Kingdom work.

- Whole, restored, open relationships are critical to an effective, durable partnership.

- The natural tendency for relationships is to drift—from lack of positive attention, to indifference, to misunderstanding, to lack of readiness to admit a problem, to a point at which, even admitting a serious problem, the parties are unwilling or unable to bring about the needed restoration.

- Facilitators or facilitation teams must be ready to take initiative and risk and to address relational brokenness with directness yet sensitivity.

- All of us following Christ are called to a ministry of reconciliation and restoration.

God calls us to *personal* wholeness, transparency, and relational health with him, with ourselves, and with others. But he also calls us to be *active agents of reconciliation with others.* Being a believer is not passive!

Consider these scriptural principles:

- Forget having an open personal relationship with God unless you have an open relationship with your friends and colleagues. Your prayers may go no farther than the ceiling if you're in a broken relationship. Matthew 5:21–24, 18:15–17, 2 Corinthians 2:5–11, and 1 Peter 3:7 point to action.

- The definition of being a part of the "people of God" is that monitoring and acting on relational issues is a central priority. (Colossians 3:12–17)

- As a body of believers, reconciliation and restoration of relationships through the power of Christ is our mission. (2 Corinthians 5:18–19)

This brings me to the next aspect of the God design particularly relevant to partnership development and effectiveness.

RELATIONSHIPS: UNITY AND DIVERSITY

"Different isn't the same as bad," the sociologist said to his class, "It's just *different!*"

The lifeblood of partnerships may be restored, open, healthy relationships. But the heartbeat of every effective, lasting partnership is that it focuses the power of Kingdom diversity in a unified process and vision. Partnerships celebrate the diversity and empower the focused integration of the whole range of available Kingdom resources. All gifts, personalities, individuals, and ministries have potentially valuable roles in a coordinated strategy that is well beyond the potential of any single individual or ministry.

The great power of the God design of unity and diversity can be experienced through an effective partnership in ways that are rarely experienced in other forms of witness.

But isn't it remarkable how, as humans, we gravitate to the familiar—not just in home, habits, food, and recreation—but also in relationships? The tendency to withdraw to our own safe haven of familiarity is powerful.

PARTNERSHIP IN PRACTICE: A charged atmosphere pervaded the first meeting to explore cooperation. There were Lutherans, Pentecostals, Baptists, Episcopalians, Brethren, and independents in the room. From extremely different backgrounds, they all claimed to be committed to the same vision.

Some heads were down, in fear that a photographer would show up. Others were asking themselves, "Who are these people? Can they really be believers?" Still others were secretly saying to themselves, "I've never met with people from backgrounds like this. How will I possibly tell the guys back at the office?" Organizational leaders later admitted that they had wondered, "How will I ever explain this to the home office and our constituency?"

Days later, when God had helped the group build trust and an environment of honesty, all admitted they had never dreamed they could openly communicate in such a diverse group—much less actually accomplish something of lasting value!

The God design in Genesis clearly had diversity at its heart. The plants were different—a mind-boggling, impossible-to-catalogue, array of wondrous diversity! The animals were different—and Adam got to name them! Day and night were different. They became the markers of time. The night sky spoke of staggering diversity in creation. And Eve, though essential companion to Adam and even made of his flesh, was *so* different from him. She "completed" Adam, gave him friendship and human intimacy, and was co-author of the future nations. In man's second generation, Cain and Abel personified diversity: one a hunter, the other a tiller of the soil.

Staggering, remarkable diversity came from the hands of the same Creator—a creativity and diversity that should stimulate worship and wonder for those who acknowledge that Creator!

Now, fast forward from Genesis to the New Testament. Should we be surprised that the pattern of God's diversity and unity continues?

In partnership development and ongoing operation, we find ourselves constantly faced with the tension between our desire for unity in purpose and process and our own highly individual desires—and similar desires on the part of others.

Jesus' remarks, at times seemingly contradictory, point us to this tension, which he understood and which we will always experience.

On familiarity and safe places, he said, "Foxes have holes, and birds have nests, but the Son of Man has no place to lie down and rest" (Matthew 8:20 GNT). But the same Jesus said: "Do not be worried or upset. . . . There are many rooms in my Father's house, and I am going to prepare a place for you" (John 14:1–2 GNT). In short, Jesus understood the value of familiarity and "safety," but he also understood there are some times the mission calls us into places of risk and discomfort.

In pushing people to declare themselves, Jesus said: "Anyone who is not for me is really against me" (Matthew 12:30 GNT). But when Jesus' disciples expressed concern about others not in their group healing in his name, Jesus responded with the opposite perspective: "Don't try to stop him . . . because no one who performs a miracle in my name will be able soon afterwards to say evil things about me. For whoever is not against us is for us" (Mark 9:39–40).

While Jesus called for clear allegiance, his heart and mission were open to the most complete diversity of followers.

Consider these three aspects of diversity in unity:

1. Jesus' readiness to include everyone consistently got him in trouble with the religious establishment of the day. He was ready to listen, accept, and seriously

respond to a staggering range of the human family: lepers, prostitutes, religious leaders, politicians, military personnel, civic authorities, widows, and children. The spiritually, physically, and mentally broken and destitute were all welcome at his feet. His message was for all. There's no record of Jesus' shrinking back from *anyone* who approached him! Whosoever will, may come. What magnificent words!

2. God designed diverse ways of communicating his extraordinary message of love and redemption.

- People would tell the story to others with completely different styles of life and communications (Matthew 11:2–19).

- Some would be assigned completely different but vital roles by the Holy Spirit (1 Corinthians 3:3–11).

- Other individuals not only played different roles but also were part of a bigger plan that played out over a very different timetable (Hebrews 2:2–4).

- The same good news, while for everyone, needed to be addressed to specific audiences in specific ways (Acts 15:1–11).

3. When the church, the body of Christ, began to emerge, it was another illustration of God's penchant for parceling out different roles to different people—all to the same end!

- Romans 12:3–21 outlines the glory of the diversity of the Holy Spirit's gifts within the church and then circles back to our original theme: In this diversity it's all about unity, relationships, and how we treat each other because of Jesus' power and love.

- 1 Corinthians 12:12–31 is a wonderful litany of the God design for unity and diversity in the church, headed by the Lord Jesus. But, again, it's all a prelude to chapter 13, which is the centerpiece of the New Testament's message on relationships and love!

- In Ephesians 4:1–16, the message of unity and diversity in God's design for the church is, again, intertwined with the message of reconciliation, love, and transformed relationships!

We all know that, in one sense, it's just a lot easier to "do your own thing" and not worry about what others are doing, how they are doing it, what our relationships should be, or what impact all this is having on the majority, non-Christian community.

If you have come to the place where the challenge is too great to go it alone and you're serious about partnership, taking time to think, pray, and take action on relationships is a great place to start.

Share your ideas and response to this chapter, tell your own story, or get connected with more partnership resources at the book's website
www.connectedbook.net

5

THE GOD DESIGN—
SPIRITUAL CHANGE
A PROCESS NOT AN EVENT

Core Idea

Scripture and life experience make clear that spiritual change occurs over time. Whether it is a single individual who turns to Christ or a community that is transformed by the power of the gospel, it is a process, not just an event. What appear to be "decisions made in a moment" are almost always based on preceding events and influences. Quick results on tough spiritual issues are very rare. The God design almost always involves multiple people and multiple forms of communication over a period of time. Effective partnerships help raise awareness of this process, can effectively link people committed to a common vision, reveal how the different parts fit together, help monitor progress, and provide encouragement to everyone along the way.

Let me say it straight out. The main points of this and the following chapter contrast sharply with much of traditional Western Christian teaching and practice on strategies for witness and service. When I have shared these ideas there is frequently agreement. Some people even have real "aha" moments of new understanding, and in many cases there is enthusiasm and a sense of encouragement. But the issues discussed in the next few pages are among the many points on which we've allowed our culture to thoroughly influence our assumptions about the gospel and how it is to be lived and presented.

The Western cultural perspective of individualism and quick results powerfully affects our view of Scripture itself, how individuals come to Christ, how discipleship occurs, and how effective strategies of evangelism and service are carried out. Effective partnerships challenge all that.

But let's allow Jesus to open the discussion.

> You have a saying, "Four more months and then the harvest."
> But I tell you, take a good look at the fields; the crops are now
> ripe and ready to be harvested! The one who reaps the harvest
> is being paid and gathers the crops for eternal life; so the one
> who plants and the one who reaps will be glad together. For
> the saying is true, "Someone plants, someone else reaps." I
> have sent you to reap a harvest in a field where you did not
> work; others worked there, and you profited from their work.
> (John 4:35–38 GNT)

This well-known passage is a kind of parenthetical exchange between Jesus and the disciples during the encounter with the Samaritan woman. The first verse or two are often used to inspire us to consider the readiness of hearts all around us and the urgency to share the *good news*. While urgency and motivation are critical, notice how the "now" of the early part of the passage is uniquely balanced with a process-oriented, big picture, longer-term emphasis in the remainder of the passage.

What kind of Kingdom vision is God putting on your heart? Is it the people of your neighborhood, or a vision for the poor and homeless of your city? Maybe it's a desire to take the *good news* to refugees settling in your area. Or you may sense a burning concern for a little-known "unreached people group" somewhere in Asia.

Joining hands in a strategic partnership with others is the best means for realizing the vision and addressing the all-important spiritual process.

More on how all this relates to good partnership practice just a bit later. But keep this in mind: You are not alone. First, God has a heart for the same people. He has already been working in their hearts in various ways—ways you may know nothing about. In addition, events are happening every day in the lives of these people; they are touched by others and by communications of many kinds. You minister to and connect with lives that aren't static but are moving, like a river.[1]

The people you want to reach and serve are on a journey. The different members of a partnership can play many roles, touching lives in your audience in different ways—pointing them to Jesus and ultimately seeing their spiritual maturity. But to realize the full potential of what God can do, we need a new respect for the importance of the roles of others. Realizing that significant change may take time and that participation by others has value can bring us balance and new hope while *never diminishing the urgency of the vision.*

PARTNERSHIP IN PRACTICE: It was a very up-market apartment in a trendy building in a large East Coast city. The reception was crowded with dozens engaged in animated conversation over their drinks and hors d'oeuvres. I was introduced to a striking woman who, in the course of our conversation, said she had recently become a believer. Always interested in how people make the journey into the Kingdom, I asked if she would tell me her story.

She had been raised by religiously indifferent parents. But an aunt who was a committed Christian, with her parents' permission, had taken her to Sunday school and church regularly throughout elementary and junior high school. A memorable part of those Sunday outings was lunch or ice cream after church, she recalled. The aunt reminded her niece that she prayed for her every day. In time, the aunt moved away. But she wrote her niece and kept up the prayers.

Eventually the young woman went to university, obtained an advanced degree, and moved up rapidly in her field. Along the way, she married, but the marriage ended in divorce. In addition, she was having problems on the job. In short, what had been the good life was looking bleak.

"One night in my apartment by myself, I was sitting with a drink in my hand, surfing the television channels. Suddenly I came across Billy Graham preaching at some crusade. I'm not sure why, but I continued to watch. At the end, he looked right at the camera and asked viewers to follow him in saying a prayer to accept Jesus as savior. He said, 'If you're hopeless, Jesus can change your life and give you hope.'"

"Well," she said, "I prayed the prayer and, in short, my life has been changed. Not some magic thing. Just the realization that I was set free, forgiven for my sins and failures, and given hope."

There had been hundreds of conversations between the aunt and her niece, hundreds of prayers by the aunt, and all those Sunday school and church visits followed by lunch or ice cream. There had been all the ongoing letters of support and prayer. Here is the question: Who was the evangelist? Billy Graham, who never met the woman? Or the faithful aunt?

Many lessons can be learned from such stories. You probably know of or have experienced similar stories yourself. How about your own spiritual journey? Sometimes the journey involves dozens of influences we can actually remember: people, books, movies, and circumstances. Whatever your journey, it probably reflects the input of many who have been part of bringing you to where you are today.

A KEY PARTNERSHIP PRINCIPLE:

Significant spiritual change occurs over time. It usually:

• Involves more than one person and more than one form of communication.

• Acknowledges that different people in our audience are at different stages in the spiritual process.

• Allows strategic partnerships to put all available Kingdom resources to work, since different forms of service and witness are appropriate for different members of the audience.

• Means that individuals touched by a ministry at one point on their spiritual journey can be consciously linked or referred on to another because the partnership empowers this kind of coordination and effectiveness.

Jesus' incisive interaction with his disciples in John 4 by the well in Samaria, quoted at the opening of the chapter, serves us well here.

• First, we need to respect the fact that others are or have been involved in the spiritual outcomes we're praying and working for in others.

- Second, recognize that each person has a role that, when faithfully played, will be used by God.

- Third, consider the blessing when we acknowledge the Lord of the harvest actually links those who "sow" and those who "reap" for his glory—each playing a vital role.

A further look at God's communication can be helpful as we work in partnerships. Consider how his communication for spiritual change in individuals and in communities has been and continues to be a process. Understanding this part of the God design is vital but often misunderstood. Clarifying this helps us see the value of effective partnerships—how they can empower God's people working together to deal with an otherwise seemingly impossible Kingdom vision.

Early passages in the New Testament book of Hebrews sum up the history of God's communication with man. They suggest that, through history, many times, in many ways, and with ever-greater specificity, God communicated to us—concluding with Jesus and the coming of the Holy Spirit.

The sequence of events started very early. God communicated directly with Adam and Eve. Those communications, before sin, were open, clear, and full of trust and hope. Man's sin clouded communication with God, resulting in the saga of Noah, the flood, the tower of Babel and, eventually, as the redemption story began to unfold, the call of Abram out of Mesopotamia. With Abram's faith, a remarkable journey began, in which he would become Abraham and the father of a great nation, whose people would be in number "like the stars in the night sky." The journey led to Canaan, to Egypt, to the wilderness, back to Canaan, through priests, Kings, and prophets.

Finally the journey led to the coming of the magnificent promised Lamb of God, the Messiah, Jesus Christ. Here's the passage from Hebrews:

> In the past, God spoke to our ancestors many times and in
> many ways through the prophets, but in these last days he has
> spoken to us through his Son. He is the one through whom
> God created the universe, the one whom God has chosen to
> possess all things at the end.
>
> The message given to our ancestors by the angels was shown
> to be true, and those who did not follow it or obey it received
> the punishment they deserved. How, then, shall we escape

if we pay no attention to such a great salvation? The Lord himself first announced this salvation, and those who heard him proved to us that it is true. At the same time God added his witness to theirs by performing all kinds of miracles and wonders and by distributing the gifts of the Holy Spirit according to his will. (Hebrews 1:1–2, 2:2–4 GNT)

One could imagine that the God who is capable of all things could have chosen at some point in early history to greatly simplify and shorten the process of revelation and redemption. Following man's catastrophic decisions in Eden, and to break through the sin and mess man had made, God could have stepped in and "solved the problem" in pretty short order. But he didn't.

While the history of man's journey played out, God's communication was always true. It became increasingly diverse, increasingly specific, increasingly complete, and increasingly personal. But, while made up of many parts, it was a process, not a single event. In the great saga of Jesus, God finally came *looking like us*. Jesus said that he didn't come to set anything aside but rather to fulfill the Old Testament. Yet here he was, right in front of us! God himself! It was absolutely perfect, complete communication.

But even with Jesus' death and resurrection, there were still more chapters ahead in the process of God's revelation, communication with us, and provision for *our* spiritual journey.

The dramatic fulfillment of Jesus' promise to the disciples about the coming "helper," the Holy Spirit, was played out in Acts 2—the famous scenes of Pentecost. Standing before the huge crowd, now pretty shaken and confused with the amazing events that were underway, Peter put matters in perspective when he said that they should not be fearful or confused but, instead, joyful. These developments were something God had planned in his salvation communication strategy all along. In making his point, Peter quoted the famous passage from the prophet Joel:

> This is what I will do in the last days, God says:
> I will pour out my Spirit on everyone.
> Your sons and daughters will proclaim
> my message;
> your young men will see visions,
> and your old men will have dreams.
> Yes, even on my servants, both men and women,

I will pour out my Spirit in those days,
and they will proclaim my message.
I will perform miracles in the sky above,
And wonders on the earth below.
(Acts 2:17–19a GNT)

By now, you are likely asking yourself, "What in the world does this have to do with partnership? This is old history. Jesus has come. The Holy Spirit is with us today. What difference does this make in the everyday strategy of working with others in partnership to touch people's lives with Jesus' power and love?"

Go with me just a bit further. I think it will become evident how all this ties together. As it does, I think you'll be as excited about the God design as I and others involved in the partnership movement have become.

For a long time, the church has accepted that God communicates in many ways and, through these communications, gives individuals an opportunity to respond.

In Romans 1, the Apostle Paul suggests that God is *always* communicating—*always* drawing us to himself. Only our sin blinds us, confuses our minds, and hardens our hearts. Romans states that *no one* has an excuse because if eyes are open and hearts receptive *God can be known*. It is a stunning statement.

Ever since God created the world, his invisible qualities, both
his eternal power and his divine nature, have been clearly
seen; they are perceived in the things that God has made. So
those people have no excuse at all! (Romans 1:20 GNT)

Theologians call it general revelation. Simply put, God's eternal and invisible character can be "decoded" through his visible creation! Or, said in reverse, God's visible and transient (according to Revelation) creation is a giant decoding system for man to see and come to understand God's eternal and invisible character. Heady stuff![2]

But in his grace, God does not rely on just such general revelation. He does not even rely on the remarkable kaleidoscopic array of Old Testament witness.

Always gracious, always taking the initiative in redemption, God makes the ultimate sacrifice to demonstrate his love. He sends his own son. He sends a messenger that looks like us, is tempted like us, eats and sleeps like us, and, yet, is transcendent. Then God complements creation and the magnificent work of Christ by giving us further resources through the ongoing presence of the Holy

Spirit. And, finally, empowered by all this, Jesus *sends us*, in his power, as his representatives, out into the world (Matthew 28:19–20). Now we both *carry* the message and *are* the message! As the Apostle Paul describes:

> All this is done by God, who through Christ changed us from
> enemies into his friends and gave us the task of making others
> his friends also. (2 Corinthians 5:18 GNT)

So where does this get us? And how does all this relate to effective strategic partnerships? Here's a kind of recap of the thoughts to help us focus:

- God may "reveal" himself to us in a memorable event or moment. He's done it millions of times. He will do it today with many. But God's typical pattern is to communicate with us over time, giving us many ways to hear, learn, and respond.

- God uses many forms of communication to help us see, hear, and understand. He's a multi-media communicator! Think of rainbows in the sky, burning bushes, talking donkeys, still small voices, plagues, pillars of fire and cloud, miracles, voices from heaven, prophets, and the Scriptures themselves. His creativity is extraordinary!

- God has given his church today a remarkable diversity of voices, gifts, and ways to communicate his power and love.

- When praying for God's work in a community, a city, an ethnic group, or on an overseas mission field, durable partnerships, operating over time, can help coordinate and make the many channels of God's communication far more effective than if we all just "do our own thing."

Let's be honest. Particularly in the West, we want simple solutions and quick results. Even in our personal financial planning, professionals are always urging us to resist trying to get rich quick. Rather, we're encouraged to take the longer-term view, to "buy and hold." Not surprisingly, the desire for immediate results pervades every nook and cranny of our thinking. Its functional influence on our view of redemption is powerful, whether we're praying for an individual life, restoration of a great city, or freedom through the *good news* for a Satan-bound unreached people group. We want the results now.

The combination of our desire for quick results and the Western tendency toward individualism has created frustration, ineffective strategies, and unrealistic expectations. As a result, millions have yet to even hear of Jesus, much less give their lives to him! Individualism means you go it alone, ignoring or minimizing the value of others and the creative roles they could play. Desire for quick results means we make unreasonable demands on people and the decisions involved in their journey from darkness to light.

Why is it important to understand that real, lasting spiritual change is almost always a process, not just an event? Because life is a journey. Our savior, Jesus, "even though he was God's Son . . . *learned* through his sufferings to be obedient." (Hebrews 5:8 GNT, emphasis added) On that journey, partnerships help God's people work together, celebrate each other's roles, and witness to Jesus' ability to make us truly human—in relationship.

Bruce Barton, one of America's advertising copy writing legends and a founder of the ad agency Batten, Barton, Durstin, and Osborne, wrote a book, now out of print, titled, *The Man Nobody Knows*. It was Barton's effort to look, as a layman, at Jesus' communications through the eyes of a modern, professional communications specialist. Here is my paraphrase of a simple but powerful illustration from Barton:

How do you get on a moving train? Do you approach it from right angles? At best you'll be embarrassed. At worst you'll be injured. No, the only way to get on a moving train is to come alongside, approximate the speed of the train and, then, all you have to do is step on.[3]

Barton's point is powerful and simple. In our effort to share Christ, we often:

- Ignore the fact that the train is already moving.

- Appear to care less what direction it's taking.

- In effect, ask the individual we're hoping to influence "to get off the train" so we can talk on our familiar turf, in terms familiar to us.

Of course "today is the day of salvation." Of course the message is urgent. Of course it is vital that we urge people to make a decision to turn *from* their old ways and *to* a new life in Christ.

In a metaphor that is foreign to city folks today but was clearly understood in New Testament times, Jesus introduced the imagery of the farm worker, the planter, in Matthew 13. It is a parable about the process of planting seeds and the types of "ground" (hearts) the seed falls on. But in the passage about the harvest at the beginning of this chapter, John 4:34–38, Jesus turned the metaphor into a means for understanding our strategic roles in working together—under his direction. In it he summarized how he and the Holy Spirit work in individual lives: some plant, some water, and some reap. Each one is doing God's work. Each *is important.* And, standing around his throne someday, they *will rejoice together!*

Jesus outlined the principles of spiritual change; then others elaborated on them in other sections of Scripture—particularly the apostle Paul. The diagram below helps graphically illustrate the process of spiritual change that is suggested in the passages we are examining.

**Evangelism / Discipleship
Process Not Event**

GROWTH OF CHURCH

- Active in Evangelism
- Faithful Life Bearing Fruit
- Growing Maturity
- Babe on Milk

GROWTH IN CHRIST

- - - - - - - - - - - - - - - - -

POINT OF COMMITMENT

- - - - - - - - - - - - - - - - -

- Reaping
- Watering
- Planting
- Stone Clearing
- General Revelation

DOES NOT KNOW CHRIST

At the bottom of the diagram are the early stages—the stone clearing and the planting. Further up is the watering. Still further up are the reaping and discipleship stages. Some may complain that the diagram is far too simplistic. I contend that, while the journey may be complex and extend over a great period of time for some, in any audience we are seeking to influence with the love and power of Christ, these key elements are always present. Subsets may be proposed, further refinement of the elements can be added, but, in the end, being aware of *and strategically taking these basic elements into consideration* is a major challenge and a discipline all too often ignored.

Effective partnerships link everyone in the process—each of us using our gifts, being faithful, and celebrating the joy of being part of God's plan.

Of course, God's general revelation, referred to earlier in this chapter (Romans 1:19–20), continues throughout all this—if the person has eyes to see and a heart to understand. All efforts we make to share the love and nature of Christ should take advantage of or build on the powerful, self-evident revelations God makes of himself every day he faithfully keeps the sun coming up over the horizon!

By the way, the church usually prefers to invest her resources in activities dealing with the middle to upper half of the diagram. Why? Because that's where

1) you can see the "results" and

2) existing Christians can grow in Christ, have fellowship, and "enjoy" the blessings of the Christian family.

The bottom half of the diagram is where the going is tough, often with little visible results.

In the next chapter, we look at other diagrams that help unpack this idea of spiritual change as a process. They also illustrate how effective partnerships are ideally suited to empower this kind of process, realizing the greatest impact in the shortest period of time.

But one more look at the New Testament's agricultural metaphor:

From the parable of the planter and Jesus' use of the metaphor with the disciples in John 4, the Apostle Paul takes the image a step further. In the church at Corinth, he was faced with factions who favored one preacher or teacher over another. Here was Paul's response:

> When one of you says, "I follow Paul," and another, "I follow
> Apollos"—aren't you acting like worldly people? After all,
> who is Apollos? And who is Paul? We are simply God's
> servants, by whom you were led to believe. Each one does
> the work which the Lord gave him to do: I planted the seed,
> Apollos watered the plant, but it was God who made the plant
> grow. The one who plants and the one who waters really do
> not matter. It is God who matters, because he makes the plant
> grow. There is no difference between the one who plants and
> the one who waters; God will reward each according to the
> work each has done. For we are partners working together for
> God, and you are God's field. (1 Corinthians 3:4–9 GNT)

Tough words. But from this passage we see several things.

The mother who prays for her children as she washes dishes, the godly teacher who acts and speaks like Christ in the classroom, and the individual who "calls for the decision," whether over a cup of coffee or from a platform in a stadium, are all important. Everyone is part of God's plan of evangelization and salvation. All should be celebrated and encouraged in faithfully carrying out their God-given roles. And—great news—all will rejoice together in the harvest!

Particularly striking and reassuring is that remarkable line, "There is no difference between the one who plants and the one who waters; God will reward each according to the work each has done." (3:8 GNT)

So we see that the real issue is *faithfulness*. Are we doing everything we can, in the power of God's Spirit, to put our assets, our gifts to best use in his work in helping others come to know him or grow in him?

We know from passages like Romans 12, 1 Corinthians 12, and Ephesians 4 that the Holy Spirit has distributed a wondrous range of gifts among God's people. The apostle Paul described Apollos, himself, and God as partners—using the gifts the Holy Spirit had given them to see Christ released to the fullest in the life of each Corinthian believer.

Effective partnerships of God's people, whether in your neighborhood or in some technically complex international radio and television strategy, empower us to join hands, acknowledge each other's roles, plan for the sowing, watering, reaping, and discipling, and actively monitor how well the different elements are working together.

PARTNERSHIP IN PRACTICE: For hundreds of years the tribal group had been Islamic. For nearly a hundred of those years, pioneer missionaries had faithfully shared the good news. Yet only a scattered handful had believed. While working in the country, a Christian organization agreed with the government to help drill vitally needed wells in the villages, many remote, of this tradition-rich tribe. On the edge of the desert, water was critical. Throughout their history, these people had had to hand carry water, often polluted, for hours each day. This water, from rivers or other secondary sources, kept them alive.

It was a huge, challenging project. But when it was complete, wells were operating in hundreds of villages. Village leaders testified, "The traditional Muslim leaders only wanted our money and a share of our crops. You Christians have brought us the most important thing we've ever needed—water."

But when the Christian leader of this project was interviewed, he said, "Some in my own organization kept asking, 'Where is the evangelism in your project?'" He went on to say, "I thought I was doing evangelism all along!"

Just about the time the well drilling project was complete, a partnership of over a dozen international and local Christian ministries was born for this tribal group. Today, seven or eight years after the launch of this partnership, an international prayer initiative supports the partnership; the Jesus Film is complete and in wide circulation; the New Testament is finished and has been published; literature production is being coordinated; literacy is being taught, empowering education and Scripture reading; local-language radio programs are on the air; and clinics are meeting physical needs.

A decade after the well drilling began, the partnership is helping coordinate a wide range of Christian service and witness. In a wonderful turn of events, long-term Christian missionaries are moving into those same villages to live there and provide vital educational and agricultural services and witness in the name of Christ. The credibility given to the gospel by the wells opened doors. More of these tribal people are turning to Christ, and a small church is beginning to develop.

Looking back, it is now clear that the faithful, often lonely, work of drilling wells in extreme heat and hardship not only gave these people water to live each day, but was a God step on the journey to opening their hearts to the eternal, living water of his life.

These people are turning to Christ as a result of a process through which God revealed his love through many—over time. And all in the partnership, those praying around the world, those supporting from home, and those working in the field, look forward to rejoicing together when, in faith, together with the majority of this tribe, they will all stand around Jesus' throne singing praises to the Lamb!

Take a moment and think about your own vision. Even though the circumstances may be sharply different, do elements of this story parallel your own situation? All Kingdom visions involve trying to encourage spiritual change, a spiritual journey. Your vision or project is no different. What can you learn and apply from this story?

Spiritual change is a process. Frequently, different people with different gifts, often at different times, are involved in that process. It's the God design. Effective partnerships integrate the pieces to address the whole challenge. They acknowledge the different places members of the audience may be at in their spiritual journey, help identify the different gifts available, work out ways the elements can be linked together, encourage everyone to be part of monitoring progress, and share good news of spiritual progress.

As we conclude this chapter, a final, critically important note needs to be sounded.

No amount of brilliant planning, strategy, or coordinated, partnership-based execution is sufficient in itself. Healthy, effective partnerships take great energy, commitment, quality work, and tenacity. But hundreds of times I've had to remind myself and my colleagues that that kind of effort isn't enough.

"Without prayer and the work of the Holy Spirit, all such efforts can crumble between our fingers or be nothing more than 'a noisy gong or a clanging bell'" (1 Corinthians 13:1 GNT).

When faced with the greatest challenges, Jesus spent long nights in prayer. He spoke and acted only as he heard the Father speak and saw the Father act (John 5:17–47). Jesus reminded his disciples, when they tried and failed to represent him, that the greatest challenges can only be addressed by prayer and fasting (Matthew 17:14–21).

We must employ the highest level of discipline, make the most cogent case, show the greatest compassion, and develop and carry out the most durable, effective partnership strategy. But spiritual change that brings an individual from darkness into light and washes away sin is solely the domain of the Holy Spirit. Anything else is short-term manipulation, not spiritual transformation.

> It was not because of any good deeds that we ourselves had done, but because of his own mercy that he saved us, through the Holy Spirit, who gives us new birth and new life by washing us. God poured out the Holy Spirit abundantly on us through Jesus Christ our Savior, so that by his grace we might be put right with God and come into possession of the eternal life we hope for. This is a true saying. (Titus 3:5–8a GNT)

Our partnerships will only have lasting, eternal significance as they are rooted in prayer and an awareness that our planning and work can, ultimately, only be empowered by the Holy Spirit's work—in our lives and the lives of those we seek to reach and serve.

 Share your ideas and response to this chapter, tell your own story, or get connected with more partnership resources at the book's website
www.connectedbook.net

6

THE GOD DESIGN—
UNDERSTANDING
LIFE-CHANGE DECISIONS

Core Idea

We've seen that spiritual change is a journey, not an event. Life-changing spiritual decisions may appear to occur in a moment, but they are usually composed of a variety of elements that are also related and call for God's people to work together. Partnerships can help link people at various stages of the journey. Any audience we are seeking to reach or serve for Christ is made up of certain predictable elements. The journey an individual member of the audience takes toward Christ is similarly made up of predictable elements. Understanding these elements, widely documented in Scripture, can transform the effectiveness of a strategic partnership.

In the previous chapter we looked at the idea that God's communication, in history and in individual lives, is a process, not an event. While a person may acknowledge Christ in a defining, watershed "aha" moment, getting to that point is always a process, whether the person or an observer is aware of it or not. And, most certainly, that person's future growth in Christ-likeness will also be an unrelenting process.

Using Jesus' agricultural metaphors from Matthew 13 and John 4, here is the diagram we introduced in the last chapter.

Evangelism / Discipleship
Process Not Event

GROWTH OF CHURCH

↑
• Active in Evangelism
• Faithful Life Bearing Fruit
• Growing Maturity
• Babe on Milk

GROWTH IN CHRIST

- - - - - - - - - - - - - - - - - -

POINT OF COMMITMENT

- - - - - - - - - - - - - - - - - -

↑
• Reaping
• Watering
• Planting
• Stone Clearing
• General Revelation

DOES NOT KNOW CHRIST

To help us further understand why working together in partnership is important, let's add another dimension to this diagram. This dimension is clear in Scripture, critical to our understanding of the spiritual change process, and central to effective partnerships.

Take a random sample of the audience you are seeking to reach or serve for Christ. Whether it is a student group in the colleges and universities of your area or a remote tribal group, the change you have in mind *almost certainly involves a journey or process in the thinking of the audience*. The work and prayer you and your colleagues undertake is targeted at helping the audience move *from* one attitude, lifestyle, belief, or action *to* another.

If you check audience attitudes toward the basic ideas you are proposing, you will almost always find three broad categories of response:

- The resistant or antagonistic. They are the ones who most oppose your ideas. While a person's negative position may be born out of genuine conviction, frequently these people have the most invested in their current way of living or thinking. Often they appear to have the most to lose if change occurs. They may lose power, prestige, security, or privileges. Realize, too, that frequently these individuals mask their real attitudes and respond with patronizing, false messages of affirmation. Think of the Pharisees and Jewish leaders of Jesus' time.

- The indifferent. They are likely the majority of the audience. Along with others in their group, they simply "go along" with the belief or lifestyle because they, their family, or their peer group always has. Maybe life hasn't been very easy or all they wanted. Some may say it hasn't been all that bad. But in any case, they don't see any need to "rock the boat." Besides, the possibilities of real change are remote. Who wants to take the chance of trying to change? They already know how the system works, and though they may complain about things, they have little motivation to risk change. Think of those who heard Jesus in the synagogues, by the seashore, or on the hillside. People may have found him interesting, possibly fascinating, in some cases even compelling. But with no sense of urgency, they never took that step of faith to follow him—into a new world.

- Seekers. These are individuals, possibly small groups within the larger group, who are dissatisfied. The lifestyle, the beliefs, the "system" of living and thinking that surrounds them has not met their needs. Those may be physical, emotional, or psychological needs or other real, powerful motivators. Frequently these people have the least to risk if they try something new. Often their perceived need gives a sense of urgency to their search. In short, they are ready, if not eager, to hear about alternatives. In the best of cases, they are actively looking for change. Think of Nicodemus, the Syrophoenecian woman, the leper in Mark 1, the thief on the cross who believed, and a couple of dozen others like them in the four Gospels.

- Believers. Of course, there are individuals who, possibly even secretly, have already made a decision to follow the new pattern of thinking or living. In some cases they have declared their decision and have already moved on to associate with a group of people who hold the same new beliefs or who are living a different lifestyle. Think of the twelve, the seventy, those who made up the new church in Jerusalem, Antioch, and, eventually, around the rim of the Mediterranean.

Now, let's take the same earlier diagram and see how these four categories of people usually align with the spiritual process.

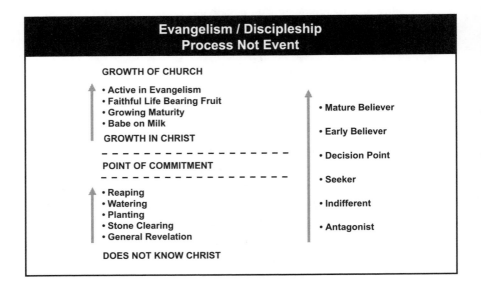

**Evangelism / Discipleship
Process Not Event**

GROWTH OF CHURCH
- Active in Evangelism
- Faithful Life Bearing Fruit
- Growing Maturity
- Babe on Milk

GROWTH IN CHRIST

- - - - - - - - - - - - - - - -

POINT OF COMMITMENT

- - - - - - - - - - - - - - - -

- Reaping
- Watering
- Planting
- Stone Clearing
- General Revelation

DOES NOT KNOW CHRIST

- Mature Believer

- Early Believer

- Decision Point

- Seeker

- Indifferent

- Antagonist

No surprises, right? It is just as you expected. With the antagonists and the resistant, you have to patiently "clear the stones" out of the field. With the indifferent, you have to patiently "plant" and "water." With the seekers, there is the opportunity to "reap" the harvest—help them make the decision for change. With the believers, there's the joyful possibility of helping them grow in their new Christ-based life of faith.

A KEY PARTNERSHIP PRINCIPLE:

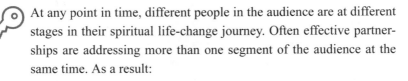

At any point in time, different people in the audience are at different stages in their spiritual life-change journey. Often effective partnerships are addressing more than one segment of the audience at the same time. As a result:

- We need to focus some part of our strategy on antagonists and the resistant while at the same time making provision to challenge the seekers to action and disciple those who have become believers.

- We begin to see more clearly that everyone's role in the partnership is important.

- Linking the work of different people or diverse ministries together to address these segments of the audience not only makes sense, it greatly expands our ministry capacity.

- The big vision or long-range objective(s) of the partnership can be kept clearly in mind while addressing and seeing breakthroughs on vital, intermediate steps.

You and your partnership colleagues:

- May be trying to bring Kingdom-valued reform to prisons and the lives of ex-offenders.

- May have a vision for providing Kingdom-minded tutors for every scholastically challenged child in your school district.

- May have a vision for coordinating all the evangelism and discipleship literature being produced for a major international language group with only a few believers.

Think about it. In every one of these cases you will encounter antagonistic, resistant people, many who are indifferent, some who are actively looking for change, and some who may already be convinced. With some you may need to do real stone clearing. With others you'll need to plant or water the ideas. Others may be ready for reaping. There may be some who really need to be *discipled* or encouraged. Keeping these factors in mind as a partnership will play a big part in realizing your vision *and* generating a sense of accomplishment among your partners!

From your own experience, keep in mind something else you already intuitively know: Circumstances in people's lives are not static—changes are occurring constantly. Sometimes the changes are minor, sometimes catastrophic!

- Despite intense need, some people may never open their hearts to change.

- Some individuals make the spiritual journey slowly, coming to faith or commitment to the new belief or lifestyle only after years of consideration.

- It is also possible that circumstances may move an individual from being an antagonist to a seeker "overnight"—or at least in a very short period of time.

Partnership Case Study: Apply the Principles

Let's say you and some others have been working on a vision to serve and reach "at-risk" kids in your community. Some are runaways, some are living on the streets, some are into the drug culture, many are in tough home circumstances, some are in gangs, some in trouble with the police and other authorities, and some just aren't making it in school.

You face a real challenge. You have to try to connect and build confidence not only with the kids, but with other groups who are involved: the police, school authorities, parents, community youth agencies, local churches, and the list goes on. These people are gatekeepers, rule setters, authority figures, resource providers, and, in some cases, strong turf defenders! In a later chapter we discuss in detail and make practical suggestions about how to identify, communicate with, and bring these other groups along as allies—even resources.

But for a moment, think just about the kids themselves. Think about the two diagrams above. You know that when you look at all the kids, some are hard, resistant, and possibly even antagonistic. Many are just going along. Indifferent. Yet, there are some who *know* they're in trouble, know they've got problems, and, in a trusting relationship, would welcome help.

You and the others interested in these kids realize that no single ministry, church, agency, much less a lone individual can take on the challenge. It's too complicated, too big, calls for too many resources, and requires too much staying power. There's only one answer: form a durable partnership that looks at the *whole problem* and tries to mobilize *all available Kingdom resources* in the community. In chapter 10, "On The Way: Exploration," you'll see that in the early stages you don't have to address *all* the issues or have *everyone* involved. In those early stages, limited, high-value, achievable objectives are vital!

As you think about the kids and possible strategies to serve and reach them with Christ's love, the diagrams in this chapter may help you analyze the situation, think creatively, and prayerfully set near- to medium-term objectives that will really make a difference.

Again, keep in mind: Your partnership doesn't have to try to reach all of the kids initially. Even if you break the challenge down by age, geography, or some other key factor, consider that you may want to focus on "antagonists" or, possibly, "seekers." As you learn to work together, gain experience, and begin to see progress, you will naturally begin to see new or additional areas for the partnership to serve.

PARTNERSHIP IN PRACTICE: In a West Coast city, a partnership involved a commercial radio station, a book club designed for seekers, a network of lay Christian counselors, a group of local churches, and hundreds of ordinary believers in the region who were committed to an innovative approach to evangelism. Their objective? See adult members of the community, primarily in the 25–45-year-old age range, come to know Christ and get integrated into local fellowships.

The partnership saw the radio station and the individual believers as working together to do "stone clearing, planting, and watering." The book club was designed to facilitate "watering" with the "indifferent" and "seekers." It offered listeners attractive paperback books on current topics with more information about Jesus, allowing them to think and consider matters further as they read at their leisure.

The counseling service was designed to be available to seekers who knew they had issues and wanted to talk. Though there was never any pressure, callers to the counseling service knew they were going to hear about God and how he could make a difference in their lives. After the initial call, they had the option of continuing to make contact by phone or meeting with a counselor in person. It was frequently in these phone calls or personal counseling sessions that "reaping" occurred.

The local churches were seeker friendly and ready to welcome and help individuals who emerged through the various other communications channels of the partnership.

By the way, the radio station was no ordinary Christian station. It offered adult, middle-of-the-road pop music combined with news and sports. It was a commercial station supported by advertising. There were no traditional Christian programs or explicitly Christian music. But every hour the station carried short, ten- to thirty-second "God spots" that talked about life, personal challenges, and how Jesus can make a difference. About every three to four hours, one of these "God spots" was replaced with a commercial for the counseling service, which was called "People Who Care."

Late one night a man called the counseling service. His first words were, "My best friend, a stock broker, died today of a brain hemorrhage. He was only 34. What does God have to say about that?"

It turns out that the caller, a young, successful banker, had been listening to the radio station for over a year. He reported hearing the "God spots" but never having really thought much about them. Yes, he had requested one of the books offered by the book club—one on a famous athlete who was a believer and who told his story in a best-selling paperback. But until his friend died that day, life had seemed pretty good. Everything was status quo.

Later, in personal counseling, the man made a commitment to Christ and got into a local church, where he began to grow spiritually.

In the meantime, the radio station and the ordinary believers in the community who were committed to the initiative continued to plant and water with people on the moving train of their lives.

We will come back to these themes again and again throughout the book. But, finally, another diagram may help us see that spiritual change is a process.

The components shown in this diagram are almost *always* part of the decision-making process whenever an individual makes a significant life change. And every effective partnership strategy acknowledges and takes these stages into consideration.

Stages of Life Change Decisions

1. Information

2. Reflection

3. Reinforcement

4. Motivation

5. Conviction

6. Decision

7. Action

8. Recommitment[1]

I unpack the meaning of these steps in more detail in the next pages.

The diagram on the opposite page helps illustrate how each element leads into the next, particularly as a person makes key, life-changing decisions.

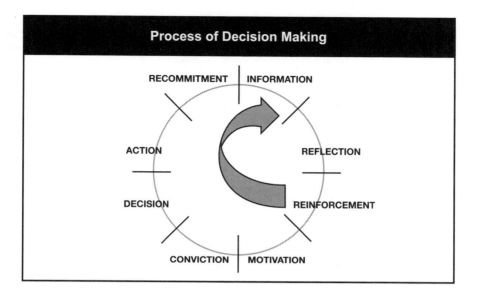

Process of Decision Making

RECOMMITMENT · INFORMATION
ACTION · REFLECTION
DECISION · REINFORCEMENT
CONVICTION · MOTIVATION

Caution: Any time you try to describe a human journey of the heart, mind, and spirit with a diagram, you are immediately on questionable ground! The categories are not the same for all; the transitions between at least some of the stages in the journey are frequently imperceptible—even to the one on the journey. By their nature, diagrams are cold, impersonal, and seemingly formulaic. The issues, feelings, and other powerful forces at work in a person's life on such a journey are anything but cold and formulaic! Throughout this book I use diagrams only to clarify the elements of a particular subject. This may help us pray and work together more sensitively and effectively. Having raised this caution, fifty years of field experience, a lifetime of studying "The Book," and consistent interaction with others on the journey verify that the main point being made here is absolutely valid and should be taken into active consideration as partnerships work together.

Let me briefly elaborate on each one of these stages in the journey. As you work through these, refer back to the diagram and think about your own life or the lives of some of the individuals your partnership is seeking to reach and serve.

1. Information: To make any important decision you must have *some* data on which to base your decision. Even leaps of faith are made in reference to what the individual already knows, has experienced, or thinks is true.

2. Reflection: Before making a decision, an individual thinks about or reflects on the data he or she already has that is relevant to the decision at hand. This reflection takes into consideration what we know, what we have experienced and, frequently, *who* we know and the potential relational implications.

3. Reinforcement: You may hear an outrageous story on the radio one morning and not believe it. But if later you also read the same story in the newspaper and then have a person you trust relate the same news to you personally, you begin to take the story more seriously. Three independent sources sharing basically the same story make it more believable. Friends may play an important role. A peer group can be particularly influential.

Note that the diagram suggests an individual may cycle through the information, reflection, and reinforcement stages repeatedly, possibly over many years, before motivation (sense of need) and conviction move him or her to action.

4. Motivation: Without motivation, individuals remain, at best, indifferent to change—to God's message. But with the right motivation, they can move to an active seeking mode. A sense of personal need moves people to consider actually making a change. Building on the information and experience they have to date, conviction of the Spirit, physical need, family problems, employment crisis, or other personal needs finally bring them up short.

5. Conviction: An individual comes to believe (have enough faith) that the proposed change will actually make a difference. Without conviction, motivation will never become action.

6. Decision: Having the information, the motivation, and the conviction, it is time to move—to actually act. Take the risk, the leap of faith. Conscious consideration about whether to act may take a long time. In other cases the commitment to action may appear to occur almost on the spur of the moment.

7. Action: This is when the talk becomes the walk. Words become deeds. All that has gone before, the invisible world of processing experience and information, is now translated into tangible action.

8. Recommitment: All of us, having made a serious commitment, usually revisit that decision again and again, reviewing and reaffirming the choice we have made. This revisiting the decision we have made and action taken usually has the effect of strengthening our resolve. In spiritual decisions, further exposure to Scripture, the affirmation of fellow believers, and the confirming work of the Holy Spirit in our lives powerfully strengthen the commitment we've made.

All effective partnerships seek change. We hope to see people, individually or as a group, move from one way of thinking and/or living to another. For that change to occur, *everyone* in the audience will move through these stages. They may or may not be consciously aware of the stage-by-stage nature of the journey. For those of us seeking guidance through communication, prayer, service, or other means, it will take great Spirit-directed sensitivity to be aware of what's happening in our audience.

All this brings us to the helpful reminder: In eternal, Kingdom-oriented decision making, we may be given the opportunity to play a significant part in a person's progress along this journey. But in the end, *it is the work of the Holy Spirit that brings real value to our efforts, touches the inner heart, and changes lives.* Anything else would find us squarely in a program of propaganda and manipulation.

Look back at the diagram on the process of evangelism earlier in the chapter. For individuals to move from antagonism or resistance to being active seekers open to taking action, they will, eventually, go through the first seven of these steps: Information to Action.

So, how is this relevant to your partnership? I'm certainly not suggesting you can know where everyone in your audience is in terms of spiritual change and decision making. Only God knows that. But we can use these tools to help us think and pray more effectively about reaching and serving our audience; help us identify various elements of our audience—their attitudes to change and potential for spiritual *decision making*; help us ask what may be the most effective strategy in communicating with them; help us identify which of our partnership's resources are best suited to communicating or serving people at different points in the process; and help us coordinate our efforts—acknowledging and celebrating the different roles different partners can play.

Finally, three brief stories from the Gospels illustrate that the people in your audience are on a journey, and their decisions are influenced by many factors.

Nicodemus (John 3:1–21, 7:50–53, 19:38–42)

Though best known for his nighttime encounter with Jesus in John 3, Nicodemus' story is a classic illustration of the spiritual journey we have been considering.

When we meet him in John 3, he is clearly not antagonistic or indifferent; he's actively seeking truth. But it is equally clear that his fear of his peer group, the Jewish religious establishment, requires his contact with Jesus to take place under the cover of darkness. Jesus challenges him on all the information he has as a Jewish religious leader, suggesting that it will take something other than his current understanding to enter the Kingdom.

The question remains: "Is Nicodemus really open to change? Is he ready to move on? Will he actually *act* on what he knows and his growing awareness/understanding of the truth?"

When Nicodemus next appears in John 7, he has moved out from under the cover of darkness and, *in his peer group*, is actually defending Jesus. Based on the categories suggested in this chapter, it seems we can make a fairly convincing case that, for Nicodemus to take this professional risk, he already has or is moving toward real conviction of a belief in Jesus.

Remember, these incidents did not take place back to back. A considerable amount of time was involved. Nicodemus had a lot of history before he ever met or even heard of Jesus of Nazareth. Then, from John 3 through the exchange in John 7 and the events of John 19, Nicodemus probably saw Jesus many times, heard him speak, watched him perform miracles, and observed his encounters with the Pharisees and Sadducees.

In addition, hundreds of stories about Jesus were floating around Israel, and particularly Jerusalem, during his three years of public ministry. Apart from his direct contact, Nicodemus was exposed to Jesus' life through countless conversations with friends, colleagues—over meals in homes, at cafes, and in the more formal sessions of the religious leadership. In short, he had a *lot of exposure to many messages* about the one claiming to be the Messiah.

Finally, in John 19, Nicodemus goes public—identifying with Jesus by teaming with Joseph of Arimathea to remove Jesus' body from the cross and place it in the tomb. His initial fear-driven spirit has been replaced by a commitment and belief in Jesus so strong that he is prepared to accept any downside implications within his peer group. Remember, it was Nicodemus' colleagues who put Jesus on the cross!

What motivated Nicodemus to make this journey? He moved from a safe place as a member of the establishment to one that now, at the very least, meant he would be considered a dissenter and an embarrassment within his peer group.

Unlike many of the other personal encounters with Jesus recorded in the four gospels, it looks like Nicodemus' journey really was a journey of the mind and heart. To all appearances he had a comfortable life. He had, apparently, a nagging sense or call in his heart to know and live the *full truth*. It was a motivation powerful enough that, when combined with the compelling life message of Jesus, Nicodemus' spirit said "yes" to the Spirit.

The Leper (Mark 1:40–45)

He lived by a strict social code. Apart from the wretchedness of his physical condition, he was a lonely outcast—on the dark fringes of society. Humanly, you could sum up his case as hopeless. Then Jesus came to town.

But the man was a Jew. And as a Jew, he knew the law and the tradition of great prophets who had great power. He had heard a lot of the same stories that Nicodemus had heard. The news about Jesus traveled fast and far over the Palestinian countryside.

In contrast to Nicodemus, who seemed to have much to lose if he cast his lot with Jesus, the leper had nothing to lose. His only way to go was up! In short, the risk was low and the potential gain was enormous.

All three accounts of this story, in Matthew, Mark, and Luke, say the man was proactive. He came out of the crowd (you can imagine the crowd shrinking back from the leper) and threw himself down in front of Jesus and begged for help.

So we have a man with a lot of information. He's given the information considerable thought. His conception of Jesus' healing powers has been reinforced many times through countless stories. And *he is motivated!*

Dogged every waking moment by his miserable condition, the indifference of this hopeless outcast changed to a man urgently seeking help—*begging* Jesus to deal with his case.

Jairus (Mark 5:21–43)

It was the middle of the day, in broad daylight, and in front of his own parishioners. Here he was, a leader of Capernaum's synagogue throwing himself down at Jesus' feet and begging him for help.

Jesus and Jairus must have known each other reasonably well by now. After all, this was Jesus' adopted hometown. As one of the leaders of the local synagogue, Jairus had encountered Jesus, probably dozens of time (see Mark 1).

Jairus was part of the religious establishment that found Jesus to be a real pain in the neck. Not all that far from Jerusalem, Capernaum's synagogue leaders certainly knew the party line on Jesus. Plus, Jairus had had to put up with all the questions from his own people about Jesus and his authenticity. Not only had Jairus most likely met Jesus many times previously, they'd seen each other in the streets, and Jairus had heard all the stories. Jesus and his disciples were always coming and going out of the seaside fishing village. Every time Jesus and his disciples came back to town, stories of extraordinary events swirled around them.

Life had been pretty good for Jairus. He had a respected position, status within his community, a reasonable living, and a family. But now he was in real trouble.

His 12-year-old daughter was dying. The trouble had only developed recently. And with the kind of edgy relationship Jairus and Jesus had likely had up to that point, Jesus probably wasn't Jairus's first choice when his daughter initially fell ill. Jairus had the usual round of choices: the local doctors, prayers and oblations, the folk remedies of the day, and possibly other more exotic options. But by now, the mourners were already at his house. Time was running out, and Jairus' options were fading.

Then, following yet another remarkable trip, this one dotted with storms at sea and an extraordinary encounter with a demon-possessed man, Jesus and his disciples arrived back home. Instantly a large crowd gathered. But for Jairus, there was no time for discreet meetings at night. He was desperate. So, in broad daylight, in front of everyone, he fell at Jesus' feet. Before Jesus had left town on his last trip, maybe Jairus had thought he had things under control. But now Jesus was the court of last resort.

The wonderful story of Jesus' readiness to help, his encouragement to Jairus along the way, even when friends came to say, "Forget it, she's already dead," and the fabulous ending always touch my heart.

In the early stages of this relationship, Jairus was, at best, indifferent. He was comfortable, with no apparent needs. In fact, there is a very good chance that Jairus was plainly antagonistic and resisted acknowledging Jesus' unique character. After all, Jesus had upstaged Jairus in his own synagogue, and Jesus was the one everyone in Capernaum and all the surrounding countryside was talking about. Jealousy? Probably so.

Jairus took all his Jewish cultural background, his personal experience, all the additional data he'd informally collected from the countless stories told around town, and the attitudes he'd picked up from leaders when he traveled up to Jerusalem. Ready to trade his privileges, his reputation, and, potentially, his relationship with the Jerusalem power elite for his daughter's life, Jairus plunged ahead on his conviction, into action.

Cultural values, peer group pressure, personal identity, sense of security, personal values; the value of his daughter's life outweighed all the other "goodies." What a roller coaster! What a step Jairus took.

CONCLUDING CONSIDERATIONS

So, we ask ourselves:

- Do we have the vision, the patience, the love, and the creativity to establish and maintain a relationship, to keep on communicating with the antagonists and the indifferent in terms they understand until they become seekers?

- Does our strategic partnership have an approach that will engage and continue to hold our relationship with these members of the audience?

- When the sense of need surfaces, are elements in our partnership prepared to respond at the seeker's point of need?

- Do we have both the capacity and the will to mount and sustain a partnership that goes the distance?

One man was on an intellectual and spiritual quest. Another was plagued by the horrific reality of his decaying body. The third was driven to save a precious daughter's life. All were on a journey that linked heart and mind. But had we met these three earlier in life, we might never have dreamed their stories would turn out as they did.

That is the remarkable potential in every strategic partnership of God's people. Empowered by prayer and love, you can encounter people where they are. You can establish and maintain a relationship. You can challenge individuals and encourage change. And, while continuing to share the story of hope and change in Jesus, you can be patient, ready to respond when the individual is ready.

 Share your ideas and response to this chapter, tell your own story, or get connected with more partnership resources at the book's website
www.connectedbook.net

PART THREE
Behind the Scenes

7

VISION

PARTNERSHIP'S DRIVING FORCE

Core Idea

As in all great accomplishments, great vision motivates effective partnerships. Vision is the driving force! Without it, no lasting, effective partnership is born, much less sustained. Vision provides focus, motivation, a gauge for evaluation along the journey, and a basis for fulfillment at the end. Partnerships are born when the vision is too big, too complex, or calls for resources too great for any individual or single ministry. Partnerships are not first about structure, or money, or theological statements. They are about *vision*. Born out of God's character, vision of *what can be* is a driving force for his people and the church.

How wonderful it is, how pleasant,
    for God's people to live together in harmony!

It is like the precious anointing oil
    running down from Aaron's head and beard,
    down to the collar of his robes.

It is like the dew on Mount Hermon,
  falling on the hills of Zion.

There is where the Lord has promised his blessing—
  life that never ends.
  Psalm 133 (GNT)

The growing complexity of the world creates such a challenge that more and more leaders, whether in Christian ministries or international businesses, acknowledge the need to work together. That's good news, because it was God's design from the beginning!

These days it's almost the "in" thing to talk about working in partnerships or strategic alliances. But do we really know what's involved? What is the real motivation for developing a partnership rather than going it alone? And what will it take to keep the partnership alive over the long haul—the time needed for the collaboration to realize its full potential?

It doesn't have to be the multibillion-dollar challenge of bringing a new breakthrough computer chip to market that brings businesses together. It doesn't have to be the enormous challenge of a comprehensive strategy for reaching an unreached people group of over fifty million with the love and power of Christ. It may be the challenge that is in our own backyard.

PARTNERSHIP IN PRACTICE: I was sitting over coffee and sandwiches with a pastor from our little town, population 38,000. We had been talking about our town, its charm and its needs. As the time to go grew near, I asked the pastor, "If Jesus were really let loose in our town and the qualities of his Kingdom were experienced, how do you think the town would look differently in, say, five years?"

There was silence for a moment, and then the pastor responded honestly, "You know, I guess I've never really thought of it that way."

We talked for several more minutes about how he and the elders from his church might creatively approach this question at their next retreat. But I was most struck by his concluding remark, "It seems to me that whatever that vision would be, it'd be too big for a single church like ours. I think, somehow, all the churches would need to work together."

Vision's the thing. But vision's first test is to what extent there's a realistic understanding of the challenge. For instance, a vision of seriously touching even a small community of 38,000 like ours with the love and power of Christ is simply beyond the scope of any individual, any church, or any ministry. Period.

So what's *your* great dream? What have you and your friends or colleagues been dreaming? Of course there always seems to be a role for the lone entrepreneur—the single visionary who takes an idea and turns it into reality. Equally obvious, when carefully examined, is that such entrepreneurs *never really do it all alone.* They always have to call on a gifted, committed team of people to help them realize the vision.

But the more complex the task, the more vital is a partnership approach. Want to turn dreams into reality? Combine vision with an effective, durable partnership approach and you're well on your way!

Previously, we referred to the architecture axiom that often helps bring other, non-architectural challenges into focus: "Form always follows function."

In other words, it is the vision, the *what,* that drives any worthwhile endeavor. The *how* always comes later. And it is the *what,* the great vision, that inspires people to believe the impossible dream, to commit extraordinary resources, to take great risks, to think "outside the box," and to personally invest their time and energy far beyond the normal.

A KEY PARTNERSHIP PRINCIPLE:

 Partnerships are durable, effective, and usually strategic when they are driven by a great vision—a vision that is clearly marked by the following characteristics:

- Greater than anything that can be accomplished by a single individual or ministry.

- One all participants agree is a "God idea," a high priority, and not someone's private agenda.

- One that, in the early stages, can be broken down into high-value, achievable elements that will give participants experience working together, growing confidence, and a sense of achievement.
- Made up of objectives all participants see as highly relevant to their own ministry vision and mission.

Hope of accomplishing something that seems impossible can motivate, supply excitement and anticipation, and provide great fulfillment when the vision is realized. Ultimately, it is this hope and vision that inspire individuals to come together and work through all the issues necessary to form and sustain an effective partnership.

Oh yes, in an effective partnership you may save money—be more efficient. Yes, you may meet new colleagues along the way and enjoy new levels of fellowship. True, the collective witness and service may be more credible and effective. But it is always the end *vision* that brings members together, that drives them on, and by which they measure their progress, month by month. And in the end, it is the vision that holds the potential for fulfillment—realization of hope.

PARTNERSHIP IN PRACTICE: (I briefly touched on this story in my introduction but want to share it in greater detail here.) Fourteen people filed into a room in the old hotel. They were from eight different ministries. All were focused on reaching and serving three nearby countries with a total population of sixty million, essentially no church for hundreds of years, and a church that at that time was tiny and struggling.

For months a neutral facilitator with a vision for the potential of cooperation had held private talks with the leaders. Though it took time, the various leaders did agree to come together for up to four days to carefully examine one question: "If we want to see hundreds of thousands of the people in these countries follow Jesus, is there anything we need to do together rather than continuing to work independently?"

Missionaries had worked faithfully in these countries for decades. A handful of courageous national believers were meeting in small house churches. But the question the leaders had come to prayerfully consider clearly was a humanly impossible dream. It was a God-sized dream and well beyond any single ministry.

They threw themselves into three-and-a-half days of seemingly endless work, prayer, and discussions—frequently till late in the evening. Finally, the group identified nearly twenty issues vital to such a breakthrough. Each of them was clearly beyond the capacity of any single ministry. Knowing they couldn't do everything at once, the group agreed on one most vital joint action objective for the first twelve months.[1] The vision, though staggering in size, now seemed possible through a doable, strategic first step. Commitment to working together in partnership was born.

Just the joy of coming to this first key moment of success caused the group to spontaneously break out in a hymn of praise! A great vision gave birth to a partnership that has endured to this day. It's a partnership that now, years later, is seeing breakthroughs consistent with the original impossible dream. God demonstrates his blessing when his people dwell in unity.

As a boy, growing up on the Mexican border, I would often travel to the interior of Baja California—far off the beaten track. More than once I heard this expression from locals:

"If a man does not know where he is going, how does he know when he arrives?"

God has vision. It is his nature for his vision to work itself out—in his creation, in his restoration of that creation, and in how his people, made in his image, live and work most effectively. His vision is beyond our comprehension. But that part of the vision that he *has* made accessible tells us all we need to know.

God's Vision—Creation

God's vision was to take a world filled with darkness, chaos, and loneliness and turn it into one of light, order, creativity, and intimate, fulfilling fellowship. What a vision! In short, God had a clear idea of where he was going and, therefore, knew when he had arrived. Genesis 1:31 records that "God looked at everything he had made, and he was very pleased" (GNT). What a complete sense of fulfillment!

God's Vision—Redemption

When Adam and Eve's decisions shattered the God design and alienated them from their Maker, God's vision again addressed what seemed to be an impossible situation.[2] Colossians 1:20 says: "Through the Son, then, God decided to bring the whole universe back to himself. God made peace through his Son's blood on the cross and so brought back to himself all things, both on earth and in heaven" (GNT).

Again we see the long view, the great vision, knowing where you want to go. It's the vision that helps you find a way and keeps you on course. The Father's vision included his Son's extraordinary work of redemption.

JESUS' VISION—OBEDIENCE AND THE CROSS

The prophet Isaiah records: "Their insults cannot hurt me because the Sovereign Lord gives me help. I brace myself to endure them. I know I will not be disgraced, for God is near, and he will prove me innocent" (50:7 GNT). In this picture of Jesus facing the cross, the older translations suggest, "Therefore have I set my face like a flint, and I know that I shall not be ashamed" (KJV).

Jesus knew exactly why he had come. He knew what he was to do. And he knew when his earthly part of the grand plan of reconciliation was complete. In John 17 we read Jesus' amazing statement: "I have shown your glory on earth; I have finished the work you gave me to do" (17:4 GNT).

God gave Abraham a vision of fathering a great nation. To Moses, God gave a vision of a new land, a set of life-changing new commandments, and a new life for the suffering people of Israel. The prophets had visions of doom and cried to their people for repentance and change. Jesus infused his disciples with vision and gave them the accompanying power, working together, to change the world. And in the stories of the gospels we see that as people came to him, Jesus restored vision and brought hope to countless broken men and women. All along the way, you hear voices of praise and joy. Tough times on the journey? Seemingly impossible challenges? Of course. But because there was vision, hope was fulfilled and dreams realized.

God's expression of love in creation, reconciliation, and our future eternal life together is driven by a vision. Against all odds—temptation, man's weakness, sin, hell, and Satan's best shot—God maintains a vision of a different future, for you and me, for those around us, and for this broken world. Do you share that vision?

For partnerships to realize great things, there must first be vision. It may be local, it may span your region or state, or it may have global impact in view. But always, vision comes first.

Later we will look more closely at the subject of setting realistic yet powerfully motivating goals and objectives. Here the early chapters provide just a brief word about vision and reality.

An old saying suggests, "Truth can never be held in one hand." Vision is much like that. Whatever the dream or vision is that God has put in your heart, you will need two hands to hold it. One hand always keeps the great vision alive, burning in your heart, driving you on. The other hand asks: "What is the first thing I need to do? What is the first, most important step on this journey? What do I or we need to do *today* to make the vision a reality?"

In the beginning, God set the example. He didn't accomplish creation in a single day. Genesis chronicles the day-by-day outworking of the grand vision. For his own reasons (so we could have an example?), God worked toward this great vision one mind-boggling step at a time.

In a sense, Abraham never experienced the realization of the full vision. But having been given the direction and promise by God, he moved forward one step at a time, powered by faith. What he did see was consistent with God's promise, and that was enough.

When Jesus said in John 17, "I have finished the work you sent me to do," within a short distance of the garden where he was praying were broken lives, widows in poverty, a bankrupt religious system, an occupying army, and disciples who, in the next few hours, would all flee—only to regain their conviction and determination well after the cross.

What is the vision Jesus has placed on your mind and deep in your heart? It's only as that vision continues to burn in your heart that you will press on when strength is low, fatigue is high, discouragement and criticism arise (and they will), resources seem inadequate, good plans go awry, and the longed-for dream seems elusive.

Effective partnerships are about doing the possible today to realize the impossible vision tomorrow.

Share your ideas and response to this chapter, tell your own story, or get connected with more partnership resources at the book's website
www.connectedbook.net

8

PRAYER

OFTEN OVERLOOKED, NEVER OVERDONE

Core Idea

Spiritual breakthroughs are not a game of guns and money. No human effort, expenditure of resources, or brilliant strategy will alone produce lasting spiritual change. Our partnerships must be informed and empowered by God's Holy Spirit in order to be effective. The challenges of relationships, cultural and theological differences, technical and strategic issues, and sustainability can only be dealt with in a process rooted in prayer.

Identifying the impact of prayer may seem elusive. But day-to-day experience in partnerships makes clear that prayer is *central* to good collaborative ministry. In a sense, of course, we are to "walk in a spirit of prayer" continuously, so that everything we do is informed by our communion with God. But we need to be proactive about prayer and its role in partnerships.

A KEY PARTNERSHIP PRINCIPLE:

Satan doesn't want us to work together. That means we're engaged in spiritual conflict. It also means effective partnerships need an *intentional* prayer strategy. Experience suggests two key elements:

- A group outside the partnership's day-to-day operation that is committed to praying for the partnership, its people, and its vision. These people must be seen as an integral part of the partnership and receive regular updates regarding challenges and progress.

- Inside the partnership prayer must be central, regular, specific, and personal. One of the most strategic parts of a partnership is a prayer task force that communicates both within the partnership and with those outside who are actively supporting the initiative.

You and friends may be mounting an initiative in your own neighborhood with a group of ministries and churches around your city, or you may be linking specialized ministries for some other strategic vision. Whatever the partnership's mission, prayer can intersect the life of your partnership in at least four sectors.

- If your partnership is focused on evangelism, prayer is an essential element in stone clearing, planting, and watering—softening spiritually hardened hearts—whether of individuals, a community, or a nation. This aspect of evangelism was covered in chapter 5, "The God Design—Spiritual Change: A Process, Not an Event." The early stages of spiritual change will never be realized without concerted prayer. Individuals only come into the Kingdom through the work of the Holy Spirit and prayer, never through strategy, no matter how brilliant.

- Prayer is essential to healthy relationships, and your partnership must be built on relationships.[1] Openness, trust, and commitment to each other's best interests can only be established and sustained in the context of prayer. These transformed relationships are essential to the launch and sustaining of effective partnership-based ministry initiatives.

- Prayer is essential to building consensus around priorities and setting Kingdom goals and objectives. The understanding and appreciation of different perspectives and readiness to listen to each other and God in a partnership are central to the process. Without prayer at the center of vision-driven consensus, partnership efforts will be powerless.

- Prayer is essential to the durability of effective partnerships. Serious spiritual change takes time, requiring lasting partnerships and extraordinary spiritual staying power. At the heart of consistent, long-term effectiveness is prayer, both internal, among partnership members, and external, on behalf of the partnership's vision, people, and work!

Let's unpack these four sectors.

PRAYER IS ESSENTIAL TO SOFTENING HARDENED HEARTS

What group is your partnership looking to serve or reach with the love of Christ? Whether it is a city, a special sector of society, or a tribal group in a remote location, prayer in and for the partnership is foundational for all stages of witness: stone clearing, sowing, watering, reaping, and discipling. Prayer, particularly in the early stages of "hard ground," has a powerful impact on opening doors and hearts to Christ.

The reality of Jesus' words to the disciples, "I have sent you to reap a harvest in a field where . . . others worked," (John 4:35–38 GNT), has been demonstrated countless times over the history of the church. Frequently we are inclined to pray primarily when spiritual response seems imminent or evident. But in difficult times, the long commitment of faithfulness powered by prayer is essential.

In recent years partnerships, again and again, have found that they have inherited the results of previous workers' commitment—people who served often in loneliness and obscurity, carried on only by prayer and a sense of God's faithfulness.

Here are some examples that I have personally encountered of the powerful role of prayer overseas in places of spiritual resistance:

- Faithful but lonely witness went on in an Islamic country with little apparent results for over four decades. While this personal witness was underway, awareness of and prayer for the people group—outside the country—was mounting. Over the last decade a strategic partnership of about a dozen ministries working with local believers has seen nearly a hundred thousand swept into the Kingdom and thousands more seeking Christ in dozens of local, home-based fellowships.

- Approximately one hundred years ago, in a Tibetan Buddhist country, missionaries and their families, more than fifty in all, were martyred while seeking to tell the people about Christ. Over the following century, countless believers were moved to pray for the region. In recent years, a cooperative, partnership-based evangelism initiative has seen tens of thousands come into the Kingdom and national leadership emerge, composing hundreds of local fellowships and countless smaller, informal groups of believers and seekers.

- Active Christian witness had been underway in an influential people group for over one hundred years. As recently as ten years ago, there was not a single functioning church among that group—employing the group's language, using Scripture in their language, and led by members of the people group. An evangelism partnership for the language group was established a few years ago. The partners agreed that developing a global prayer initiative was one of their highest collaborative priorities. An Internet-based prayer bulletin was launched, along with a bimonthly hard copy version that has had wide circulation. Other initiatives on the ground are backed by these prayer endeavors. Today, churches are functioning in this people group, the New Testament is complete, and the local fellowships are led by nationals.

- The "praying through the window" initiative (associated with the AD2000 Movement), between the years 1993 and 2000, engaged over 45 million believers worldwide. Participants signed a covenant to pray daily during the month of October for a massive harvest of souls among the major language groups in and around the 10/40 Window. Focused prayer on this scale has never been known in the history of the church. The decade of the nineties saw more people come into the Kingdom and more new local fellowships established in the Islamic, Hindu, Buddhist, and Tibetan blocs than the entire first ninety years of the twentieth century. The correlation between these two realities cannot be a coincidence.

Right now, there are people praying for communities, cities, and special groups of people with great spiritual need. Partnerships, powered by those prayers, often are called to help connect a wide range of men and women committed to witness and service. In our local community or internationally, each one has a part. Yet often the critical role of prayer, a less visible but vital part of the process, gets overlooked or minimized.

Jesus' promise in John 4:35–38 is that the reaper *and the planter* will rejoice when we stand around his throne in heaven. The prayer-based faithfulness of those who witnessed and served in those hard early stages is linked by the Holy Spirit to the prayer-based faithfulness of those who come later so that, in spiritual partnership, they will *rejoice together*.

Prayer Is Essential to Healthy Relationships—
the Basis for Cooperative Endeavors

If the heart of the Gospel is restored relationships, partnership-based initiatives are a classic test bed. So much of the church's ineffectiveness worldwide is associated with our division and broken relationships *inside* the community of believers.[2] Repeated partnership experience has shown the importance of being proactive in prayer.

Some examples of prayer's role in healthy partnerships, internationally include the following:

- In an area of the world that is highly contested spiritually, hundreds of individuals were making inquiry about Christ. An inquiring individual might have been exposed to the good news via radio, Bible correspondence courses, literature distribution, or personal witness. While interest was high, a total lack of coordination of all of these elements was reducing effectiveness and seriously jeopardizing the security of many national believers. In an effort to bring coordination out of the chaos, fifteen men from eight different ministries gathered to work diligently for three days and nights.

  When they arrived, only four of the fifteen had ever met. Diversity in age, ethnic background, denominational/organizational histories, and real and perceived theological differences created fear, mistrust, and an environment in which it seemed little could be accomplished. Faced with seemingly impossible roadblocks, three or four times each day the men broke into small groups of two to three. Each time, they were asked to share personal needs as they prayed for each other and the issues they were discussing.

  By the end of the working meetings, each had prayed personally for everyone else in the group at least twice; each had *been prayed for* by all of the others at least twice; and, in the process, they had learned about one another's real needs, personal spiritual journey, and relationship to Christ. At the conclusion of their days together, tears filled the eyes of all participants. They had hammered out a multi-point action plan that has since transformed follow-up work with inquirers in that region. But many felt the most important breakthrough had been in their relationships. Despite their extremely different backgrounds and traditions, they decided to have communion together to demonstrate that they had come to know and trust each other in a new level of trusting relationships.

- Seeking spiritual breakthroughs in an Asian country that had been "closed" during most of modern missions history, seventy-four people gathered to pray and discuss the possibility of working together in partnership. Rifts in some of the relationships were so great that a special international prayer network had been established to pray for each participant individually throughout the four-day working meetings.

As in the example cited above, the group was divided into small, highly focused prayer groups each day, allowing participants to share personal needs and to develop relationships. Additionally, prayer and reconciliation meetings were arranged for each of the three nights to address the hostility present in the most extreme cases of broken relationships. (Remember that these are *believers*—committed to world evangelization!) When the wider group acknowledged that they *did* want to move forward in a partnership for the country, they agreed the proactive prayer and work on relationships had been essential to moving forward—together.

- A partnership of nearly a dozen ministries was working on a bilingual evangelism project in a very hostile social and spiritual environment. The partnership included both national and expatriate ministries that varied enormously in size. Their contribution to the partnership's efforts also varied greatly—from the significant resources donated by a major international ministry to the "widow's mite" given by an impoverished national ministry. Culture, size, ecclesiastical traditions, and perceived influence of the participants could hardly have been more diverse.

Because of these huge differences, if God really blessed their partnership, how would they ever be able to share success? Concerted prayer eventually produced a remarkably simple solution: "Everyone can claim success for all that God does." There was one stipulation: "When a ministry refers to the project and God's work through their efforts, we ask that they simply indicate, 'We are seeing these results as we work together with other ministries in a strategic partnership.'"

In many ways, the challenge of serving your local community may be just as complex, if not more so. Prayer is critical to partnership effectiveness—at home or overseas.

PRAYER IS ESSENTIAL TO DEVELOPING TRUST, CONSENSUS, AND COMMON VISION

As we have said many times already, by definition, effective working partnerships frequently bring together highly diverse individuals or ministries. Developing trusting relationships under these circumstances can be challenging enough. But to jointly hear the Spirit of God and establish a common vision and action plan can be even more challenging.

The circumstances are similar, whether your group is defining a common vision and a related action plan for the first time or an established partnership is doing an annual review and refocusing for the next twelve months. Brainstorming the possibilities in small groups and sharing them in an open forum is an essential step. However, helping the group acknowledge that it can't do everything and, therefore, needs to establish priorities, takes the need for trust and open relationships to another level. Prayer in this priority-setting process is vital.

(Note: for further ideas on setting priorities and objectives, see chapter 11, "On The Way: Formation.")

Satan doesn't want us to acknowledge his reality, much less his influence in our daily lives. But one of his central strategies is destroying relationships between believers, therefore crippling our ability to develop a common, Spirit-empowered strategy to share the *good news* of Jesus.[3]

Developing consensus is vital to generating a common vision (*what* the partnership wants to accomplish) and a shared plan (*how* you will accomplish the vision).

Prayer plays a vital role at each of these points in a partnership's development:

- Review of the facts (What is the actual situation?)

- Reflection/discussion (What do the facts mean or imply?)

- Considering the challenge/discussion (What are the roadblocks to breakthroughs?)

- Looking ahead/discussion (What are possible action steps?)

- Planning/discussion (What are the priorities, and what objectives will be established?)

- Making commitments (Who is responsible for what, and when?)

Experience suggests that the more a group can come to consensus around the key elements in each of these stages, the clearer the understanding and the greater the ownership. Pray *before* you launch into the topic. Pray as you take up each point. Then, *after* you have identified the relevant issues, pray together and ask God for guidance: Which of these points does the group agree are the most important? Taking at least a brief period of time to pray in small groups about each of these stages produces rich dividends.

You will be amazed and thrilled at what the Spirit of God does as people think *and pray* together! Should we be surprised? I think not.

Prayer Is Essential to the Durability of Partnership-Based Strategies

Westerners want instant results, whether it is through our self-help programs, investments, or spiritual strategies. Clearly, for both individuals and communities, profound change in spiritual direction sometimes seems to occur in a moment. But those are exceptions. Individual lives, like communities and nations, develop a pattern that is typically the result of a long series of decisions—good or bad.

Real, long-term change in your neighborhood, a group within your community, a whole city, or an unreached people group 6,000 miles away can only result from consistent, enduring work and prayer. Partnerships that seek this kind of change must be equally durable.

Internationally, of all the unreached people evangelism partnerships that my colleagues and I have been associated with since the mid-eighties, the majority are still active. Most still serve as the primary forum for ministry coordination in the area. Many of the other partnerships still exist but may be less robust, due to lack of strong leadership or other circumstances.

In light of the short-term, often transitory nature of cooperative efforts in the church elsewhere, what can explain the extraordinary staying power of these partnerships? In talking with my colleagues and folks involved in these initiatives, no single factor provides the explanation. It's the *combination* of the unique elements of these partnerships that provides the enduring spiritual and relational chemistry. Press hard enough, however, and, ultimately, prayer is cited as the central power point. Remember, these are initiatives that, often daily, face impossible spiritual odds, formidable relational issues, operational challenges that frequently seem insurmountable, and dreams of spiritual outcomes that are rarely even hoped for, much less realized, in the West.

Prayer is the point in a partnership at which the spiritual power is tapped. Listening to God becomes more natural, the Spirit works in hearts to deal with relational issues, and the hope of realizing the impossible dream is born—in prayer. Conscious effort to encourage the ongoing effective intersection of these wide-ranging elements through prayer is vital to the partnership's staying power.

When hope is fading, when consensus seems just out of reach, when the complexities of integrating widely diverse individuals or ministries into a common vision and action plan seem too complex, when old, unhealed relational wounds surface or fears about another ministry's motives produce caution, prayer is the consistent essential ingredient.

The facilitator or facilitation team must be constantly vigilant to the dangers of sterile processes, planning, or efforts to encourage best practices across ministry lines. Prayer puts the Spirit of God at the center where his grace, power, insights, reconciliation, and hope can radiate through a group so diverse that, otherwise, it may seem a hopeless candidate for any cooperative success.

What to Make of All This?

In meeting, talking, and praying with friends and colleagues working in partnership initiatives, we all continue to learn many lessons. However, some themes seem to recur:

- Intentional, concerted prayer is vital to defeating Satan's offensive to divide and, thereby, neutralize the church's witness.

- Intentional, concerted prayer is vital to the development of trusting, open, restored relationships—the basis for all cooperative Kingdom efforts.

- Intentional, concerted prayer is vital to bringing about consensus and developing action plans that empower lasting Kingdom cooperation.

- Intentional, concerted prayer is too frequently considered an "add-on" rather than the center of each step in planning, preparing, executing, and sustaining partnership-based ministry.

- Intentional, concerted prayer is vital if the church seeks the power and refreshment offered as God's gift in Psalm 133.

 Share your ideas and response to this chapter, tell your own story, or get connected with more partnership resources at the book's website
www.connectedbook.net

9

ON THE MOVE

PARTNERSHIP IS A PROCESS, NOT AN EVENT

Core Idea

An effective, durable partnership involves identifying potential partners, establishing trusting relationships, and exploring and coming to consensus on the vision. Identifying key action steps and responsibilities, successfully meeting initial objectives, and moving on to realize the vision follow. Developing such partnerships takes time. Understand your partnership's development as a process, not an event, and you've taken a big step toward seeing your dream come true.

INSTANT PARTNERSHIP, LONG-TERM FAILURE

My colleagues and I had just been talking with a small group of ministry leaders who were hoping to launch a partnership for an important project in their region. They all understood clearly that, working individually, they would never reach the vision.

Highly motivated, the group naturally wanted to get going. Impatient and a bit frustrated, they felt that too much time had already been lost. The following exchange between one of the local leaders (LL) and a partnership facilitator from our team (PF) pretty well summarizes the tension often felt when people start thinking about a partnership approach:

LL: Along with these other folks, I've been thinking and dreaming about this idea for a long time. The others here agree on moving forward. Why can't we just get started? For instance, the others and I have wondered if we shouldn't just call a meeting and present the idea to other ministers in our area.

PF: It's great that you folks have a common vision for this project. But let me ask: How many other ministries might be interested in the idea or, eventually, join the partnership?

LL: I honestly don't know, but I imagine, knowing the kind of project we're talking about, it could potentially be a number of people and, who knows, maybe fifteen to twenty organizations. We know some of the key people, but not all of them.

PF: Do you have a sense of how the leaders of those other agencies feel about the project you're discussing? Or how they might feel about working together with other ministries?

LL: No, I don't. But, I'm sure it probably varies from person to person.

PF: Based on what you know, which of these leaders or agencies do you think it would be most important to "sell" on the idea? Which ones need to have a sense of ownership and be enthusiastic about it?

LL: Again, I have some ideas. But I think we'd need to actually go out and talk with them to find out.

PF: You're absolutely right. You know, my colleagues and I have a saying, "Many times the quickest way to kill a partnership is to call a meeting—too soon!" We'd really encourage you to make your first step meeting one on one with others who may be interested and listening to them. Take the time now, and you'll be thankful later.

PARTNERSHIP IN PRACTICE: Mary-Jo had a vision. She was concerned about her community and what seemed, at least to her, to be a disconnect between the local churches and the community's needs. For months she'd reflected, "Wouldn't it be a lot better if all the churches in this neighborhood worked together, rather than just 'doing their own thing?'" It sure seemed to make sense.

Mary-Jo talked to her pastor, who had some reservations but felt on principle that he should probably encourage her. With this backing, Mary-Jo got a list of all the churches in the area, sent out a letter to the pastors, and called a meeting to discuss the possibilities. When the night of the meeting arrived, only four of the thirteen churches she'd contacted showed up. Only two of the attendees were senior pastors!

Like many others who have held similar dreams, Mary-Jo's vision of a partnership among the churches died quietly. The lack of patient relationship building, careful listening, and consensus development among the potential partners doomed the vision from the start. It was Mary-Jo's vision, not the churches'. The churches had never acknowledged a need to join hands for more effective witness and service. Possibly most telling, the churches couldn't see how their own congregations would benefit from linking with others.

Those of us from Western cultures often want quick results. But think of:

- Doing your own landscaping vs. developing a city park that will serve thousands of children and adults.

- Building a do-it-yourself dinghy vs. designing, financing, and constructing a large cruise ship that will carry hundreds of passengers on luxurious ocean voyages for years to come.

- Planning your personal two-week vacation vs. organizing and funding your local college orchestra's European performance tour.

You can think of dozens of similar comparisons.

Having seen many partnerships among people and ministries emerge as long-term, effective strategies (along with a few significant failures along the way!), it is clear to me that durable partnerships usually go through four phases. Whether you have a vision for your community, city, special interest group (e.g., immigrants, homeless, athletes, kids), or overseas language group with no effective witness for Christ, the phases are essentially the same.

Exploration: The time and energy invested in identifying the potential partners and exploring their vision, interest, and readiness to at least prayerfully talk about collaboration.

Formation: The critical, "go/no-go" phase in partnership development. It's when potential partner ministries say, "We agree the only way we can accomplish this vision is by working together." Or they say, "At least for now, we don't think so."

Operation: The phase in partnership development at which talk turns to action. Goals are set, roles defined, and time lines and the basis for monitoring and evaluation agreed upon. Once there is consensus on the vision and the core plan, the emerging partnership moves forward.

Maturation: The partnership begins to see real, tangible outcomes. Relationships begin to mature—both inside the partnership and with the community outside. Confidence in the process increases and objectives begin to enlarge. Continued attention to communications and expectations is vital.

But before thinking more about partnerships as a process, let's look at a partnership development diagram. It is the classic partnership "life cycle," predictable but full of powerful implications.

Partnership Life Cycle

• Continuity / medium-term outcomes
• Wider ownership / increasing objectives

MATURATION

• Initial outcomes
• Initial limited / positive objectives

OPERATION
- - - - - - - - - - - - - - - - - -
FORMATION...GO / NO-GO
- - - - - - - - - - - - - - - - - -

• Identify / train faciliator or team
• Develop consensus
• Identify opportunities / needs
• Identify partner ministries

EXPLORATION (ALLOW TIME!)

In part 4, "On The Way" (chapters 10–12), I look at these phases in considerable detail, provide illustrations, and break the process down into understandable steps you and your friends can take for greater success.

Invest the time and energy each of these phases deserves, and you can be richly rewarded. Expect this to happen overnight, and you are headed for big disappointments!

THE HOT DOG STAND AND THE SKYSCRAPER

For a moment let's move from Kingdom partnerships and consider the case of the hot dog stand and the skyscraper.

Establishing a hot dog stand involves a number of important factors like vision, modest start-up capital, good equipment, quality ingredients that make a great hot dog, license from the city to sell, high-traffic location, right sales price, a person to run the stand who loves making and selling hot dogs, and a simple but effective system to keep track of expense and income. Best-case time line, from idea to operations on the street? Maybe one to four months.

Constructing a skyscraper with hundreds of thousands of square feet of prime office space is a project of entirely different magnitude. It involves preliminary planning, interim funding, site acquisition, architectural design, engineering, review and approval by environmental and building departments, long-term financing, initial marketing to prime tenants, and, finally, the construction—from groundbreaking to completion of interiors right up to the top floor. Best-case time line, from initial idea to first tenant move-in? Probably three to five years.

A profitable hot dog stand:

- Requires one person with a dream.

- Takes modest resources—space, money, and technology.

- Requires an important but limited range of skills.

- Has, at best, a medium-term life expectancy.

- Offers limited revenue potential.

- Operated effectively, may offer personal satisfaction to the operator and, hopefully, many customers. But the community served will be relatively small.

An effectively executed skyscraper project:

- First requires one person with an expansive, long-term vision.

- Next calls for a range of influential people to buy into the dream. Champions have to include the developer, the architects, the bankers, the contractors, and, ultimately, the leasing company.

- Takes significant financial capital, space, and technology.

- Must bring together people with a blinding array of specialized skills and experience. Hundreds of individuals are needed just to construct, not to mention occupy and operate, the building.

- Has a long-term life expectancy.
- Offers significant return on capital.
- Operated effectively, can reflect responsible space utilization and provide a productive working environment for thousands of people.

Here's another fascinating parallel between building a skyscraper and launching an effective partnership. Once groundbreaking for the skyscraper finally takes place, construction work goes *down, not up!* A big hole is excavated, a large fence placed around the site, and for months, maybe over a year, people drive or walk by saying, "I thought they were building a skyscraper here." Developers will tell you that once construction of a real skyscraper comes back up to ground level where the public can begin to see the building going up, the project is probably over sixty percent complete! The long years of planning, site acquisition, engineering, environmental clearances, financing, and constructing the foundation represent well over half of the total time involved!

Building a good skyscraper is clearly a complex process that cannot be accomplished by calling a meeting! But in the end, tenacious commitment to the vision of the building can provide major returns on investment.

Risk, Faith, and Partnership Development

But you may say, "The partnership I have in mind may not be a hot dog stand, but it certainly is no skyscraper!" No matter what issue or challenge you're trying to address, effectively launching the partnership to realize your vision is a *process*. It means a lot of time-consuming, "invisible" work. Doing that invisible work and preparing the right foundation is your key to longer-term success.

Experience shows that an effective partnership of individuals or ministries can accomplish things that the member could never achieve doing it alone. But larger vision takes significant commitment and time. Launching an effective partnership is often an act of faith—and demonstration of willingness to take risks. You have to *believe* that investing time and resources now will produce far greater Kingdom returns in the future.

Based on what you know, are you ready to make that investment, take that risk? Consider the parable of the stewards in Matthew 25 and Luke 19.

The *minimum* the master expected was his money back *with interest.*

The texts suggest that the slacking servant knew about the bank and the interest it paid as well as the master did. Instead, as you will remember, he played it safe and buried the money in the ground. When his master returned, he was judged on what he *did know* but *didn't do*; putting the money in the bank would have been an essentially risk-free strategy. The other two stewards who doubled their master's money were aware of the potential in the money they'd been given, had a good grasp of their master's expectations, knew the rough timetable they were working on, had an associated sense of urgency, understood what their investment options were, and took risks well beyond just putting the money in the bank! When he returned, the master's preference between these two approaches was clear.

What assets has God put in your hands? He is looking for people willing to trust him and take risks with the assets he has given them!

A KEY PARTNERSHIP PRINCIPLE:

 If you know your long-term dream eventually has to involve others, take time now to assess what the vision may involve. Then make the choice to risk slowing down and working through the steps to develop a healthy partnership. Keep the vision alive. But don't plunge ahead and end in disappointment.

Does it all seem complicated? Look like the potential payoff is too far down the road? Keep reading. The chapters just ahead give you, your friends, and colleagues the practical tools to take the journey, successfully, one step at a time.

Ready to jump in?

Share your ideas and response to this chapter, tell your own story, or get connected with more partnership resources at the book's website
www.connectedbook.net

PART FOUR
On the Way

10

ON THE WAY
EXPLORATION
(PART ONE)

Core Idea

! We usually don't choose to take the long road. Life is a journey on which, all too often, we look for shortcuts. Getting God's people to work together in partnership is no different. All of us wish there were an easy way to overcome barriers, build relationships, develop trust and common vision, and see wonderful outcomes. But, the early, Exploration stage of a partnership is no place for shortcuts. Make your strategic investments of time, prayer, and energy here, and you will see rich dividends later. This chapter shows you what's involved and how to do it.

In the vital Exploration phase of partnership development, a lot of time is spent one on one. You'll be asking questions and *listening*, expanding your personal base of information, and multiplying relationships. You'll also be broadening your understanding about the realities of the vision you have in mind and the perceptions of *others*. Remember, an individual's *perceptions* are usually his or her *reality*—even though their perceptions may be quite different from yours!

During this phase you'll also need to identify who will serve as the partnership's facilitator or facilitation team. Later, an entire chapter will be devoted to this key person or group of people. You may be that person. Or you may be instrumental in finding him or her. It's extremely helpful for the longer-term facilitator to be involved in these early stages—meeting people, getting a good sense of the issues, and helping design the process.

In any case, the facilitator(s) must be patient, tenacious, and committed to the vision. This person needs to demonstrate the spirit of a servant while bringing the partnership to life and keeping the fires burning. This "honest broker" must be a person of integrity who will keep on, despite all discouragement. The facilitator is a prophet, servant, and a resource person who must be trained, nurtured, and encouraged.

PARTNERSHIP IN PRACTICE: The Exploration phase of a particularly challenging international partnership I worked on went like this. In the early stages, with colleagues, we identified approximately twenty ministries that either had already done something on this project or had said they were interested in doing something in the next two to three years. Because the project was located in a country in which the borders had been closed to outsiders for a long time, only a handful of people had personally visited the project location.

Over a period of eighteen months, I visited the top leaders in sixteen of these ministries. One of the great challenges was that these ministries were scattered from Finland to Holland, from Germany to Australia, and from the U.S. to the U.K.! Great skepticism and interpersonal problems meant that, in many cases, I had to meet multiple times with the same leaders to build relationships and an initial level of trust.

This was not a matter of driving across town for a cup of coffee with an interested party. These were expensive airplane trips. Once there, the meetings often took three to four hours. Before the Exploration phase was complete, dozens of these meetings had taken place. During this time, I could tell absolutely no one about this quiet, behind the scenes work, except those I was calling on. Before any leaders were invited to a meeting to discuss the project and a possible partnership approach to it, nearly $30,000 had already been invested in phone, fax, airfares, hotel, taxi, and food bills!

Imagine having to write up a progress report on an initiative like that. Yes, quiet, behind the scenes progress had been made. But there certainly wasn't much to show for all this investment of Kingdom resources—at least not yet. Talk about a journey of faith!

You could say, "But I just want to do something here in my hometown. I don't need to do all that complicated stuff!" Absolutely true. However, remember that, while each person I called on had an affiliation with some ministry, each was, first and foremost, *an individual*—a real person with emotions, hopes, dreams, families, and a history. And if you're thinking and praying about a partnership of God's people in your hometown, you need to spend time with people—first as individuals. If they are with an organization or ministry, their personal feelings may be intertwined with their ministry's agenda. We'll talk more about those challenges later. But first, they are people.

Your partnership Exploration journey probably won't be so arduous. But done prayerfully and carefully, it will always take the same level of commitment and patience.

Potential Resource:

✓ You might like to review sections of chapter 5, which explores the process of change. There always has to be "stone clearing, planting, and watering" before "reaping" can occur. By exploring a potential partnership, you are proposing change. It's a process and takes real patience.

Your Key Action Points

- You will have your prayer team in place.

- You will get to know who is doing what.

- You will identify the most influential and knowledgeable people in the field (as you know, they aren't always the same!).

- One on one, you will talk with, listen to, and get to know these leaders, their background, vision, and current involvement in the issue that concerns you.

- You will expand your knowledge, your network of relationships, and your personal credibility.

- You will identify the potential partnership facilitator or form the facilitation team (see the next chapter, "Formation"). It's vital for them to be involved in these early stages and get the training they need for their important role.

Here's how the process looks with the main points in diagram form:

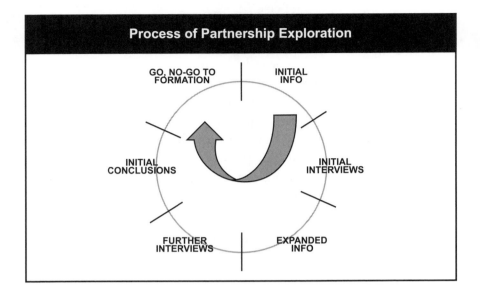

Process of Partnership Exploration

GO, NO-GO TO FORMATION

INITIAL INFO

INITIAL CONCLUSIONS

INITIAL INTERVIEWS

FURTHER INTERVIEWS

EXPANDED INFO

A KEY PARTNERSHIP PRINCIPLE:

In effective partnership development, someone at least has to be acquainted with everyone!

Why? Someone has to be acquainted with all the main issues. And someone has to know where the historical, relational, and operational land mines are located! The facilitator or the facilitation team needs to know as much as possible about the history, relationships, players, current feelings and relationships between the players, and what they think about the vision under discussion.

This information and this relational "bank account" are major assets. Make the investment now, and it will pay major dividends.

Particularly as you move into the next phases of your partnership's development, you want to *minimize* the surprises and *maximize* the consensus. No matter how diligent you've been, count on it—there will still be plenty of surprises!

Whether your vision is for your neighborhood or community, a whole city, or a group of people somewhere else in the world who need Jesus' love and freedom, investing the time in this first phase, Exploration, will pay huge dividends as you move forward.

So how do you actually go about this key phase called Exploration? Who does it? What are the main steps? How is it done? What are key indicators that you're ready for the next phase of your partnership's development? Let's take a look.

WHO DOES THE EXPLORATION?

The simple answer: the person with the burning vision for the partnership and its potential.

This is not something that can be farmed out to someone else—neither well-meaning volunteers nor even paid staff. The vision has to be strongly felt, a conviction deep inside, for a person to play this critical role.

So if you're the person with the vision, you are likely the one to do this all-important groundwork. But before you say, "Whoa! No way. I don't have the time or the ability," consider a few things.

Depending on your time availability and the urgency of the vision, there may be alternatives.

- You may be able to work on the project part time, meeting with potential partners (individuals or ministries) as you can. It may take a little longer, but you can assure continuity of vision and approach.

- If you have a friend or colleague who has the same vision and same commitment, you may be able to split the work and speed up the process.

- If you have a small, preliminary working group of people who are fully behind the vision and share your level of commitment, you may be able to select two or three people to serve as an Exploration team. In turn, these "explorers" can meet regularly with your working group, report on the feedback they get and fine-tune their interview process.

If more than one person is involved in the Exploration, each one must be saying the same thing, taking the same approach in the meetings/interviews, and be looking for and ready to report on the same kinds of information.

See chapter 13, "The Partnership Facilitator: The Vision-Powered Servant Leader." It's full of suggestions for identifying this key person or facilitation team and effectively preparing and nurturing them for the role.

When you actually get into the Exploration interviews, it's very easy to get sidetracked. It may seem obvious, but it is vital that you stick closely to your objectives and planned approach. I cover some of the challenges you will face and approaches to take a bit later. See particularly the suggestions in "How's The Exploration Done?" later in this chapter.

CONTINUITY IN LEADERSHIP

The person or persons doing the Exploration phase *must be active participants in leadership or facilitation when you get to the critical Formation, go/no-go phase of the Partnership*. That's why it's important to identify this person or team early.

The knowledge base you build, relationships you establish, and trust you or your explorers develop all come into play at the crucial partnership Formation point (next chapter). Potential partners will be face to face, talking and praying about the possibility of working together on a common vision. They need to be working with individuals they have already met and come to know.

THE MAIN STEPS IN EXPLORATION?

1. *Be knowledgeable about your topic.* Not an expert. Certainly not *the* expert. But in doing the Exploration interviews with potential partners, ministries, or individuals, an important part of your credibility will be your own knowledge of the topic. Whether you meet with senior pastors, ministry leaders, or community agency personnel, they all have had to deal with too many well-intentioned but uninformed people with a new idea! Get as many facts as possible about the problem that has inspired your vision.

For the sake of illustration, let's suppose you want to launch a partnership for ministry to street kids in your city. You need a *pretty good idea* of their current situation: How many there are, who they are, their demographics, what services are currently offered, who is providing the services, how services are funded, and where gaps and overlap in service may exist. Possibly most important, you should know what previous efforts, if any, have been made to encourage cooperation in working with street kids—and what became of those initiatives.

You can immediately begin to see that if more than one person is working on this Exploration phase, actually interviewing/talking with potential partner agencies, each one has to be working from the same knowledge base. Impossible? No. But it means that coordination, full information sharing, and mutual feedback are critical.

2. *Find out who is* already *involved.* If you feel you've already developed a good understanding of who is doing what, great. If not, you need to know which individuals, agencies, ministries, churches, and so on, are currently trying to deal with the challenge of street kids. You not only need names, addresses, and phone numbers. If you're talking about ministries or community agencies, you also need to know the names of the leaders. In the "How's It Done?" section on the next page, I strongly recommend that you always start with the leader. More on that later.

A Key Partnership Principle:

If at all possible, it's important that your partnership or network team include individuals who represent the group you are trying to serve or reach. Trying to develop a partnership to reach or serve the street kids in your city? Better have some who have "been there, done that" in your discussions and planning. Hoping to change the way ministries coordinate their efforts? Better make sure leadership from those ministries is involved. It may seem obvious. But many times this key principle is overlooked—particularly when language, cultural, or social circumstances are natural barriers. The conscious effort to include these people will pay rich dividends.

Beyond names and contact information, you need to know at least something about what a particular individual or organization does. Demonstrate that you have taken the time to learn something about them and the role they play. It's another step in establishing your personal credibility. (We've all dealt with a salesperson who tries to sell us something by pretending to be interested in us, but who clearly doesn't *really* know anything about us and obviously cares just about as much!)

So before doing your first face-to-face Exploration interviews, you need to have an initial database of information about who is involved and, generally, what they are doing. Phone books, local government agencies, pubic libraries, Internet Web sites, and Internet search engines can all yield valuable information. If you feel you already have a fairly thorough idea of who is working in the field, fine. Experience suggests that the Exploration process can expand your understanding, strengthen your credibility, and deepen relationships. So if you know you need more information, think of the obvious sources first.

PARTNERSHIP IN PRACTICE: Over the years I have found that an honest, interested approach can yield a treasure of information. From my days as a journalist, it's called the "front door" strategy.

Let's take the street kids challenge, for example. Even if you think you want to engage the wider community, it is usually important for a core group of individuals, churches, and/or local Christian ministries to come to consensus about the need first. A natural question is, "Which local churches or Christian ministries already have initiatives for street kids under way?"

Among the explicitly Christian groups, you might want to talk with the leadership of Youth for Christ, Young Life, or other Christian youth agencies in your area. It would also make sense to contact the youth or urban ministry staff of three or four key churches, especially ones that you or others know have a commitment to ministry outside their four walls—in the city. When you call, use the same approach with each. Seeking information from multiple sources helps you get a more complete, objective idea of what's going on.

In the general community, you might try calling the police community relations department. Simply indicate you're an interested citizen and ask if 1) they have a list of agencies or organizations working with street kids, or, 2) lacking a list, they could give you the names of two or three groups they know are actively working with street kids.

There may be a juvenile crime prevention group in the city. Look for a Youth or Youth and Family Services department or agency. The local United Way could be a valuable source of information.

When you make these initial "who is doing what" calls, I strongly recommend not raising the issue of partnership or cooperation. At this stage, you are just trying to become as knowledgeable as possible. Even mentioning the word "partnership" now will probably raise questions you're not ready to answer—particularly on the phone. You don't want to needlessly raise barriers to a face-to-face meeting. This is not deception. Your vision will emerge at the right time. Remember, men and women in a growing love relationship may think about the possibility of marriage for quite a while before they actually talk about it!

The vision and goals of your project may differ sharply from those of a partnership focused on street kids. The appendix suggests further resources and sources of information. You may find it helpful.

3. Based on your initial round of information gathering, *decide which individuals, organizations, or ministries are your first personal interview priorities.* As you conduct the interviews, keep in mind that you are likely to uncover new information about these individuals or ministries. That new information may, in turn, expand or modify the list of those you want to interview face to face.

To prioritize your interviews, here are a couple of factors to keep in mind:

- In these initial contacts, which names have most frequently been mentioned? Are there certain leaders, agencies, ministries, or churches that people have consistently referred to?

- In your initial conversations, have you heard phrases like, "Mary Jones is by far the most knowledgeable person," or "Agency/organization X really seems to be the most active"?

Combined with any other research you have done (on websites, etc.), this kind of information can guide you to natural starting points in your Exploration process. If your vision is for your neighborhood or community, this initial round of interviews may involve only a handful of leaders or ministries. But a vision taking in a larger area or larger population group could involve talking personally with many more.

If your vision is reaching and serving a town or large city, you face special challenges. See chapter 18, "Special Cases, Special Opportunities—Partnership: The Challenge of Cities," for specific suggestions, ideas, and illustrations.

4. Once your Exploration interviews are complete, *use the information you gather to make a decision about moving on* to the next phase of partnership development—Formation. The next section, "How's It Done?" will help clarify the types of information you or your exploration team will gather, some of the challenges you may face, and the outcomes you can expect.

How's It Done? —The Exploration Interviews

It may seem strange, even counterintuitive, particularly with a vision that may be burning in your heart, but remember: In this phase of partnership development, your goal is *not* to convince ministry leaders to be part of a partnership! Your goal is to collect information, build relationships, and *seek positive consensus around two very simple but central questions* (using the street kids challenge as the example):

1. "Do you think there is anything that *might* be accomplished more effectively with street kids if the various interested groups worked together rather than each one doing its own thing?"

2. "If there *are* other agencies/ministries interested in exploring possible areas of greater collaboration in serving street kids, would you have any interest in being part of those discussions?"

If you get a positive answer to these two questions, even if the response is tentative, you have all the commitment you need—for the moment. During the interview, you may get varied responses.

- Indifferent to negative. Don't be discouraged! See ideas on what to do with leaders/agencies who say no.

- Strongly positive. That's great!

- Initially negative but, as you discuss the ideas further, turning to conditional openness.

Note that with these questions you are intentionally *doing* certain things and *avoiding* others. You are:

- Not assuming that a partnership will be born. You're exploring what people think about the idea of possibly working together.

- Not asking people to endorse a partnership, much less join one. You're exploring their readiness to sit down and talk about the potential added value of cooperation with others.

- Not defining what the primary priorities might be for a partnership if it did come together. That is something the group has to decide when the leaders meet together—if they decide to move forward.

- Not defining in specific terms how such a partnership might be structured and function. If the group meets, talks, and prays, then decides to go forward, they will have to develop a consensus about what structure is needed and how it will operate.

PARTNERSHIP IN PRACTICE: Joanna had been working as a nurse practitioner in a Southeast Asian country for nearly ten years. Medical services had proven to be a valuable practical demonstration of Christ's love for the people in this country, where so many had so little access to basic health services. She was a senior person in her own ministry and knew many of the people in the other five ministries doing medical work in the country. Through informal talks with friends and colleagues, Joanna sensed major gaps and, at times, overlap in the work of the various medical organizations. Collaboration between ministries was lacking. And as a group, their communication with the government's department of health was not coordinated.

A meeting with a ministry partnership specialist living in the region bolstered her confidence and helped her map out the initial steps of her strategy. Eager to move things along, in the first meeting she had with the leader of another medical ministry, Joanna proposed that the various ministries could work together in some kind of partnership. Even though she had known this leader for several years, she wasn't ready for his skepticism. "We're all spread too thin as it is," he said. "We don't have time for more meetings. Besides, my experience has been that most talk about cooperation really goes nowhere."

After several e-mail exchanges with the partnership specialist, Joanna revised her strategy. In the interviews with the four other ministry leaders she took a different approach. She focused on where the leaders felt there were gaps in health service in the country and the main roadblocks they faced in their own work. When she asked about their interest in sitting down with others to explore ways to address these challenges, she found them much more interested.

Joanna had recognized a key reality in partnership development: Even to consider working with other groups, people must sense some need—either in their own ministry or among the people they are trying to reach or serve. Without that sense of need, there is little motivation to seriously consider working together more closely.

POTENTIAL RESOURCE:

✓ You might like to review sections of chapter 6. It deals with *motivation* and the crucial role it plays in ministry direction and in bringing real change to individuals. Effective partnerships are only launched or sustained by *motivated* individuals.

Whatever the response in the interview, keep moving forward, stay positive, and don't try to argue about the value of partnership. Here are things that need to come through clearly and strongly to the individual you're interviewing:

- Your love for and commitment to the vision (street kids).

- Your respect for who you're interviewing, their history, commitment, and service.

- Your desire to know more about their work and their vision.

- Your sincere belief (not dogmatism!) that working together really makes sense. You believe coordinated efforts in other situations have been shown to have real, positive value to (the kids) and to the participating organizations.

- Your goal at this stage is solely to explore the possibility of partnership and facilitate the process. Ultimately, any decision about working together has to be made by those actively involved—when they meet and talk.

Does this mean you are passive? Hardly! Already, commitment to this vision and the Exploration process has taken a great deal of time, prayer, work, connections, and initiative. And you know there is more ahead. So while you're a listener/learner at this stage, by simply being there, expressing clear interest in the issue, and positively exploring the potential of working together—you are *active*!

Any "selling" of the partnership vision may be more implicit than explicit at this point. But you *are* an ambassador, an advocate for the vision.

Let's check your progress so far:

- You have done your advance research and feel fairly comfortable about your general awareness of who is doing what.

- You have decided which individuals and/or ministry leaders are your priorities for personal interviews.

- You have a pretty good idea of what you want to cover when you are face to face with these people.

- You have, ideally, identified who the facilitator or facilitation team will be. These people need to be actively involved in this process!

TYPICAL CHALLENGES YOU MAY FACE

When you make the call to set up the interview appointment, what challenges are you most likely to face?

Remember, if you are talking with experienced people in the field—those working with street kids, for example—they:

- Are skeptical of strangers with new ideas. As we discussed earlier, they've had their share of well intentioned but naive people coming to them with "hot new ideas."

- Are skeptical of talk about collaboration. They've had bad experiences; they think it's a waste of time; they are already overworked and under resourced; or they can't see any potential added value for their agency or ministry.

- Will wonder about your motivation. So much talk about partnership is really a strategy by one organization to strengthen its own private mission. Often, partnership talk is really about a private agenda, not one that serves everyone.

- Will find it hard to believe that you really are only committed to two things: the welfare of street kids and helping the various organizations become more effective, individually and collectively.

- Will question your credibility, wanting to know, "What do you know about street kids?" and, "Who asked you to take this initiative?" (See the box below on what this really means and your potential response.) Remember that, even among Christian leaders, there are often well-established ideas about others' ministries. Those perceptions may be positive or negative!

The Nuts and Bolts

When you actually sit down with the individual, it is important to ask if you can take notes as the two of you talk. This lets them know you respect them and their time, you take their desires seriously, and want to make sure you can accurately recall the main points of your discussion. Do not, under any circumstances, try to use an electronic recorder of any type. Too threatening!

So, what do you want to accomplish in these interviews? Here's a checklist:

☐ Understand the history, purpose, current activity, and future plans and dreams of the individual or the agency/ministry with regard to street kids.

☐ Get a sense of the interviewees—their personality, style, history, "call" to their work, frustrations, and hopes.

☐ Learn what they feel are the priority challenges in dealing with street kids.

☐ Discover what resources they think are needed for more effective work with street kids.

☐ Find out what they see as the main roadblocks to progress on better, more complete service to street kids.

☐ Learn from them what other individuals or organizations are working with street kids. Can they give you their sense of what these agencies actually do? (Note: In this area of the interview you want to stay focused on objective information about other people or agencies—their vision, work, etc. However, be alert because, as you would expect, most of the leaders have their own subjective idea about others working in the field: their style, the quality of their work, their reputation, and so on.)

☐ Find out if this individual or ministry has collaborated or is now collaborating with other agencies to serve street kids. If yes, what's the purpose of the cooperation and—very important—how do they feel about the results?

☐ Do they know of any other partnerships or collaborative efforts, past or present, for street kids? If yes, ask for their description and assessment of those efforts.

When you have covered this much, you will have a pretty good sense of the kind of person you're talking with, the purpose and nature of their agency or ministry, and some indication of their openness to working with others. So, at last, you come to the two key questions we covered earlier:

• Does the leader feel there is anything that might be accomplished more effectively for street kids if the various interested groups in the area worked together more fully and consistently? If so, what might that be? If not, why not? (Note: This is obviously a critical point in the discussion. Make good notes and ask questions to make sure you understand what the leader is saying. Chapter 14 on the partnership facilitator has suggestions on active listening that may help.)

• If, in the course of these interviews, other agencies or ministries serving street kids indicate an interest in exploring the possibility of working together more closely, would this leader want to be part of those discussions?

SUGGESTION:

 Before you meet, write out the key questions you want to cover. The list needs to be short—no more than six to eight questions. In the interview, those six to eight basic questions may, of course, lead to related questions or issues. But stay focused and always get back to your core questions. You want to be able to at least informally compile and compare the feedback from the different interviews. To do that you need to be consistent in your approach. This is particularly true if you have a team of explorers working with you. Everyone needs to be working from the same page with the same limited objectives in mind.

At the end of the interviews, thank the leaders for their time. Assure them that if your interviews with other individuals suggest there is interest in exploring collaboration, you will keep them fully apprised. Even if people have expressed skepticism about cooperation, ask if they would want to be informed if any further talks were planned. Most leaders, even if they are negative, want to know what's going on with others!

Process Suggestion:

You believe the issue you're concerned about is important. You believe partnership could be a key to more effective service and witness. You believe that prayer is central to enabling God's people to work together. Now is a good time to bring all of these elements together. Based on your assessment of the person and the situation, you may want to suggest closing your meeting in prayer. This is no time for pious formulas. Now is the time for honesty and candor—in what you say and how you pray. The person you've met with, his or her work, the larger challenge, and the potential for collaboration would all be natural prayer points. Again depending on your assessment of the person and the situation, you may want to invite the leader to pray with you. Or you may simply ask if you can lead in prayer to conclude your time together. Authenticity is key.

A Key Partnership Principle:

The more neutral the partnership facilitator is, the easier it will be for that person to approach others with experience in the field. It is usually very hard for staff from a ministry already engaged in the issue to facilitate a partnership's development. Many will fear that they really represent their *own organization's agenda*—not the common good.

Is it impossible for an insider to facilitate such a process? No. But, without hiding their identity, an insider has to take off their own organization's "hat" and consciously seek to be a neutral, honest broker.

"Who asked you to take this initiative?" This question addresses your credibility, experience, motivation, and organizational affiliation. Let's look at it in more detail.

"Who Asked *You* to Take this Initiative?"

Stated or unstated, this question, in one form or another, is likely to be in the minds of many you interview. Count on it! It's not personal. It's not negative. It's natural. What it really means can vary. It may mean:

- "What is your real agenda?"
- "I don't know you. I know everyone who's doing anything with street kids. I've never heard of you, so you must not have much experience in this field."
- "Why do you think you should take initiative like this?"
- "I don't like the idea of someone else taking an initiative like this. It might preempt one of my own pet projects—or threaten my own inflated sense of my leadership in this field."
- "What organization are you with? I know all the organizations working with street kids and have real questions about some of them." (Getting your organizational affiliation is a shortcut to pigeonholing you and your likely agenda.)

Don't be discouraged. Remember, *working together is worth it*. But if it were easy, everyone would already being doing it—right? You can establish credibility with these agency leaders several ways:

- Their prior knowledge and positive impression of you or the organization you represent.
- Your demonstrated knowledge and/or experience in the field.
- Your previous involvement in successful partnership development and/or knowledge of effective collaboration undertaken by others in this field.
- Your conduct—both in the initial phone contact and in the interview.

- Your demonstrated, genuine interest in them and their ministry.

- Your demonstration of integrity—especially by what you say and don't say about other relevant ministries and their leaders.

- Your faithfulness to your promises. You do what you say you will do, when you say you'll do it.

Remember: Honesty is the best policy!

A CRITICAL PERSONAL QUALITY

Have open eyes, ears, and heart, and a closed mouth. *Never* talk about others you have previously interviewed in a judgmental way. "Revealing" anything but factual information can be the kiss of death to your credibility. Rightfully, the person you're interviewing expects that the things the two of you discuss will be the same things you'll discuss with others. Why should they be open and honest with you if you betray their trust? It often takes weeks or months to prove your integrity, as a person waits to hear from others what you've said about them!

THE CHALLENGE OF ORGANIZATIONAL AFFILIATION

Embedded in the question, "Who asked you to take this initiative?" are established ideas that individuals working in the field have about *others* working in the field. The "others" may be individuals, ministries (churches, agencies, and so on), or a combination of the two. You may be fortunate and already affiliated with an agency or ministry that is known to be competent in the field—and neutral. Finding both qualities in the same organization is rare. But if that is the case, you probably have a good base from which to work. On the other hand, what if that's not your situation?

If you're not affiliated with a known, respected, neutral agency or ministry:

- Check around for one that might share your vision and could become the home base for your efforts. If you ask diplomatically, people knowledgeable in the field may agree that there's one agency or ministry in the city or region who fits this description.

- Check with others about existing networks related to your area of interest that may already exist. Those networks may specialize in fields like youth, media, urban, or ethnic ministries. It may be that pastors are already meeting regularly in your area. You might want to explore the potential of presenting the vision to the pastors. In this case, your main agenda may not be getting their actual involvement in a partnership. Rather, at this stage you may seek their endorsement of exploring the partnership idea among other individuals, churches, and ministries in the area—and using their pastor's group as your base of reference. If you're working internationally, the networks may be focused on evangelism and church planting; Scripture translation, production, or distribution; or relief and development.

- In this early phase, if you and maybe a few of your friends are the only ones committed to the vision, say so. Ideally, you have this vision because you've been involved with the work for some time and see unrealized potential for ministry. If so, better to just say, "I've worked as a volunteer for x years with xx organization and have gotten to know a number of people in the field. I've seen how, in other cities and other types of ministry, collaboration has often been very helpful. As I talked with a few others, we felt it would be worth exploring the potential for more collaboration in ministry (to street kids) here in our city."

Again, honesty is the best policy. Better be up front, because in ten to fifteen minutes of talking, an experienced person in the field will know whether you know what you're talking about or not anyway. Honesty itself greatly strengthens your credibility.

It may seem obvious, but the scale of the area or complexity of your vision tends to dictate whom you need to interview. If it's your neighborhood, the number you need to talk with may be limited. But if you're dealing with a big project—a city, an unreached people group, or another complex initiative—you can't interview everyone. Therefore, it is all the more important to identify *key or influential* parties.

A KEY PARTNERSHIP PRINCIPLE:

You don't need to have *all* the players ready to talk about possible cooperation. But you do need *a few* of the leaders or ministries already recognized as credible and competent in the field. I have found that if you have thirty to fifty percent of the more influential people, you have a good start. The initiative will become linked to their credibility. If the partnership moves forward, the others looking on will eventually be drawn in.

PARTNERSHIP IN PRACTICE: In a partnership I facilitated, the wider group kept bringing up a certain agency they felt should be involved. However, the leader of the agency was known to be quite independent. I got stuck with the assignment of going to visit the leader in person to encourage the participation of that ministry in the partnership process. On my first visit I was hospitably received, shown every courtesy, and told, "That idea of working together for this project is good for some, but we are very clear on what we are doing. Thank you for coming—and do come back any time."

I felt I had been patronized and the larger group's efforts trivialized. But over the next two years I made two other trips to visit this ministry, encouraging their participation. Each time I got the same reception and the same answer. Then, at the beginning of the third year, one of the partnership's task forces was holding a meeting on a topic that fell in the reluctant agency's area of primary activity. After the task force sent out notices for the specialized working meeting, no one was more surprised than I when the reluctant agency's leader for that kind of work showed up, was personable with everyone, and contributed effectively in the meetings. Following that, the agency became a long-term, active part of the partnership—something that never would have happened if we had not made the patient commitment to communicate with and relate to them in the early stages.

Signposts of Success

OK, take a deep breath! Where are we in the process? Here's a short checklist. You have:

- ☐ Identified most of the individuals, agencies, or ministries relevant to your field of interest.

- ☐ Identified the partnership facilitator or facilitation team and helped them get the training they need.

- ☐ Put your prayer team in place and engaged their active involvement.

- ☐ Identified the individuals and ministries that seem to be the leaders in the field because of their size, reputation for quality work, available resources, or innovation.

☐ Personally interviewed at least the majority of these key people.

☐ Developed an initial personal relationship with these leaders so that you are known to each other and your motivation and vision are established. (You will have to keep on demonstrating your pure motives and neutrality. Be patient! It's a process, not an event!)

☐ Compiled the main points of your findings and identified key concerns/ issues that the people and/or their ministries have in common.

☐ Come to a much more complete understanding of the perceived challenges and roadblocks in your field of interest.

☐ Learned a great deal about how the existing leaders feel about the priority issues—and about each other!

☐ Developed a fairly clear sense of which leaders feel greater cooperation might have value and are willing to invest some time in seriously exploring the possibility.

☐ Have met with your core group of friends and/or colleagues who are committed to this vision with you. Together, you have reviewed progress to date, prayed about it, and decided on next steps.

Have you made it this far in the process? Have some of the key players indicated their desire or readiness to meet and explore possible cooperation? Great—and congratulations! You have completed one of the most challenging and often discouraging stages of effective partnership development.

Make sure those committed to the vision—colleagues, your prayer support team, and others—know how things have gone. They need to share the fulfillment of knowing that God has brought you this far!

As you move forward, you will never regret the investment of time and energy you have made in this Exploration stage. Ready for the next step? The Formation stage is potentially the most challenging of all: intensive, stimulating, and rewarding.

Get your prayer team, review your vision, and press on!

 Share your ideas and response to this chapter, tell your own story, or get connected with more partnership resources at the book's website
www.connectedbook.net

ON THE WAY
FORMATION
(PART TWO)

Core Idea

This is the critical "go/no-go" phase in the life of partnership development. It's when potential partner ministries say, "We agree, the only way we can accomplish this vision is by working together." Or, a time when they say, "At least for now, we don't think so." You can know in advance what is most important to give your partnership the best chance of being launched on solid ground—and with realistic, positive expectations. This chapter gives you a look at both the big picture of "why" but also provides the vital nuts and bolts of "how to."

It's when potential partner ministries say, "We agree, the only way we can accomplish this vision is by working together." Or when they say, "At least for now, we don't think so." You can know in advance what is most important in order to give your partnership the best chance of being launched on solid ground—and with realistic, positive expectations. This chapter gives you a look at both the big picture of "why" but also provides the vital nuts and bolts of "how to."

In the Exploration phase we have just covered, you will have developed information and relationships that are invaluable. You're poised for the big next step: "Will they or won't they?" It can be a heart-stopper. The process of partnership development can also be tremendously rewarding, both for the facilitator and for the other participants.

Building on the information and relationships you developed in your Exploration efforts, you're now at the key "go/no-go" phase.

THE ESSENTIAL SUCCESS FACTORS

Further on, I unpack each of the elements that will help you achieve a successful launch for your partnership. First, here's a checklist of the essentials for success:

☐ Enough of the "influentials" are going to be in these initial working meetings to lend the meetings credibility. You don't need everyone, but you do need a number of the people or ministries with recognized effectiveness to bring their credibility into the Formation process.

☐ Everyone clearly understands the objectives and expectations for the first round of discussions. If everyone knows the agenda and has had a chance to give input, the trust factor goes up, along with your likelihood of success.

☐ Your initial meeting/discussion time is long enough to allow you to develop a base of common information and relationships among participants. Trying to cut corners for busy people will come back to haunt you!

☐ You make a point of building trust. Building "equity" in your "trust account" will greatly strengthen your ability to serve and facilitate the process. Word will spread that the partnership and its leadership have integrity.

☐ You have pursued careful planning and facilitating of this initial face-to-face meeting. Don't leave the plans or execution to chance or the last minute. Careful, detailed planning pays off—big!

☐ Before you get to the vital "go/no-go" question, you make sure your participants have at least general agreement on the points outlined in the section later in this chapter on building trust.

PARTNERSHIP IN PRACTICE: Everyone Jack had met in the Exploration phase had said, "Yes, we're genuinely committed to connecting local churches and the needs of the schools in their city." Some were doing tutorial programs; others were providing teacher's aides. Still others were helping promote foster parent and "big brother" initiatives. Everyone seemed convinced it was a powerful way to connect the love of Jesus with the practical, budget-restricted needs of their local schools. Some schools had resisted the local churches' involvement—afraid of church-state issues. Others, however, had welcomed the churches' readiness to help.

Jack had spent a lot of time meeting individually with leaders. But when it came to that first face-to-face meeting about possible collaboration among the churches, leaders showed up reluctantly. Some, it seems, were prompted by guilt; Christians "ought" to be working together. A few felt they might be left out if others agreed to cooperate. A few were just curious.

Jack worked hard, getting as many as possible involved in establishing the meeting's objectives and agenda. Well into the meeting process, flip charts from small-group work lined the walls of the room. But frustration flared, in spite of the best efforts of Jack and his team. A few hours into the process one person said, "I'm not sure we're getting anywhere." Another commented, "When are we going to get to talk about real, practical action options?" It was difficult for the facilitation team to convince the participants to be patient and press on—getting to know each other and agreeing on the core elements of the challenge in church-school linkages.

Finally, two hours before the meeting's scheduled conclusion, the group had identified six issues that could only be accomplished if they worked together. Now it was down to seeing whether they could develop consensus around one or two of the issues as priority action points.

As this and the following chapter unfold, we will see what you and your team, like Jack, need to do

- to put the meeting together
- to keep hopes alive and participants focused during the most discouraging moments

- and, near the end, to see the whole group achieve what seemed to be impossible—a common commitment to move forward in partnership on key issues.

THE PARTNERSHIP FORMATION MEETING

Let's assume that your vision has become increasingly clear. You have a vision for a particular neighborhood, community, group of people in your city or, possibly a collaborative effort overseas. Further, you know it makes a lot of sense to bring Kingdom resources together in some kind of cooperative, partnership approach to a long-term strategy. A natural step in such a process would seem to be, "Let's get at least the main players together to talk and pray about it and see what interest exists."

As I've previously noted, twenty years of experience shows that often the quickest way to kill a promising partnership vision is to call a meeting of the potential players too soon! In your eagerness to get the interested parties actually talking face to face, it is easy to call such a meeting prematurely.

What is so important about this formation meeting? After all, isn't one well-run meeting similar to most others? Good question!

To respond, in the remainder of this chapter and the next, let's explore several key elements of such a meeting.

A "PRE-MEETING" CHECKLIST

☐ Have you identified most of the key resources related to work in the area/people you want to serve or reach? They may be individuals, agencies, churches, or specialized groups. They may be locals or outsiders who are active locally.

☐ Have you identified who is currently funding work in your area of interest—if anyone? Money and its influence are always an issue.

☐ Do you have a fairly clear sense of each person or agency's history, traditions, vision, agenda, primary experience, attitude toward cooperation, and history of relationships with other organizations? Can you sit down, confidentially, with a third party and recite the main points of this information—giving you confidence that you really do know it?

☐ Do the key leaders you have met with agree at least on the basic need for an exploratory meeting? Remember, as you have talked with these people in advance, many operational, funding, relational, tactical, and philosophy issues will have emerged. The Formation meeting must not get lost in details.

- ☐ Are the parties ready to meet and explore one key question like: "If we want to see real next-level breakthroughs, is there anything we might do better together than if we continue to work separately?"

- ☐ Does everyone coming have a clear, realistic understanding of the meeting's objectives? Have valuable but limited expectations been established so that the potential for realizing them is high?

- ☐ What level of trust do you sense between the agencies and their leaders? If there are problems, what are the causes or histories? Do these issues need to be resolved before an effective meeting can ever occur? (See the section on building trust later in this chapter.)

- ☐ Have you allowed enough time after reading through this chapter to work through these steps?

Rushing a partnership Formation meeting can be counterproductive, increase frustration, and give the impression that you are "railroading" ideas. Many major partnership or network initiatives take two to four days of concentrated work together on this first meeting. Can you do it in a day? Do you need two days—or more? Realistically, how much time will the participants commit to this endeavor?

Note: This sort of pre-meeting process minimizes the "surprises" for a facilitator, increases his/her understanding, enhances relationships and credibility with the main players, and goes a long way toward establishing a preliminary level of consensus *before the meeting ever starts.*

PARTNERSHIP IN PRACTICE: The "Exploration" work on one partnership uncovered a landscape littered with broken relationships. Intense bitterness, lack of trust, old grudges, and animosity were everywhere. It was an extreme situation. However, most of the parties said the vision they were trying to achieve was so important that discussing some kind of collaboration was probably worthwhile. It was just that they didn't want to work with "those people!"

The partnership facilitation team sensed that they could never achieve real Kingdom collaboration unless, somehow, the problems in broken relationships were addressed. But at the same time, no one was ready to come to a meeting *specifically* to talk about or work on those relationships! Somehow, the issue of relationships had to be dealt with in the process of addressing objective topics, such as the region's needs and the potential for working together. The facilitation team dealt with the relational issues in four ways:

- An international prayer team was asked to pray, confidentially, on the days of the meeting, with an emphasis on restoration of relationships.

- Morning devotions focused on the power and importance of the gospel message of restored relationships.

- Prayer times always included a segment during which small groups were directed to pray for each other's needs—getting to know each other better and coming to see the "human" side of their colleagues.

- Three teams of two people each, experienced in reconciliation and relational counseling, were made available, and individuals with known relational problems were asked, privately, if they would meet with one of these teams to talk and pray about the issues. Most of these sessions took place late at night—sometimes going until five o'clock in the morning!

These relational issues were addressed specifically but quietly and without any public fanfare. Almost all agreed that without this element, the partnership never would have formed and developed a basis for fruitful ministry many years into the future.

Trust—A Central Element in Partnership Success

In launching your partnership, keep in mind that the partners, leaders representing their organizations or ministries, must ultimately have trust in two core elements:

- The people: you, as the partnership facilitator, your facilitation team, and, finally, a growing trust of the other partners.

- The process: how the partnership operates, their sense of ownership of the process, and the fact that negative surprises are minimized and good experiences maximized.

We will look at these points in greater detail, but here are the six key elements that always have to be present to develop and sustain trust:

1. Common vision: Vision is the *what* of our dream. What major outcome are we hoping for in the area, among the people, or in the project for which we plan to build the partnership?

2. Common values: Values determine *how* we will realize our vision. They help us define the strategy, tactics, and qualities of the initiative that we feel are vital to realizing the dream.

3. Holding each other's best interests at heart: Are we committed to each other's organizational and personal success and health? Is each member's relationship with the partnership going to result in a genuine "win-win" situation? Or is the relationship only based on convenience and selfish motivation?

4. Competence: Can you perform the task, fulfill the promise, or provide the resources you have committed to provide? We have all been disappointed by individuals who made promises without the ability to follow through on them.

5. Reliability: You may have the capacity to fulfill your promise, but *will* you? Possibly more disappointing than promises than *can't* be kept are those that *could be* met but for a variety of reasons *simply aren't.*

6. Faithfulness. It is commendable to fulfill your promise once. But in a partnership, long-term reliability has a huge impact on trust. Will you *continue* to provide resources, show up for planned meetings, meet your commitments, perform on time, or demonstrate other aspects of long-term commitment to both the vision and your colleagues in the partnership?

Based on helping dozens of partnerships and networks launch effectively, here is a way to look at the key elements of building trust during your Formation meeting.

PROCESS OF BUILDING TRUST

The following diagram contains the key elements in your Formation meeting(s). Over time, facilitated by prayer, the building blocks shown can help build a basis of 1) Common information/understanding, 2) Trust—in the vision, the leadership, and the process of the emerging partnership and, 3) Mutually agreed-upon specifics for future action and responsibilities.

Well-intentioned partnership facilitators or facilitation teams frequently assume that everyone in the room or around the table is working from the same experience

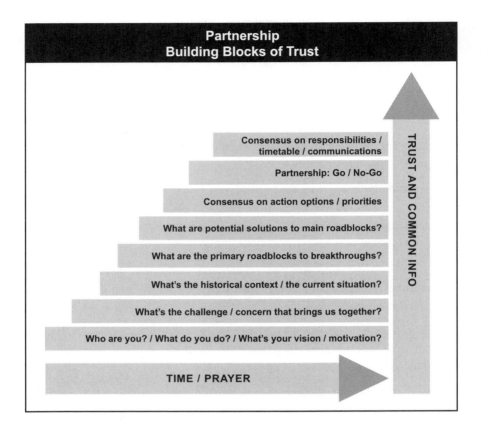

**Partnership
Building Blocks of Trust**

Consensus on responsibilities /
timetable / communications

Partnership: Go / No-Go

Consensus on action options / priorities

What are potential solutions to main roadblocks?

What are the primary roadblocks to breakthroughs?

What's the historical context / the current situation?

What's the challenge / concern that brings us together?

Who are you? / What do you do? / What's your vision / motivation?

TIME / PRAYER

TRUST AND COMMON INFO

and information framework. That is usually a false assumption and, untested, can lead to broken dreams, serious misunderstandings, and no partnership!

A person who is a native of a country doesn't *necessarily* know why natives do what they do. A resident of a city may not know the nature and real makeup of that city. A person committed to ministry with a particular group of people doesn't *necessarily* know their history, context, and other critical information.

If you take time in the beginning to help people get, at least approximately, on the same page, you will be glad you did later.

Working with others on a partnership is a lot like taking a journey together. As with any journey, people want to know the destination and whether there is a road map. As they proceed, they naturally want to know, "Where are we on the road map?" People want to know where they are going, at least the approximate route they are taking, and how they will know when they have arrived. Helping the group review its progress (where it has come from and where it's going) is a key role of the facilitator.

Partnership Recommendation:

✳ As you work your way "up" through the elements on the preceding "Trust" diagram, pause before moving to the next point and recap what you have covered so far. Focus particularly on those points where there has been agreement. If there are outstanding questions, remind the group of the method they have agreed on for dealing with those items (like having a small group work on the issue in a special subcommittee or task force, reporting back to the larger group later with recommendations). This will give the group a sense of momentum and confidence, as members see growing agreement. A big part of your undertaking is breaking what may be a complicated challenge down into parts that most participants understand and agree on. It is only the vision *based on the accepted common ground* that allows you to move forward.

Now let's unpack the diagram, element by element.

WHO ARE YOU? WHAT DO YOU DO? WHAT IS YOUR VISION/MOTIVATION?

Suggested Format: Individuals share their own stories (define specific time limits and allow brief questions)

Your focus may be a city in India or one in North America. It may be an unreached people group in a remote area overseas or a specialized realm of ministry such as young people, media, sports, or health services. Frequently, as you may know, many of the players have *heard* of each other but don't really *know* each other. In the partnership Formation process, building trust and shared information is vital. Here are some things that will help:

- Have participants tell something about their personal background—place of birth, previous pursuits, current role, and job responsibilities. Having them summarize in one minute their personal and family situation and/or personal interests—outside their job—gives the others a more complete picture of each participant as an individual.

- Then, have participants give an overview of their organization—a brief history, its primary objectives, its primary services, products it may have produced related to the topic under discussion, some idea of its size and staff, and its interest in the topic you are there to discuss.

- Finally, have participants share their vision for the field, project, area, or people that the group has come together to discuss.

When this approach is taken, most participants in partnership Formation meetings have significant "aha" moments, as they learn things about people and their organizations that they never knew—or seriously misunderstood.

In some international situations, this process has required twenty to thirty minutes for each person and can take several hours. In other, often Western, situations you may need to limit each person to five to ten minutes. Even then, it will take time, and the temptation is to take shortcuts. Don't do it!

WHAT'S THE CHALLENGE/CONCERN THAT BRINGS US TOGETHER?

Suggested Format: Main challenge/big vision written out in two to three brief sentences (on a white board, flip chart, or overhead). Have a brief plenary discussion to affirm this.

This is the central issue. What motivated you even to dream of building a partnership for ministry? What outcome was *so* important, *so* challenging, that you knew it could only be done *together* rather than by any single ministry? As you have visited with community, ministry, or organizational leaders in the Exploration stage, what vision have people consistently agreed needs to be accomplished—more fully, sooner, or more effectively?

What is God laying on your heart? What do you sense he is laying on the hearts of those you've met and talked with? Here are some examples that have helped motivate partnerships.

- In your neighborhood it might be: "The kids in our area need a recreation center with a positive moral atmosphere and positive Christian role models. How can we provide that?"

- In your city it might be: "How can our suburban churches really connect and consistently be involved with Christ's love for the urban homeless of our city?"

- Or it might be: "There are so many good things being done by churches and Christian organizations in our city, but there's no way to get information on these programs by category, date, or location. Most people don't know how to 'plug in.' Couldn't we be more effective if we shared and coordinated our information?"

- In your state it might be: "Teachers face a really challenging task, with increased loads, higher expectations, and tighter budgets. Could an alliance be formed among Christian teachers to sponsor initiatives, provide faith-based models in the classroom, and encourage and support teachers and young people?"

- In an unreached people group it might be: "Good work has been done here for a long time, but still there have been no breakthroughs. Could it be that we would see new opportunities, find potential joint action points, and encourage each other if we could work together on key issues, rather than separately on everything?"

When you meet for the first time, it's important to get this question or vision up in front of the group by means of a white board, overhead projector, or similar tool. Make sure everyone understands that this is a *provisional* statement of the challenge—that the group itself will continue to examine and refine it as the discussion proceeds.

What's the Historical Context/ the Current Situation?

In developing effective Kingdom collaboration, regardless of the focus of the partnership, participants will have widely varied knowledge and perceptions about the context in which you are working.

Suggested Format: Panel discussion by three to four individuals knowledge-able in the field, followed by discussion.

A Key Partnership Principle:

No partnership or network can effectively be launched, much less sustained, without a commonly agreed upon base of information and assumptions. This "common data set" involves history, social/spiritual context, information about organizations and their leadership and teams, understanding of roadblocks, and so on.

The following illustration may seem exaggerated, but it clearly makes the point.

Partnership in Practice: Imagine you have a spacecraft bound for an observation mission around a distant planet. It will take two years for the spacecraft to arrive, once launched from Earth. If the rocket's angle of launch is even one-quarter of a degree off, where will it be two years from now? Every second of the spacecraft's travel takes it farther and farther off course—unless there is a correction capacity built in. In short, a common understanding of the challenge you are discussing and praying about is vital to developing an effective long-term solution—and monitoring your progress along the way.

In another case:

PARTNERSHIP IN PRACTICE: Organizations had been working in a spiritually resistant country for a long time. Most everyone knew at least one or two other people or agencies working somewhere in the country. Despite the country's complex social, political, religious, and economic history, there was no regular, consistent orientation for newcomers to the country. When the partnership Formation meeting was held, the group held a panel discussion of four different missionaries. Each addressed a different aspect of the country's historical and current situation. As the panel members shared their information, the wider group was encouraged to contribute information or ask for clarification. At the end of that section of the Formation meeting, a high percentage said they had found the session very helpful; almost everyone acknowledged they had learned something significant in the process. Was it comprehensive? Of course not. But did it give all the participants a chance to hear the same material, interact on it, and consider the implications? A resounding yes!

A KEY PARTNERSHIP PRINCIPLE:

Sharing this information contributes to a common "data set" that becomes an invaluable "vocabulary" and set of assumptions participants will draw from as they move forward. Where their experience confirms what has been said, they can indicate that. Where it doesn't, they can use the common information as a point of reference.

PARTNERSHIP PROCESS SUGGESTION:

After each of these steps, make sure to summarize and recap the main points. Review the highlights of what has been said. Ask if there is agreement on the main points, while acknowledging that you are not attempting to be comprehensive. At this point often people will want to get in "their bit" that they feel was not heard or understood. That's fine. But, usually, that "bit" doesn't change the essence of what has been said and agreed upon by the wider group. However, it's important to give individuals opportunities to make their point.

The tremendous benefit of investing time in sharing and agreeing on the broad strokes of this information is that it builds confidence within the group:

- That there are no hidden assumptions or pieces of information missing.

- That you are all working more or less "off of the same page" of information, even though you will not agree on every detail.

- That the process is open and healthy and that the both the process and its leadership can be trusted. That no one is hiding a private agenda point that will lead to later unpleasant surprises.

Go back up to the five illustrations in the section, *What's the Challenge/Concern That Brings Us Together?* Those five visions represent a huge range—from the need for a recreation center for kids to the dream of seeing an unreached people reached for Christ. Each has a history. Each has a current context. The more we know about those, the more effective our thinking and planning will be.

In short, we all *think* we know the history, context, and current situation. The truth is, we can all learn more. By doing this *together,* we serve our objectives and build confidence in our relationships and the process.

Developing Consensus: What Are the Primary Roadblocks to a Real Breakthrough?

Suggested Format: Small group discussion with reports in a plenary session.

Let's begin to really examine the challenge. Get back to your main vision. Again, look at those same five illustrations given earlier in the section, *What's the Challenge/Concern That Brings Us Together?* Each of these visions has a unique set of challenges. But what *are* those challenges? Are they policies, circumstances, institutions, lack of awareness, lack of people, money, other resources, or turf issues? *Which challenges are the most strategic or should have the highest priority in your consideration?*

Note: The next chapter, "Key Elements of Successful Partnership Meetings," takes you through the details of this kind of meeting and gives ideas for handling small working groups, feedback, and so on.

As the Trust diagram on page 145 suggests, in going through this process you are getting to know each other and the real nature of the challenges you face. You are also building relationships and confidence in the group's ability to listen and work together.

As your small groups report back to the whole, it's vital to get their feedback up in front of everyone. Make sure you have plenty of white board space or flip chart paper or the ability to document on your computer projection system.

PARTNERSHIP MEETING SUGGESTION:

Old-fashioned flip chart paper is often the best medium. As ideas are shared they can be posted around the meeting room, often in sequence, and remain available for immediate reference as your discussion and work go forward. White boards have to be erased, and even computer documentation is able to display only one page at a time, requiring large type and much scrolling up and down to find work the group has done. The flip charts become good documentation of key meeting points—the basis for helping develop reports about your work together.

You want to encourage people to think as creatively as possible in small groups. It's important to give these groups very specific instructions on *how* to work—not what conclusions to reach or ideas to develop. The goal is for members to do their own thinking but to work toward the same *type* of outcome. You want to help the group communicate and work together effectively. Using the same *approach* is important, even though the *content* they produce may be different.

For example: "In light of our primary vision, identify what your group thinks are the three most significant challenges or roadblocks."

PARTNERSHIP SUGGESTION:

Here's a great opportunity to check back on chapter 8, "Prayer: Often Overlooked, Never Overdone." Each round of consensus development in this way provides a wonderful opportunity to pause and pray in small groups. Have people pray for each other's individual needs and for guidance as they make choices about action. I often have them first pray silently, asking the Holy Spirit to guide their choices and recommendations. It is always encouraging when the group sees that consensus about their vision is growing—that it just might be God who is actually guiding them!

Say you have six groups of three people each. In the above illustration you might think that the groups would come up with eighteen different points.

A KEY PARTNERSHIP PRINCIPLE:

If the group of people you are working with has any real experience with the subject under discussion, their ideas will tend to cluster around certain common themes. You can predict with reasonable certainty that the eighteen people working on a single question such as that posed above will identify only eight to ten issues—not eighteen. In fact, it would not be surprising if they came up with only six to eight. Their common history and understanding about the matter under discussion accounts for this. This is true in virtually every consensus-building process you will use in partnership development.

As the small groups report to the group they can identify points shared by different groups. This will produce the shorter list mentioned above.

The problem, of course, is that this group has never worked together on solutions before—never jointly addressed any of these issues or challenges. So we need to press for outcomes that are manageable—objectives that can be realized. This means we probably need to narrow the list still further!

PARTNERSHIP IN PRACTICE: A company building automobiles involves an incredible variety of disciplines. But all those disciplines must share an absolutely clear focus on producing an automobile. Until the team members have successfully demonstrated their ability to work together and produce one kind of automobile, they can't think about producing five different models. Henry Ford first built only the Model T (and only in black!), then the Model A, and so on. It was only after twenty years of company history that they brought out multiple models at the same time.

Later, if the partnership goes forward, you may want to encourage new individuals or organizations to participate, bringing their own perspective and experience to the partnership.

In the initial list of roadblocks, the group probably developed a raw list of perhaps six to eight. The next key issue is prioritizing these. Some issues are real but just a nuisance. Others are strategic and, in effect, create a "go/no-go" situation for your vision. The challenge is for the group to decide which is which.

At this point, it is vital to go through the process of small group discussion, feedback, and summary again. Two or three rounds of this may be necessary to finally get your list of priority roadblocks down to one or two—the problems that, if resolved, could have the greatest impact on reaching the group's longer-range goal.

DEVELOPING CONSENSUS:
WHAT ARE THE POTENTIAL SOLUTIONS
TO THE PRIMARY ROADBLOCKS?

Suggested Format: Small group discussion with reports in a plenary session.

OK. So the group has narrowed the most critical challenges down to one or two and has agreed to work together on the next steps toward realizing the main vision.

What's next? Now the creative thinking really begins! We need to think, discuss, pray about potential *solutions* to the priority challenge(s) we have identified. What are the potential responses to these roadblocks or creative actions we could take? What might be the most strategic action steps?

Again, to get the best results, it is worth the time to brainstorm a list of options in small groups. (You may want to mix people into new small groups at each stage, allowing them to get to know more people and giving a fresh perspective to group thinking.)

Here is another way to ask the question: "If we could accomplish one thing over the next six months, what would have the greatest impact on dealing with these primary roadblocks and realizing the bigger vision?"

Help the group go through the same process described previously. By discussion, prayer, and feedback, whittle down the suggestions for the most effective action steps to one or two ideas.

Keep in mind that, like the automobile manufacturing illustration, the group needs to walk before it runs. They need to identify a crucial roadblock or challenge, then develop and actually carry out a strategy to deal jointly with that challenge. This is a *huge* step forward and vital to both practical progress and a group sense of success.

You may need to go back through the brainstorming, reporting, consensus building process two or three times. The second time, if you have six to eight issues on the board, ask the small working groups to pick *just one*. "If we could successfully address just one of these, which do you feel would, in the next six to twelve months, *most influence* realization of our vision?"

When groups report back this second time, you will find the list will shrink to three to four key issues. It is remarkable to watch the group develop consensus. This process is vital to their understanding and ownership of the process and its outcomes. By the way, it will also do wonders for your confidence and that of your team as you facilitate the process!

In the next round, do the same thing, but this time say, "We have to get this down to one to two issues that would have the greatest impact if we could solve them." Again, give the groups one vote each, this time choosing out of only the three to four problems left on the board.

A KEY PARTNERSHIP PRINCIPLE:

Group meetings that work on processes like this develop their own personality and emotional atmosphere. As facilitators, we need to work actively to be positive, constantly engage the group, calling on those who may be less forward. Make sure the group knows where it is in the process and what progress it has already made. Referring back to the road map is always helpful.

Here's a reality check for you. It is normal for participants in partnership Formation meetings to go through highs and lows in their emotional/psychological stages of engagement. Often these stages involve:

1. Curiosity and anticipation.

2. Interest and engagement.

3. Growing frustration (at the slowness of the process or inability to see how it all relates to practical outcomes).

4. Re-engagement (tentative or whole-hearted).

5. Ownership, fulfillment, and celebration of positive outcomes.

The critical point, of course, is the transition through stage three. Helping the group see the importance of their work, the progress they have made, and how it relates to their objective is vital to keeping the group's hope and energy alive. Keep referring to the road map. And keep reaffirming what the group has agreed on so far. We all need perspective and encouragement—particularly when dealing with people we may not know well, when working in a process that is "foreign" to us, and in a process that we may feel we don't control.

The group needs to see the clear connection between achieving this near- or medium-term challenge and accomplishing the BIG vision that will probably take longer and involve other key steps along the way. *We need to walk before we run. And in walking together, we have to have joy, fulfillment, and a sense of accomplishment.*

At this stage in the Formation meeting, the group faces the following:

- Greatest danger: Letting the big vision dominate and having the group set near- to medium-term goals that are hopelessly ambitious. Outcome— likely failure, despair, and lack of faith in the vision and the potential of partnership.

- Greatest opportunity: Helping the group identify near-term goals that are clearly important as steps toward the big vision. Defining what success means in reaching those intermediate goals, and affirming the strategy within the group.

Your partnership's sense of success and fulfillment comes, at least in part, from the meeting itself and, in the months ahead, the work you achieve as you move forward together.

The following diagram suggests two possible approaches. Model 1 almost always brings failure. Model 2 is a simple approach that produces real results, a sense of success, and, with that, hope for realizing the big vision and the value of the partnership.

Unpacking the Diagram

Model 1

Motivated by a real love for God and the people, area, or project, people come together with big dreams. They set large objectives and decide to move forward. However, they have never worked together and have little experience

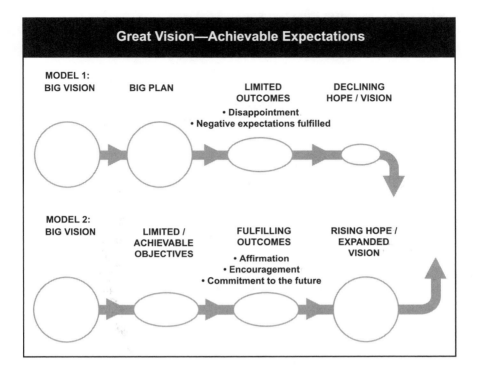

Great Vision—Achievable Expectations

MODEL 1:
BIG VISION   BIG PLAN   LIMITED OUTCOMES   DECLINING HOPE / VISION

• Disappointment
• Negative expectations fulfilled

MODEL 2:
BIG VISION   LIMITED / ACHIEVABLE OBJECTIVES   FULFILLING OUTCOMES   RISING HOPE / EXPANDED VISION

• Affirmation
• Encouragement
• Commitment to the future

in collaboration. The big objectives are daunting and, eventually, the projected timetable for the initial phase of the partnership begins to slip, time eventually runs out, and little has been accomplished. Disappointment is high, and "I told you it wouldn't work" remarks are made (or thought!). The group's confidence wanes, its vision declines, and hope diminishes.

Model 2

Motivated by a real love for God and the people, area, or project, people come together with big dreams. But, they realize they have never worked together before—that they need to walk before they can run. So they set valuable but limited objectives that they believe are genuinely achievable over the next four to six months. As those committed to carrying out the objectives move forward, they see good results and communicate them to all the partners. Everyone sees how these limited, short-term objectives are an important step in realizing the bigger dream. As the group reviews their progress and what they've learned, they are encouraged, hope rises, and they are ready to make a larger commitment—strengthened by their early successes.

These limited, achievable objectives must always meet two key criteria:

- All participants must be able to say, "This is something that is vital to reaching our common objective, and it is something that none of us could ever do alone." It needs to be clear that this vision is "a God thing"—something everyone believes he wants done.

- These same individuals must be able to say, "If we achieve this objective, I can see how, in the not too distant future, it will help my vision or my ministry achieve its vision/mission."

In short, initial objectives you set or challenges you decide to address must clearly be something that can *only be done together*. The goal has to capture everyone's imagination, but everyone who represents a ministry or organization must also be able to see the specific, potential value for the organization's mission. It's a simple equation: Unless these two elements coincide for all the players at the table, they will ultimately opt out of the process or question the partnership's relevance for them.

OK. Where are we? We've gotten to know each other. We've defined why we're talking—the big vision (even though it may only be defined in general terms). We've talked about the context of the vision. We've defined key roadblocks and prioritized which we feel are most important to address. And we have identified action points we feel should be priorities as we move forward.

Now we've come to The Moment!

PARTNERSHIP: GO OR NO-GO

If you have made it this far, you have come a long way. Great progress! Your vision, dreams, and hard work have set the stage for the group to review the potential of the work they've done together. As a group, you have learned a lot, developed a base of information, and shared a process that will have helped build your confidence.

Based on:

- What you know about each other,

- What you know about the big vision,

- What you know about the context and current situation,

- What you believe are the primary roadblocks or challenges involved, and,

- What you believe are priority action points.

it is time to take stock of where you are. First, it is important to briefly review the main points you have covered. Focus on the areas of broad agreement. A key part of facilitating a process like this is helping the group recognize their progress. It is easy for a group, in a sense, to get lost in all the discussion.

So you come to the key question. Based on all you know and have done so far, . . .

*Do group members think it makes sense to move to the next step and explore how they might work **together** to address this opportunity, rather than continuing to work separately?*

Before asking that key question, allow at least a few minutes to address any outstanding questions or comments.

It is important for participants to understand that at this point they are:

- Not making a binding commitment—either as individuals or for their organization.

- Not deciding on the specifics of an action plan or the structure of a collaborative initiative.

- Not deciding "who is in charge" or how much the initiative will cost.

The group will deal with those important matters later. What they *are* saying is, "We believe this challenge is worth working on *together,* and we want to look more closely at what it will take to do that."

Meeting Process Suggestion:

✳ Here is another natural point at which to pause for prayer. Remind each other of the big vision, its importance, and how much it would mean to achieve a breakthrough. Trust God to speak to people. They will respect you for it, and they will have greater ownership of the outcomes.

Make the process as simple as possible. A voice vote or a show of hands is often best. Don't drag this out. All you are asking at this point is, "Based on all we've done and learned, does it make sense to move forward and take the next steps in exploring collaboration?" Based on feedback in the main sessions as well as in the hallways during coffee or meal breaks, you should have a fairly accurate sense of what the group is thinking. Their response should not be a surprise.

If the consensus is yes, there are a couple of important next steps that we will discuss below. If you have progressed this far and the participants have agreed on the main points until now, it is unlikely they will turn back. Their own work and agreement will encourage them to move forward.

But if for some reason the consensus is no, here are a few suggestions.

- First, know that your work is not necessarily in vain. If you have come this far, the group has to have already explored, understood, and agreed on many key issues.

- It's probably worth the effort to take some time to identify the "sticking points"—the questions, doubts, or "why nots" in people's minds. They may be issues that simply have not come up until this key moment. These points may be clarified easily or referred to a smaller working group.

- Ask the group if they would be willing to go forward with the next steps and wait to make their decision (in effect, reserve judgment) on the potential of working together. Frequently more information and detailed planning can help resolve anxiety or questions in participants' minds.

Let's assume the group says, "Yes, we want to move forward—to take the next steps and see what God may show us." Even if the group's affirmation is tentative, the investment everyone has made so far deserves serious further work.

MEETING PROCESS SUGGESTION:

In a process like this, a sense of momentum is a great thing. This is hard work—for everyone involved. If your group has been working well together and has a sense of direction, it's valuable to keep pushing forward. But depending on your meeting schedule, if you have to break, this is a good time to do it. You may need to break for an hour or longer—perhaps overnight. Whatever the needs of the group's schedule, before you break and when you come back to resume action, *make sure* to recap where you are on your process road map. You want to maximize the clarity and minimize the confusion.

Developing Consensus:
Action Responsibilities and Timetable

Suggested Format: Plenary session that moves to work by an action task force.

At this point you are getting to a level of detail that a large group normally can't address effectively. Whether you have fifteen or fifty, now is a good time for the group to identify a smaller task force that can work through details of the next steps.

At this point, these are the main things that need to happen:

1. Participants should contribute input on resources, contacts, strategic ideas, and other items that could be relevant to action priorities the group has agreed on. Everyone needs to be able to offer ideas and resources in order to have a sense of ownership.

2. The smaller task force—possibly as few as four to six people—can use this general input and the will of the group to come up with practical next steps for action. The following methods of identifying these people are arranged in ascending order, according to their likelihood of success: ask for volunteers; have the group suggest or nominate members; have members of the advisory group (with your input) make recommendations based on their assessment of participants' interest and abilities.

3. Make sure the larger group knows:

- What action (in principle) the task force will be taking.

- What they can expect in the way of feedback.

- That no steps will be taken without the larger group's awareness and affirmation.

- Who will be responsible for communication to the group.

- What the timetable will be for communication.

- How they will know they have successfully completed this first step of working together.

- When the larger group will meet again.

4. The action task force needs to agree on:

- Who will do what.

- Who in the task force will coordinate the group's efforts and communication.

- Their timetable for action.

- Who will be responsible for reporting back to the larger group, about what, and when.

On Organization and Structures

How the group organizes itself is one of the most important steps in the life of an emerging partnership. Remember, you are always dealing with *individual people*. A certain dynamic exists in a neighborhood initiative in which those individuals are speaking for themselves, not some organization. As soon as the participants represent their personal interests *and* the interests of an organization, the dynamics usually change significantly.

In part five, chapter 16, "Effective Partnership Structures: Form Follows Function," I give further ideas, models, and ways to organize the initiative for effectiveness. But here, a few comments allow us to recognize the challenge we have at this point.

Some individuals, leaders, or organizations have had experience in trade associations, business alliances, professional societies, or other kinds of collaborative initiatives. Others have had little such experience. It is often particularly challenging when you move from the business or professional sectors into the nonprofit area—particularly religious nonprofit organizations.

These three issues always come to mind, both for individuals and organizational leaders, in discussions about how a collaborative effort will be structured:

- Decisions. Will my/our independence be curtailed? How will decisions be made in this new alliance, and who will make them? (The Formation process they've just been through should provide the best possible model of what they can expect.)

- Money. What kind of financial commitment will be involved, and will I/we retain control over that commitment? (Reference to how action steps have been discussed already may help people see that no "top-down" decisions or ultimatums will emerge.)

- Identity. Will I/we be able to retain our own identity, and how will this affect our relationship with our constituents? (The tone of openness and full ownership by the group in the Formation process should help people sense that their individual or organizational identities are respected and will not be minimized in any new initiative.) See chapter 15, "Building Hope: Meeting Expectations and Sharing Credit."

A Key Partnership Principle:

The challenge is always to develop a structure that will meet the essential needs of the partnership's vision, while allowing individuals or organizations to retain their own identity and freedom in other sectors of life and ministry.

Dozens of partnerships have found they can operate very effectively based on consensus, with very limited rules guiding their joint efforts. Others work from a middle ground and use a memorandum of agreement or other document to give structure to their alliance. Still others develop more formal structures with membership, decision-making procedures, and other elements that define how they will work together.

But until your task force has a chance to work, think, pray, and get back to the wider group, serious consideration of such details is probably premature.

Wrapping up Your Formation Meeting:
Reflection and Celebration

The Task Force needs to meet immediately and plan its next steps, in light of the larger group's expectations. Getting down to very practical action points, they will have to agree among themselves on how to call on the wider group's ideas and resources.

Finally, before the larger group disbands, take some time to get feedback from the group on how well they think they worked together. The next chapter suggests ways to evaluate your meetings. Take time to celebrate and praise God for what he has done with and through the group and to pray for breakthroughs as you move forward together.

A lasting, effective partnership depends as much on confidence in *the process* as it does on confidence in the *people* who are leading it. The next chapter builds on what we have covered here and provides additional key elements for successful partnership meetings.

Signposts of Success

☐ The majority of the potential participants with whom you had met prior to the meeting and who had committed to attending actually showed up.

☐ The group stuck with it and worked through the process, step by step.

☐ Relationships were cordial, and any sticking points were resolved as you went along.

- ☐ Participants affirmed the value of joint prayer times.

- ☐ The group developed a growing sense of purpose and genuine unity.

- ☐ Participants established limited, valuable objectives, planned action steps, and agreed on a realistic timetable.

- ☐ Participants identified and determined additional people or ministries to invite that could contribute significantly in the future.

- ☐ A small team of respected individuals was identified to serve as an ongoing task force and, along with the facilitator or facilitation team, to help move the partnership forward.

- ☐ An ongoing communications plan has been established and participants know what to expect, from whom, by what date.

Congratulations on your vision and perseverance that has brought you to this point. *Remember, if it were easy, everyone would be doing it.* Satan's activity and our sinful nature, busy lives, and private agendas all work against Kingdom collaboration. But Christ is faithful, and his Spirit will give you the strength and joy to press on.

God bless you—and may your partnership launch be wonderfully success-ful—a great experience for all involved. Having invested your prayers and energy, you deserve that encouragement!

 Share your ideas and response to this chapter, tell your own story, or get connected with more partnership resources at the book's website
www.connectedbook.net

12

ON THE MOVE

KEY ELEMENTS OF SUCCESSFUL PARTNERSHIP/NETWORK MEETINGS

Core Idea

! Meetings that effectively help God's people work together do not just happen.

They are the result of very careful attention to detail before the meeting, during the meeting, and after. A partnership formation process like that discussed in the previous chapter is a dynamic balance between meticulous work before and during the process and looking to God's Spirit for guidance minute by minute!

This brief chapter shares some of the experience gained over the years that can help you succeed and reduce the potential for frustration or, even worse, failure.

Let's be honest. Most of us dislike meetings. I dislike meetings. For me and, possibly, you, meetings have a bad reputation. Often my frustration is high, and practical output seems low. That is particularly true of meetings in which a disparate, fragmented group of people are trying to "get it together" around a topic of mutual interest. Most of us don't want to get involved in something that, right at the front end, seems likely to fail. In short, most of us have been to our share of boring, bad meetings. Who needs more of that? I trust the ideas shared in this chapter will raise fulfillment and reduce frustration in your partnership meetings. Trust me, it is possible to have really good, productive, fulfilling meetings!

This chapter walks you through some key principles and practical suggestions. I have used the partnership Formation meeting we discussed in the last chapter as the primary model for these suggestions. But you will find many of these principles valuable for any partnership-related meeting you or your colleagues facilitate.

Pre-Meeting Action

We assume that you have gotten to know everyone you are in touch with in this process—probably face to face. They know you, your vision, and your role, and they will not be surprised to hear from you. Better yet, you have told them in your personal meetings to expect to hear from you again, soliciting their input on the process.

Here are some recommendations for helping potential attendees have a sense of participation and ownership early in the process:

By e-mail or fax:

1. Circulate a draft agenda. *Remember: You are doing this because people have already agreed the challenge is so big that it would be worth at least seriously exploring the potential of working together.* Stay focused, but make this agenda general—a framework for your planned meeting (see the example later in this chapter). Don't try to list specific issues. The group will want to define those themselves as they work together.

- Indicate the meeting is their meeting and that the goal is to advance Kingdom priorities, not private agendas.

- Request their comments on the agenda, indicating that all feedback will be welcome.

- This input can go a long way, both for your insights as to the potential participants' ideas and in giving them a sense that they are being heard.

2. Identify and obtain a commitment from four to six mature, insightful participants who can serve as a meeting program advisory committee. They should give input (as above) like everyone else. But they will serve, informally, as a forum

for feedback and counsel during the meeting, listen to what is being said in the hallways, and give the participants a sense that the proceedings have a broad base of wisdom and leadership. Participants should be encouraged to go to any of these people with ideas, questions, or suggestions. It should be clear that this is just a temporary, informal group designed to help the meeting be as effective as possible.

3. Revise the draft agenda based on participants' input.

4. Arrange for a prayer network that will pray specifically for:

- The participants as they prepare to attend; for safety, open minds, etc.

- The participants and leaders during the meeting; for open relationships, truth spoken in love, spiritual insights, practical and lasting Kingdom outcomes.

- Protection from Satan's divisiveness and for evidence of Christ's power from beginning to end.

- A sense of joy and thanksgiving among participants during and at the conclusion of the meeting.

- Clear, practical next steps in post-meeting action.

PROCESS RECOMMENDATION:

It is *vital* to make the following things clear in pre-meeting communications and at the outset of the actual meeting:

- The principal reason for the meeting is to encourage information sharing and to explore possible cooperation on a task that has already been agreed is far too large for any single agency or ministry.

- No preconceived ideas have been suggested as to whether such cooperation will take place or, if so, what form it should take.

- The group itself will discuss openly and prayerfully whether any such ongoing cooperation or partnership would be beneficial and, if so, for what purpose and in what format.

- The process of discussion will be open to all participants.

A KEY PARTNERSHIP PRINCIPLE:

Investing quality time at the Formation meeting helps you and your partners lay an essential foundation for good relationships and strengthen the partnership's later work. It establishes healthy patterns and increases confidence.

Meeting Process Check List: Suggestions For Success

☐ To help participants focus and accomplish all they can with the time they have, arrange for the formation meeting to take place in some kind of retreat or conference facility—well away from their usual office facilities. No phone calls, except on breaks!

☐ Working through the issues outlined in this process will take considerable time. Maybe you can do it in a day or two. But many partnership or network Formation meetings take three or four days. Keep in mind the scale of the vision and the potential long-term impact if you are able to really work together effectively. Serious collaboration takes time. Many new partnerships and networks fail at the Formation stage because they try to rush the process.

☐ You may need to break the Formation stage into two or more parts so that a break of a few days or a week will allow busy leaders to return to their responsibilities. This will depend, of course, on whether the participants come from a fairly small geographical region or have to travel great distances. In most cases it is certainly less expensive and far more efficient to have one complete working session—whether two, three, or four days.

☐ If you do have to break the Formation stage into two parts, make sure: (A) The same people attend both parts. New people in part two will not be up on the information or relationships. They will raise issues the group has already covered or agreed on and, in doing so, frustrate the larger group. (B) Take time at the start of part two to carefully review key elements of what occurred and what was agreed on in part one.

☐ Have the group agree on ground rules regarding taking or making phone calls and participating in the meetings. If everyone is not on hand almost all the time, chances are lower for achieving the kind of success and wide ownership you and the other participants want.

☐ Have clear objectives—know the outcomes you desire. But in the spirit of a servant, allow important issues and decisions to arise from within the group. Make sure participants feel full ownership of any outcomes. In short, make sure you are a facilitator and not a manipulator!

☐ Encourage participation proactively. Often those with excellent ideas are less forward in sharing them. Call on those who haven't participated—just don't embarrass anyone.

☐ Almost every meeting has someone who talks too much or someone who wants to discuss an issue that is peripheral or too complex to address in the larger group. When this occurs, here are some ideas: (A) Say, in front of the group, "Let's talk on the next break and see if we can't work through this." (B) Suggest that your advisory group meet with the person on the next break to talk about the issue further. (C) Refer the question or idea to a smaller working group that can take the time over a break or meal to work through the idea with the individual.

☐ Keep providing feedback for the group. Don't assume that because you are all in the same room, everyone is hearing the same thing or getting the big picture. Keep reviewing where you are in the agenda, the overall meeting schedule, what has been accomplished so far, and where the meetings are headed.

☐ Return to and use the agenda as a "road map" and make sure to ask if everyone understands and agrees on where you are and what the group has accomplished so far. Confidence will rise if people are being consulted and if they know what is happening, what to expect, and where they are going. The more participants have participated and agreed along the way, the more likely they will be ready to make a commitment to future action.

MEETING PROCESS DIAGRAM

It may look complicated, but the diagram that follows is actually very simple. It represents the process we discussed in the last chapter, just related graphically rather than in words. For some people, a picture is (still) worth a thousand words!

Start at the bottom of the diagram and work your way up. It walks you through the typical elements in the meeting process. Each network or partnership formation meeting will be slightly different. But the principles do not vary.

MEETING FACILITATION PRINCIPLE:

At many points in the process you may be perplexed or wonder exactly what to do next. Welcome to the world of strategic facilitation. Keep praying, privately, constantly. When you really get stuck, be honest and suggest the whole group pray about the issue—in small groups is

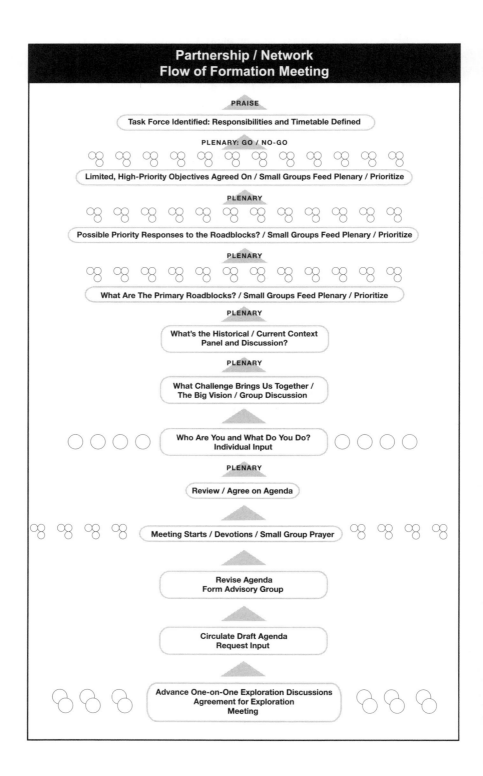

Partnership / Network
Flow of Formation Meeting

PRAISE

Task Force Identified: Responsibilities and Timetable Defined

PLENARY: GO / NO-GO

Limited, High-Priority Objectives Agreed On / Small Groups Feed Plenary / Prioritize

PLENARY

Possible Priority Responses to the Roadblocks? / Small Groups Feed Plenary / Prioritize

PLENARY

What Are The Primary Roadblocks? / Small Groups Feed Plenary / Prioritize

PLENARY

What's the Historical / Current Context
Panel and Discussion?

PLENARY

What Challenge Brings Us Together /
The Big Vision / Group Discussion

Who Are You and What Do You Do?
Individual Input

PLENARY

Review / Agree on Agenda

Meeting Starts / Devotions / Small Group Prayer

Revise Agenda
Form Advisory Group

Circulate Draft Agenda
Request Input

Advance One-on-One Exploration Discussions
Agreement for Exploration
Meeting

probably best. You will be amazed at how God's Spirit will give ideas and help the group achieve consensus on the way forward!

Unpacking The Diagram

Working from the bottom up, the diagram simply breaks down the process visually, step by step. It represents exactly the same format and process discussed in detail in the previous chapter. The circles suggest encounters between people; you may meet one on one; small groups of two or three can work together in groups that review and generate ideas, reporting back to the larger group; individuals tell their own story. You will see all of the familiar elements here that make for a successful early meeting.

Sample: Partnership Formation Meeting Agenda

General Example

Day 1

8:00	Registration/coffee
8:30	Devotions/Prayer
9:00	Background/Primary Challenge (Reason We Are Here)
9:30	Review and Agree on Agenda
10:00	Get Acquainted/Introductions: Part One
10:30	Coffee
11:00	Get Acquainted/Introductions: Part Two
12:30	Lunch
1:30	Historical/Current Context of the Big Challenge
3:30	Coffee
4:00	Primary Roadblocks or Issues in Addressing the Big Challenge
5:30	Break
6:30	Dinner
7:30	Free Time/Prayer

Day 2

8:00	Devotions/Prayer
8:30	Review Day 1/What Is Ahead?
9:00	Prioritizing the Roadblocks or Issues
10:30	Coffee
11:00	Go/No-Go
11:30	(If "Go") Identify Limited, High-Priority Action Steps
12:30	Lunch
1:30	Agree on Main Elements of the Action Plan
2:30	Prayer/Praise

Working Task Force (as defined by the wider group):

- Primary next steps
- Who will do what?
- Who will coordinate communication and feedback?
- Timetable for action and communication

Depending on the size of the group and time available, this format, shown here as less than two days, can be condensed into one very long day or expanded to cover three to four days.

SAMPLE: PARTNERSHIP FORMATION MEETING EVALUATION

Example of simple evaluation questionnaire you can use:

Please rank the following items on a scale of 1 (low) to 10 (high):

____ Facilities (lodging/facilities/food)

____ Relevance of meeting to your ministry

____ Extent to which your expectations were met

____ Effectiveness of meeting schedule/agenda

____ Potential value of an ongoing collaborative effort

____ Your interest in involvement in an ongoing partnership

Please fill in the blanks:

Most helpful aspect of the meeting: _____

Least helpful aspect of the meeting: _____

If I were to make one change in the meeting it would be: _____

_____

_____

My expectations of the meetings were: Exceeded ___ Met ___ Not Met ___

Why?_____

_____

Future meetings should include: _____

_____

What individuals/organizations should be at future meetings:

Name: _____

Organization: _____

Address: _____

_____

Your name (Optional) _____

Your organization (Optional) _____

Share your ideas and response to this chapter, tell your own
story, or get connected with more partnership resources at the
book's website
www.connectedbook.net

ON THE WAY
OPERATION
(PART THREE)

Core Idea

So, the group you've worked so hard to assemble have taken that big, first step; they've said, "Yes, we want to work together on this challenge rather than do it alone." But to get any real, lasting results, a partnership not only has to come together, it has to *stay* together. This chapter helps you consider the challenges you're likely to face and provides approaches to help you move ahead successfully.

If you have worked your way through the Exploration and Formation stages of your partnership, congratulations! To get this far in a partnership's development is a real challenge spiritually, emotionally, and relationally. The requirement of time and energy is a real test of your commitment to the vision God has put in your heart—whatever that may be. If you have made it this far, you likely want to heave a sigh of relief and relax a bit. Well . . .

If your group has said yes to moving forward, it is entirely appropriate to give thanks and heave that sigh of relief. Effective partnership facilitation is hard work—no matter how valuable the vision or goal. Those who have worked with you, those who have prayed for you and the process, and those who have taken part in the Formation have all made a commitment. But time to relax? Probably not just yet!

KEY ELEMENTS OF YOUR GROUP'S
NEXT LEVEL OF WORK TOGETHER

You need early successes. The important but limited/achievable objective(s) that your group set as their first priority *must be achieved.* All of the action priorities I suggest in the next section need to be focused on this. If group members sense that coming together in the partnership has really demonstrated its value, they will be encouraged, continue to participate, possibly even more enthusiastically, and consider more significant objectives. But failure to meet the group's initial objectives will engender disappointment, reinforce the view that Kingdom collaboration doesn't work, and make reviving interest in the partnership doubly difficult.

A KEY PARTNERSHIP PRINCIPLE:

No process is perfect. It's natural that problems will arise in achieving your partnership or network's initial vision. But many times you don't have to achieve absolutely 100 percent of your objectives (assuming you have clearly defined how you will measure "success"). What is important is that you have made strong progress, are clearly headed in the right direction, and your partner ministries and their personnel can see how progress to date will allow the group to be successful. The other critical element is that everyone in the group has been kept fully informed about how things are going—no secrets, no covering up. Active, positive communication is the core of strengthening ownership and trust in your group and its collaborative process.

PARTNERSHIP IN PRACTICE: INTERNATIONAL—The long-range vision was to see hundreds if not thousands coming to Christ in a large people group where there were virtually no believers. The partnership involved radio, Bible correspondence courses, literature, and personal witness and discipleship ministries. The group decided that a new radio program in the local language was key to opening the doors, establishing relationships, and doing the "planting and watering"—all as part of a long-range strategy that would eventually involve all the ministries.

Just designing the new radio series, recruiting production and on-air staff (some had to be trained), clearing air time, and presenting test programs to focus groups of listeners was a complex process. Original estimates were that first programs could be tested within four months and on the air in six months.

After four months the group was well behind schedule. Recruitment and training of talented people in the heart language was very challenging. But they had made encouraging progress. Everyone in the partnership was kept informed; a decision was made to have the first test programs done by the six-month mark, then to bring all the partner ministries together at that point to not only hear the programs but also to read and review the response from the focus groups.

Despite the challenges and slipped schedule, group interest remained high, everyone affirmed the decision to move forward, and all came to the six-month review meeting. At that time the group reaffirmed the vision and the next steps. Even though they had faltered in their timetable, the essence of the vision was alive and moving forward—and everyone was aware of the information and involved in the decisions.

What do you think were the reasons hope stayed alive and momentum underway?

PARTNERSHIP IN PRACTICE: Domestic—Three local Christian high school coaches had led an initiative that involved teachers, some administrators, parents, and a number of area church youth pastors. The vision was to develop a sports camp during the summer that could potentially touch every middle and high school in the metro area. The challenge was huge. Clearly, it could only be realized through a collaborative effort.

The group's Christian purpose was clear. The members wanted to expose young athletes in the area to Christ and his good news more specifically than they could on school campuses and through regular athletic programs. To get other area coaches to "buy in," the group knew the program had to offer high quality training and modeling, be "values based," and have strong, trusting relationships within the coaching community.

The partnership group decided to go forward and set two main objectives:

- Design the core curriculum of the summer sports camps and identify local coaches and parents who could teach and mentor the athletes.

- Talk personally with every area coach and get a commitment from at least fifty percent to endorse and promote the first year's camps. This coach advisory group was crucial.

One team worked on the design and another on calling on the coaches. Work went well on the first objective, but those calling the other coaches ran into resistance. A number were interested, but a couple of influential coaches were not ready to endorse the initiative.

The two task forces were meeting together every two weeks to share their progress. When the second group began to run into resistance, they openly shared their challenges. Since some coaches had shown real interest and the group still believed deeply in the idea, they called their whole partnership group back together. They identified individuals who could strengthen the task force by calling on the area coaches, mounted a special prayer initiative, and revised their schedule. For the first year they might have to alter the plan, offering shorter winter camps instead of summer camps. But again, everyone was involved, saw real progress despite the problems, and remained committed.

The group missed their first summer "window" but kept moving forward, held a couple of well-received sports camps over winter and spring vacations, and were stronger and ready with an expanded initiative the second summer.

Despite the disappointments, what kept the group going?

PROCESS VS. PROGRAM: DEFINING NEAR-TERM SUCCESS

The long-term vision frequently requires new partnerships to put in place a structure, or facilities, or a team in order to implement the core vision.

In the international example above, the group had to get the radio program underway and produce a response. It was the "point of the arrow" in their overall strategy. Until that happened, the other groups could be planning, praying, and preparing, but they could not realize their shared goal of reaching more people with the good news.

In the domestic example, the partnership needed a lot of elements in place before they could actually directly serve and influence young athletes in the sports camps. They needed a prepared curriculum; "buy in" from other coaches in the area; teaching, coaching, and counseling teams for the camps; plus facilities where the sports camps could be held.

This means it's important that we analyze the *process* our vision will ultimately require and identify those elements in our overall plan. Those pieces can be key milestones for our group, helping us identify success or suggesting course corrections we need to make.

In chapter 11 on partnership Formation, we talked about positive but limited, achievable objectives. We opened this chapter by saying it is *vital* to achieve those initial objectives—even if they are not the ultimate destination. By defining the important steps involved in *getting to* our goal, we are developing a road map for the vision. Road maps are important. They point to the destination; they help define the route, and they establish markers for measuring our progress. If this road map is in place, everyone involved can see the markers. They become points of focus for our mutual expectations and communications.

Without getting too complex, develop a road map that contains the main points and that everyone can understand. Some prefer a simple list—putting the steps in order possibly with dates for completion alongside the main points. Because different teams or task forces in the partnership or network may be working on different elements at the same time (like the sports camp project), a simple tool like a PERT chart (Program Evaluation/Review Technique) can be helpful.

Here are simple examples of these two approaches, based on the sports camp partnership:

THE LIST APPROACH

This very simple approach helps your group brainstorm and define the key elements involved in meeting your near-term objectives. Unpacking the process and "getting the pieces on the table" helps people understand who is doing what and when. The list becomes your near-term "road map" and can be used as an informal evaluation tool as you and your colleagues move forward.

Outcome	Responsible	Expected Date
Initial Meeting • Make Key Assignments • Agree on timetable	Jack and Robin	October 1
Curriculum Team 1. Define core objectives 2. Define curriculum / plan 3. Define staffing requirements 4. Identify possible staff 5. Present plan to full partnership	Hugo To be determined To be determined To be determined Full team	November 1 November 15 November 15 November 20 December 1
Coach Advisory **Development Team** 1. Identify key coaches 2. Identify additional people for the Development Team 3. Agree on group's approach to the coaches 4. Make calls 5. Check on results 6. Report results	Full Development Team Tom & Team Tom & Team Team Tom Full Team	November 1 November 5 November 10 November 15 November 20 December 1

A PERT (PROGRAM EVALUATION/REVIEW TECHNIQUE) CHART APPROACH

(Using the same numbers associated with the key outcomes above.)

This type of chart allows you to show a bit more clearly how elements relate to each other. In the chart below it might be that there is need for some kind of specific coordination between the Curriculum Design Team and those on the Coach Advisory Team. If that was the case, you might revise the chart to show how or where those connections need to be made.

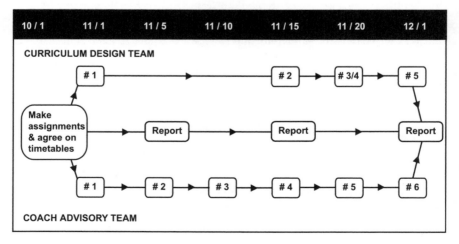

Making the Planning Work for You

Working through charts like these can help your group in a number of ways.

- It helps you to actually think through what you're doing—together.

- Everyone can contribute. Often one person will see important parts or missing pieces that the group has overlooked.

- It may help your group see the relationships between the various pieces in the partnership more clearly.

- A road map like this will help you think ahead, seeing the consequences of your group's plans or what will be needed in the next steps.

Just a reminder—keep it simple. Do the first few drafts on a white board or flip chart so you can move things around easily. Once you've got a plan you feel comfortable with, you can take it down in some form that can be duplicated and shared. But stay flexible. You can't afford to chisel it in marble! There will be too many variables! Expect change, and you'll be rewarded. (Some fairly simple computer programs will help you make these kinds of charts, but unless your group is really into technology, stick with the simple approach.)

Are We Meeting Our Objectives?

None of us gets involved in developing a ministry partnership just for the fun of it! You have a vision. It is a high priority and can make a real difference—if the potential players are willing to join hands.

What was the original dream God gave you? Have you thought through what success will look like? Many collaborative efforts break down simply because there is or was no clear agreement on the destination for the journey!

Almost all partnerships have both objective elements that are frequently *quantitative*—they can be counted or measured—and subjective elements that deal with more *qualitative* issues and outcomes. Qualitative elements include relationships, policies, processes, organizational structures, and opinions. It is helpful to have your team discuss these elements—always remaining ready to modify your approach once the group actually gets underway and you start experiencing the reality of both process and program results.

In the early going, meeting your objectives is often heavily oriented toward process rather than program outcomes. The reason? A fair amount of process work is usually required to put the key elements of the partnership in place before you can start working specifically on the vision that originally motivated you. The two case histories we just looked at are good illustrations:

Case #1: International

At first they had to get their main communication elements in place. This was before they could ever speak to the "audience" and prayerfully look for spiritual response. For this group, medium-term success combined both *process* and *program* success. Here are examples of outcomes they might have looked for:

Element	Process	Program
Design radio program	X	X
Test radio programs	X	X
Radio program production	X	
Develop Bible correspondence course	X	X
Identify relevant literature	X	
Identify personal follow-up team	X	
Radio programs on the air	X	X
Initial response to radio programs		X
Begin correspondence/follow up		X
Evaluate initial phase of project	X	
Key elements of project revised	X	X
Identify task forces for		X

- Radio
- Bible correspondence/literature
- Personal follow-up

Old Proverb

"Don't confuse the building that *houses* your work with the *work itself.*" While the building may be important functionally and aesthetically, it is a *means* to an end, not the end in itself. Always keep your ultimate goal in mind. Usually that is changed lives, relationships, priorities, or human processes.

In moving to the operational phase of a partnership, it is often easy to be totally engrossed in getting the key elements of the collaboration in place. Once you have moved into the Program phase of operations—the real reason you came together in the first place—it is important to keep all eyes focused on the primary goal(s)—changed lives or the other primary objectives you had in mind from the beginning.

PARTNERSHIP IN PRACTICE: The partnership facilitation team had been working together in the meeting for more than four hours. The group was committed to a highly strategic evangelism initiative that involved a number of different ministries. Months before, a number of key indicators had been established by the group to show whether they were on course in meeting their evangelism objectives.

But the discussion in this meeting had wandered off into a technical problem that one of the task forces in the partnership was facing. The whole group had gotten drawn into the problem and, in effect, had wasted at least two hours of everyone's time. (Two hours times eight people in the meeting equals sixteen hours of precious human time!) Spirits were lagging and, clearly, the group dissatisfaction level was growing!

I finally woke up and said, "Let's stop for just a moment and think about our primary objectives. As important as this problem is, can't we just make a few suggestions and let the task force resolve the issue? In fifteen minutes, I think we'd all feel a lot better if we could get back to the main vision and take a look at the progress indicators we've agreed on." We took a short break, and on our return we were able to move ahead with a fresh focus and renewed energy.

Case # 2: Domestic

Dreaming of influencing young athletes, an important sector of the next generation of leaders for Christ across a whole city, is a big vision. Even working together, realizing that kind of vision doesn't happen overnight. The group focused on a Christian sports camp experience for young athletes also has to deal with a mixture of *process* work and *program* outcomes to see their dreams realized. Some possible issues they will face:

Element	Process	Program
Sports camp curriculum in place	X	X
Identify coach advisory group	X	
Define the funding plan/initial funding in place	X	
Define desired outcomes (quantitative/qualitative)	X	X
Identify camp staff/teams	X	
Identify project working groups		
• Curriculum/staff	X	X
• Facilities	X	X
• Marketing/Communications	X	X
Define/identify/finalize camp facilities	X	
Marketing/communications plan in place	X	
Initial registrations	X	
Orient camp staff/teams	X	X
Hold first camp(s)		X
Evaluate first camps (objective/subjective)	X	X

A KEY PARTNERSHIP PRINCIPLE:

Keep in mind that for participating individuals and ministries, the partnership's vision and operations must meet two criteria. The partners must believe that accomplishing this vision is clearly something God wants done, and that accomplishing this vision will help them realize their own mission more fully.

MOVING TOWARD MATURITY

As your partnership begins to realize its key program goals, you will begin thinking about "What's next?" You have come a long way and worked hard to get to this point. The challenge now is to:

- Sustain and strengthen the elements in your initiative that are critical to achieving your primary objectives. You may need to strengthen the structure, increase the number or diversity of participants, or revise the approach to the main challenge you've set for yourselves.

- Ensure that communication involves everyone in the initiative so no one is left in the dark. You want a high sense of participation in the partnership and ownership of the outcomes.

- Pray and think about the next stage in the partnership's future. How can it be strengthened? How can the results be improved—qualitatively or quantitatively?

PARTNERSHIP IN PRACTICE—The Path vs. The Road: A friend who lived in Central Africa reported that a central challenge for the tribe he worked with was getting their produce to market. The main market town could only be reached by a series of roundabout trails. The trips were arduous and often so long that produce would spoil on the way to market.

Encouraged by my friend, the tribe decided to work together to cut a direct trail to the market town, reducing the journey by four to five hours. It took nearly a year to plan and then, working together, hack the new trail through the jungle. When it was completed there was both great celebration of their joint effort and access to new income.

Before long, income grew so that a few in the tribe were able to buy small motorcycles. Soon they began thinking: With the motorcycles they could not only carry their own produce but that of others in the tribe. Time to the market could be cut in half, and the volume of produce sold would probably double. But they knew that would require widening their trail to make it passable with the motorcycles. They went to work together again. Their trail turned into a path. The motorcycles were bought and the economy of the tribe grew stronger.

Three years later, the tribe decided that if they widened their trail, which was now a well-worn path, small trucks could make the journey. It would reduce the time to market still further and greatly increase the volume of produce and other products they could sell. It was a long, slow process, but they succeeded in the end. Working together, what began as a footpath through the jungle had slowly become a road, and everyone benefited.

Your partnership or network may start by blazing a rudimentary trail. Continued commitment can see that trail turn to a well-worn path that, eventually, becomes a road or even a highway enabling remarkable things to happen.

A Key Partnership Principle:

 Celebrate the milestones you reach! Acknowledge those who have made special contributions to the progress of the partnership or network. Let your success to date energize and encourage the group to continue toward the dream with even greater appreciation and confidence. All great journeys are made of incremental steps.

Emerging Structures

As your initiative matures and the vision widens, the group will need to consider how it will organize for effectiveness. Frequently the group's vision comprises a range of elements, each fairly challenging in its own right, that must be effectively linked together in order to achieve the end goal.

Collaboration can be organized in many ways, from informal awareness of each other to highly structured initiatives with constitutions, membership, and significant budgets.

I deal with these issues later in chapter 16, "Effective Partnership Structures: Form Follows Function." But at this point, here are a few things to consider.

Keep the structure as simple as possible. Don't let discussions or debate on *how* you are going to organize deflect the *focus on your vision*. The dream is what motivates people to join hands and hearts. Structures only exist to facilitate the dream and give clarity to *how* you do *what* you do.

Particularly in the early going, you probably need only a small coordinating team with a servant leader to facilitate. Then you can add some working groups to get down to the specifics of accomplishing the big vision.

In the *international* case above you could imagine the group developing several working groups or task forces that would focus on the key elements in the strategy. One group might work on the radio programs, another on literature and

Bible correspondence courses, and another on options and strategies for personal follow up. Each task force might have its own coordinator, and those coordinators, in turn, might link with the overall facilitator to serve as a steering committee.

In the *domestic* case we've cited, one task force might focus on building relationships with the city's coaches, another could focus on building the curriculum and identifying possible sports camp staff, and another might work on marketing and facilities. Linked with the overall facilitator, their coordinated efforts all point in the same direction.

In your partnership, issues or opportunities may arise that are clearly related to the main objectives but need special focus or concentration. Be flexible and engage the widest range of people possible in order to explore new options for service, outreach, or innovation in ministry. The main point is to make sure everyone is clear about objectives, timetables, and communications. Collaborative initiatives often go wrong when members (people, committees, task forces, or working groups) work on something the wider group doesn't understand or doesn't believe is a priority; don't achieve their objectives on schedule, through poor planning, execution, or inattention; or fail to communicate what they are doing with the wider group.

COMMUNICATING: WHO ARE THE CRITICAL AUDIENCES?

In chapter 15, "Building Hope: Meeting Expectations and Sharing Credit," I deal with four key constituencies that every partnership has: audiences that we need to keep in mind and in the flow of information if our initiative is to be successful.

As you get underway with your partnership, here's a quick look at those groups:

- The group you are trying to reach or serve. In the international and domestic cases cited in this chapter, who would those people be? Your initiative must listen to these people carefully if you want to serve or reach them effectively.

- The leadership of the organizations or ministries participating in your partnership or initiative. These people who give their approval and continue to affirm their team members' participation in the initiative need to know that the whole enterprise is bringing added value to the mission for which they are responsible.

- The people who are praying, investing financially, or in some other way supporting the partnership. What are their expectations? What do they think the initiative's all about? Can you report to them in terms they understand?

- The people in the partnership or network itself. As you dream, work together, set goals and timetables, and agree on hoped-for outcomes, expectations are raised. Anticipation can be high. These people are committing time, energy, money, and often other resources. Keeping these people informed, communicating the good and, sometimes, not-so-good news, is vital.

EVALUATION: ITS IMPACT ON CELEBRATION AND PROGRESS

We've discussed the importance of setting specific objectives on your partnership journey. Hopefully yours are limited, achievable, high-priority objectives that are essential steps on the way toward your overall vision.

One of the benefits of establishing those objectives is that they give you points of agreement for you and your colleagues by which you will evaluate your progress. The objectives become signposts or progress markers on your journey together.

In establishing these objectives we need to have first asked ourselves, "What will be different if we achieve our *overall*, ultimate goal?" You may be looking for change in individual lives, communities, institutions, or "the way things work." Your big goal may involve change or indicators in all of these sectors. Even in local communities, the fabric of our daily lives is complex—made up of people, institutions, and relationships.

But working backward from your overall goal, the plans you put in place will give you natural points along the way at which to ask, "How are we doing?"

A commitment to evaluating your progress can help in several ways. A pause to ask, "How are we doing?" is always healthy. It provides a breather and a natural point for reflection. It allows you to make course corrections, to ask, "What can we do better?" or, "How could we improve our approach?" It allows you to reaffirm your road map and overall goal. If course corrections are needed, stopping to discuss and agree on those points can be vital.

The worst possible scenario is to assume that everything is going okay. If we don't stop to ask the "How are we doing?" question, we're likely to find ourselves off course, confused, and disappointed.

Many partnerships or networks just begin to be really productive once they have been operational for two to three years. Often long-range goals involve change that is complex and takes a long time. Early in the book we discussed that one of the quickest ways to kill a partnership's potential is to call a meeting and expect that everyone will show up, that they have a common vision, and that they will agree to move forward together. *It's the "Surely you must see the world the same way I do" syndrome.*

Just as launching effective partnerships takes time, it takes time for them to mature and become productive. People have to get used to each other, build relationships, become comfortable with the shared vision and mutually accepted plans, and see that working together can actually produce positive results.

Defining and agreeing on near- to medium-term objectives, on your way to the big goal or vision, helps you and your group monitor, correct, and celebrate the progress on your journey. This means that evaluation needs to be *ongoing*.

My recommendation is that a small team, possibly just two to three people, serves as your group's evaluation team. When someone is specifically charged with this role it's more likely to actually happen! This evaluation team can help the partnership or network pause and reflect on that "How are we doing?" question, based on the objectives and overall goals the group has agreed on.

Once your partnership or network has been underway for a while, an *annual, overall evaluation* can provide the basis for both course adjustments and celebration of progress. This kind of annual evaluation can also be the occasion for the partnership or network to review its goals, objectives, and plans for the next twelve months. Reaffirming your course with the wider group's participation strengthens the partnership and the sense of ownership and participation.

Note: The appendix has a sample evaluation tool you can review and use or modify as needed for your group. Examine the questions or issues that this tool raises. The categories and questions may or may not be relevant to your specific initiative. But they do reflect the cumulative experience of many partnerships and networks—both domestic and international.

Money: How to Fund Your Collaborative Efforts

We have already agreed that the goal we want to achieve is too big for any one organization or ministry. People and their organizations need to join hands and hearts to realize the vision. It follows, then, that the funding for such projects will also be a joint effort. While there may be the occasional "angel" with a special interest in your project, the most likely sources for funding are those people, agencies, and ministries that understand the challenge and the potential in the collaborative effort and that have the long-term commitment required to make a real difference.

In chapter 16, "Effective Partnership Structures: Form Follows Function," I deal with money and partnerships in more detail. Here are a few preliminary comments.

Experience shows that the most effective, lasting partnerships or networks emerge from a grassroots concern for certain issues. They are led by people who feel strongly about effecting change. People like this are committed to doing "whatever it takes" to see the goals realized. That includes contributing resources like money.

While a number of coalitions have been formed around high visibility issues and funded by foundation grants, governmental support, etc., the sense of ownership and commitment to success is rarely the same as with initiatives that are funded from the grassroots—by those most closely connected to and concerned about the vision.

Frequently in the early Exploration and Formation stages, costs are comparatively low. There may be salary and/or out-of-pocket costs for a facilitator working behind the scenes. Frequently this person is given time by his or her organization because of the organization's commitment to both the vision and the potential for collaboration.

There may also be communications, travel, and other incidental costs. Often some person or organization covers these by loaning office facilities or part-time support staff.

As the group moves toward the formation stage, costs may be incurred for meeting places, food/hospitality, supplies, etc. These things, too, are often donated by interested or participating organizations. If cash is needed and there is no immediate source, often the group committed to the vision will, in these early stages, agree on a modest contribution by each that will allow the group to move to the critical go/no-go stage of Formation.

Dozens of partnerships are operating very successfully in various parts of the world with minimal, consensus-based organizational structures, informal memberships, and donations that pay for central out-of-pocket costs. In those same partnerships, if you look at the various collaborative projects, those projects may have operating budgets of millions of dollars.

In short, it has been consistently demonstrated that there are creative, durable, highly effective models of collaboration that can avoid many of the traditional problems associated with issues like constitutional structures, members "rights and responsibilities," dues and fees, and so on.

As you move into this Operational stage of your partnership's journey, the need for structure, funding, and defined roles (who is responsible for what) all become more important.

Conflict Resolution: It's Part of Working Together

When people work together, count on it—there are going to be differences in style, theology, lifestyle, understanding, experience, ministry approach, personality, heritage and background, maturity, and motivation. In a sense, you could say it's remarkable that we can find enough in common to work together on anything!

Partnership in Practice: For months Philippe had been meeting behind the scenes with potential participants in the network. What he had found was a very mixed scene. There was high interest in the problem the network was hoping to address. A number of the leaders had actually expressed interest in talking with others, though many were skeptical of the practical value of trying to work together.

The biggest surprise for Philippe was the depth and intensity of mistrust and broken relationships he discovered among a number of the key leaders. A couple of these leaders had, in effect, said, "If that man is in the meetings, I will not attend!"

Philippe and his team were forced to develop a comprehensive prayer strategy and team to pray for these individuals and the broken relationships. They also had to organize a special counseling and reconciliation team to come to the first working meetings. Delicately and prayerfully, Philippe and members of his team met with those who had come with strong feelings about others in attendance. In most cases, they were successful in arranging discussion and prayer times between those in conflict with one another, facilitated by neutral, experienced individuals who helped them explore and deal with the elements of their relational problems. It was vital that the discussions be kept confidential. Most were held privately in the evenings after each day's working sessions. It was hard work—spiritually and emotionally. But in the end, the team was convinced that unless they had addressed these problems, the network would never have been able to go forward. Not only were initial, important steps taken in restoration of relationships, but a precedent was set for how the network would address difficult issues like this—discreetly but directly.

Here are some of the natural points at which you can expect challenges:

- Relationships between people in the partnership or network. These problems may have nothing to do with the partnership itself but frequently, if left unresolved, can have a huge impact on your collaborative initiative. This is baggage that people bring with them.

- Differences of opinion regarding the facts or the context in which you are working. Usually this has to do with background, experience, or perspective on the challenge you are addressing together.

- Differences regarding procedures in the partnership: how your agendas or meetings are organized or conducted, who works on which task force, how the facilitation or leadership of the initiative is developed, or how the group approaches the funding needed for the joint effort.

- Differences in priority or strategic approach to the main purpose of the partnership.

- Differences in philosophy of ministry that affect the partnership's overall strategy or specific tactics. These differences can often be couched in theological terms. They may, in fact, be rooted in an organization or individual's culture, history, or worldview.

A Key Partnership Principle:

It is vital to address differences or conflicts directly and immediately. However, the *way* in which you deal with the conflict is critical. Those who are actually involved in the problem need to know that the issue is being addressed. But the number of voices heard in dealing with the issue must be manageable. Confidentiality is usually vital. Conflict or disagreement among a few can have a major psychological and spiritual impact on many who may not know the background and who, in the end, have little to nothing to do directly with the issue.

PARTNERSHIP IN PRACTICE: A conflict can appear small. But, not addressed, or addressed poorly, comparatively simple issues can become big ones.

Jason and his facilitation team had worked hard to get input on the agenda for their partnership's first working meeting. Their focus was stated thus: "There are many good things happening and wonderful resources available in our city, but a high percentage of the Christian community doesn't know about these things. How can we coordinate news and information from churches and Christian ministries to maximize participation and use of resources and minimize gaps and overlap?"

Early in the opening session, they took time to briefly review the history of the initiative and how the agenda had been developed. Then they took a few minutes to solicit further input from the group before moving ahead. Jason facilitated the first full working session, which focused on helping everyone get on the same page—giving background for what was currently happening and efforts that had been made to share information in the past.

After the opening session and a coffee break, the group resumed. But as session two got underway, one person asked, "I really wonder if we need to take all this time on this topic. Can't we just form a small committee and come up with a plan?"

What should Jason do? What would you do? How do you respond, showing respect yet keeping the group's focus? Here, in effect, was a challenge—albeit fairly mild—to all the work that had been done by Jason and his team to date and to the commitment by the rest of the group to come together. The objection probably was based, at least in part, on a lack of knowledge of the complexity of the challenge they were discussing. As is often the case, the individual was one who "didn't have time to meet" with any member of the facilitation team prior to the meeting.

Here is what Jason did. He started by saying, "First, thanks for bringing up this idea. We want to encourage everyone to come forward with ideas about what we're doing and how we do it. Second, I'd like to add that the facilitation team you've met here this morning connected over the last few months with almost everyone in the room. Together they came up with the agenda and then, as you know, we had a chance about an hour and a half ago to review it, and everyone agreed to move forward." He added, "So I'd like to suggest that we continue, based on the agenda we've agreed on. But I'd also like to suggest that Jack and Mary Ann, who are part of the facilitation team, meet with you over lunch and talk through any ideas you may have."

Jason responded directly and openly. He demonstrated respect for alternative views and showed there was a way for them to be heard. He ascribed value to the work the group had already done and expectations that had been established. And he got others involved, rather than trying to solve the problem alone.

As conflict—mild to intense—is something you should expect, be ready. Be positive. Be proactive in dealing with it. Don't procrastinate. Remember that differences of opinion are essential to the health of an effective partnership. The outcome of the conflict is often not as important as how it was handled.

Finally, in the bibliography in the appendix you will find some valuable resources for further help.

OPERATIONS: EARLY SIGNPOSTS OF SUCCESS

Here is a checklist of things you should be looking for as your group moves forward. They all indicate that you are making progress. You don't have to see them all happening at the same time, but keep them in mind as signs of health and growing maturity.

- ☐ Clear agreement on short- and medium-term objectives.
- ☐ Clear understanding and agreement on what constitutes success in each of those objectives.
- ☐ Clear understanding of the timetable.
- ☐ Well-defined and understood roles.
- ☐ Communications expectations defined and responsibilities assigned.
- ☐ Growing sense of ownership, vision, and commitment by partner agencies.
- ☐ Identification of additional priority resources needed for the effort.
- ☐ Evaluation, monitoring, and reporting system in place and working effectively.

☐ Participants organizing into functional working groups to meet specialized tasks and objectives.

☐ Individuals emerging to share leadership in partnership and working groups.

☐ Demonstrated ability to deal with differences and conflict.

☐ Growing trust and openness among partner agencies.

☐ Effective documentation program operational.

☐ Balance of participants and resources (church, parachurch, ethnic groups, etc.).

Share your ideas and response to this chapter, tell your own story, or get connected with more partnership resources at the book's website
www.connectedbook.net

PART FIVE
Working It Out

THE PARTNERSHIP FACILITATOR

THE VISION-POWERED SERVANT LEADER

Core Idea

! Every collaborative effort needs a man or woman deeply committed to the vision. But who makes the best partnership or network facilitator? Are you that person? You may be surprised! Check out the qualities of men and women, at home and abroad, who have helped God's people produce the most significant spiritual change. In this chapter you will also get a checklist of key things the facilitator needs to do and outcomes you should be looking for.

So you think God's called you to help his people work together? You have started on a remarkable journey, one filled with great challenges and great rewards. From Jesus' own mouth, here is his promise about the role you're taking up.

> You are blessed when you can show people how to cooperate instead of how to compete and fight. That is when you will discover who you really are and your place in God's family.
> Matthew 5:9 MSG

But to take on this challenging role, what kind of person do you need to be?

At a reception, my wife and I met a gentleman who had invented a device that, over the last twenty years, has completely changed the face of entertainment, information, and education—worldwide. His invention transformed huge segments of the electronics and computer industry. Later, my wife and I were comparing notes and the conversation went something like this: "If you'd seen that man walking down the street or sitting in a coffee shop, would you have had any idea of who he was or what he had done?" Our mutual answer, of course, was, "Never!" But life constantly surprises us like that, doesn't it? Despite wanting to be objective and accepting, we retain stereotypes of what people must be like to fulfill certain roles. Too often we judge the package by the wrapping!

So it's not surprising that we wonder, "What kind of people are best suited to be effective partnership facilitators? What do they look like? What kind of personality should they have? Would you immediately recognize them and their ability if you met them?"

Throughout the book so far, we've talked consistently about this person—the individual (sometimes a small group) who leads a partnership. As in all human enterprise, *people* determine the success or failure of any collaborative effort. *By* people, *with* people, and *for* people—that's the essence of partnership.

In this chapter, many of the themes previously discussed about leading partnerships come together. In chapter 16, "Form Follows Function: Money and Structures for Collaboration," I explore the wider leadership context of partnerships and how the facilitator fits into that picture and plays his or her role effectively.

A Reminder: Early in the book we made it clear that partnerships and networks are not the same. Both have unique qualities and unique, important roles. They are often naturally linked. But throughout the book, to keep matters simple, I've consistently used the word "partnership" to generically reflect the wide range of possible cooperative approaches. Wherever there is a specific reason for doing so, I've sought to point out the special relevance of strategic alliances, networks, covenants, and other specialized forms of partnership. The issues discussed in this chapter on the partnership facilitator, for instance, are equally relevant for networks, partnerships, or any other form of Kingdom collaboration.

THE TWO VISIONS

Even in a neighborhood partnership, serving as a facilitator, helping people work together, involves many roles. The frame of the car you drive provides the means for wheels, engine, and countless other parts to work together, pointed in the same direction, allowing you to arrive at your destination. In partnerships, two visions form the framework that must remain firmly fixed in the heart and mind of the partnership facilitator—the *purpose* and the *process*:

1. *The purpose.* What is it that you and your colleagues want to see changed? What is the point of the partnership? It's not the *value* of working together. Rather, what spiritual and other changes in lives and communities are you hoping and praying for *because* people will work together?

PARTNERSHIP IN PRACTICE: In the book we look at an amazing range of dreams that have inspired and motivated men and women to launch partnerships. We've already covered some of these stories—others are to come.

- A woman who wanted health ministries in a Southeast Asian country to more effectively serve the people and witness for Christ by working together.

- An individual who was committed to the street kids in his city and felt that God's people, working together, could have a much greater impact.

- A coach who wanted to touch the lives of all the high school athletes in his city developed a coalition of people and ministries to realize that dream.

- A woman who had a vision for single mothers and the struggles they face started a small group, which grew into a citywide partnership with real impact.

- An individual burdened about a "closed" country, who, after two to three years, was able to bring together diverse ministries that touched thousands of lives.

- A person concerned about the fact that radio broadcasters in his region overseas were not coordinating their programming or schedules. A partnership changed that.

- Church leaders in a U.S. city who decided to cooperate with churches in Latin America to increase their effectiveness and sense of fulfillment.

- Leaders of three student ministries on a university campus who finally decided it really would be much more effective to communicate with each other, coordinate their work, and, where appropriate, collaborate on initiatives.

- Four Christian camps in a single region who found they could serve more people and have stronger programs by working together at several levels.

What is *your* dream? Working together for partnership's sake isn't enough. There has to be a vision that attracts, motivates, and sustains people's interest. It's your partnership's *purpose*.

2. The process. You have a vision for something no single individual or ministry can do alone. That's the *purpose—the what.* But as challenging as that vision is, equally challenging is the *process—the how.* That is, developing a partnership or some other form of collaboration to realize that vision.

A KEY PARTNERSHIP PRINCIPLE:

Remember, the fundamental reason God's people don't work together is, naturally, sin. It shows in our fear, selfishness, ego, individualism, and protection of "turf." Satan works overtime to keep us divided. As a result, developing and sustaining effective partnerships takes great prayer, vision, energy, long-term commitment, and patience. It's a God-sized job! *If it were easy or natural, everyone would be doing it!*

As you dream and work toward an effective partnership, keep praying that God will keep those two elements, *purpose and process*, alive in you; the dream of the great outcome, whether in your neighborhood, city, or some distant land; and the dream of his people working together to make that dream a reality.

If the *process* is long, it may be hard for you and your colleagues to keep the *purpose* alive in your hearts. But keep in mind the hot dog stand and the skyscraper. If you are working on a partnership to do something no individual or ministry can do alone, you're probably working on something that, in principle, isn't a hot dog stand. It can take longer, but its potential is infinitely greater!

THE TWO ROLES

Just as two visions provide the framework for all you do, as a partnership facilitator, you have to consistently wear two hats. To serve the partnership best, you have to be both a prophet and a servant. Split personality? No. Important? Yes! Let's examine what that really means.

1. The Prophet. You may say, "I certainly don't feel like a prophet, and I'm not sure I want to be one!" The very word may bring to mind unsettling images: Jeremiah thrown down an empty well and sinking into the mud to die (Jeremiah 38:5–6); Elijah's life-or-death confrontation with the priests of Baal (1 Kings 18:18–40); or John the Baptist dressed in animal skins, eating locusts and wild honey (Mark 1:6).

But consider some of the roles of prophets. They help people see and think about what they don't *usually* see or think about—or don't *want* to see or think about! They call people back to their core values, like, "God's people really *ought* to be working together." They remind people of their commitments. They remind people of their priorities. They frequently help renew or focus the vision, and with that vision comes new hope. In short, they are communicators with commitment.

If God has really placed a vision in your heart, a dream of something you know is consistent with his character and the needs you see, are you willing to communicate that commitment? And communicate it again? And again? And again?

In your *role as a prophet* you hold out to people, individually and collectively:

- The vision of what can be if they work together.

- A vision for a new way of doing ministry—how the vision can be realized.

- New hope—for achieving greater effectiveness and touching more people by Christ's love and power.

In your role as a prophet you:

- Serve as an advocate, an ambassador for the vision of working together.

- Hold out the vision that it is possible to work together, that others are doing it, and that it really can make a difference.

- Encourage the group by helping them see what they've accomplished or the progress they've made.

You play your prophetic role in all kinds of settings: one-on-one appointments, small group sessions, and public meetings.

PARTNERSHIP IN PRACTICE: Three years before, I had certainly felt like a prophet—a prophet in the wilderness! I slogged around a country in Asia on four or five trips that extended over eighteen months. Finally, a group of ministries agreed to meet, pray, and talk about working together to reach a strategic group in the country.

After all that effort, the group did decide to move forward. I had to serve as the temporary facilitator, though they soon affirmed a neutral person from within the group to play that key role. But less than twelve months into the partnership's operations, I found myself with the steering committee in a meeting that got bogged down for over three hours in discussion of one detail of the partnership's work. The issue actually involved fewer than half the people around the table—but talking about it was occupying everyone's time! Was it important? Of course. Was it central to the partnership's day-to-day primary vision and objectives? No. Finally, I gently interrupted the group and said, "I know it's important that this issue get sorted out. But may I make a suggestion? Let's turn this problem over to a couple of people to review and make suggestions. Then this group can get back to reviewing the key indicators of how the partnership is doing on our primary goal—reaching this people group."

This kind of story seems so basic. But the prophetic role of the facilitator means you can't let a partnership drift, get sidetracked, or lose its focus. You can't *force* anything. The vision and commitment has to be growing in the hearts of all the participants. Participants can get preoccupied with either their own organization's agenda or some detail of the partnership that their task force or working group is addressing. Keeping the focus on the big picture is a vital role for the prophet.

PARTNERSHIP IN PRACTICE: I had already been sitting for three hours in a Paris cafe talking with a gentleman about a strategic partnership and how other leaders in the partnership really wanted the participation of his ministry. We had finally taken our coffee to a bench outside and were talking in the afternoon sun. He was pleasant but continued to suggest that either his ministry couldn't contribute anything to the group or that his group was doing just fine on its own. Finally, partly in frustration and partly out of what I really felt were Kingdom principles, I said: "You know, my sense is that the Kingdom vision of the need for God's people to work together simply isn't a priority for you. That the biblical imperatives of Jesus in John 17 that we love each other and work together and Paul's vision in Romans 12 of the various elements of the Body linked to each other, practically speaking, just don't figure into your ministry."

His predictable response was, "Oh no. I think it's important to work with other ministries!"

So I continued. "All right, I believe you. And with that in mind, I'd like to challenge you to explore an alternative approach. It doesn't mean replacing what you're doing, but expanding it. Send one of your key people to the partnership's next working meeting. Better yet, come yourself so you can meet the other leaders and make up your own mind whether there is any value."

It wasn't an easy thing to say. Frankly, it can be daunting to challenge the leadership of an established ministry—even if you have logic and Scripture on your side, and even if you do so in a quiet spirit of humility and grace! But it's often the kind of prophetic role the facilitator has to play. How did the story turn out? The leader actually came to the next working meeting, and his ministry became a growing, vital part of the partnership. They continue to be active today, and that leader is a strong advocate for the partnership vision.

---

2. *The servant.* That great passage in Philippians 2:6–7 summarizes the model for this facilitation role:

> He always had the nature of God, but he did not think that
> by force he should try to become equal with God. Instead of
> this, of his own free will he gave up all that he had, and took
> the nature of a servant. He became like a human being and
> appeared in human likeness. (GNT)

Was Jesus considered a prophet? Did he have a clear vision? Did he provide extraordinary leadership? Of course! But here we see him characterized as the model *servant.* Does this mean you are passive in your servant role as a facilitator? Hardly. Commitment to this vision takes time, prayer, work, connections, and *initiative*. You listen, you learn, you help, but the servant never loses the clarity of his or her vision. That prophetic vision is always there in the background like your North Star guiding all you do.

In your *role as a servant*, some of your key roles are to:

- Help individual ministries see where they can or do fit into the bigger picture.
- Help ministries find points in common they never knew they had.
- Help ministries integrate their work—finding ways to link with others when they've never done it before.

As a servant you also:

- Help fellow believers build and strengthen relationships.
- Help the partnership or network work well—and keep working—through effective communications, meetings, productive task forces, etc.
- Help the group monitor and evaluate its progress—providing encouragement, course correction, and reports to others.

PARTNERSHIP IN PRACTICE: In working with partnerships and networks over the years I've played dozens of behind-the-scenes servant roles. Dishwasher—helping clean up after working meetings. Logistics coordinator—arranging hotels, meals, and facilities. Prayer coordinator—in the early going, before the partnership or network had its own prayer team, recruiting and communicating with those who provided the spiritual "engine" for the work. Arbitrator—helping partner ministry-leaders reconcile or work through their differences. Counselor—listening into the wee, small hours to partnership participants as they unload personal burdens with someone they consider neutral and willing to listen. Resource facilitator—helping task forces, working groups, or individual ministries in the partnership locate and connect with the resources they need to move forward.

As the partnership or network grows and individuals or groups with the initiative emerge with various gifts, many of these roles can and should be given to others.

This increases their sense of ownership and responsibility. But keep your eyes, ears, and heart open. You'll find there will always be a need for your servant role.

PARTNERSHIP IN PRACTICE: A missionary friend had a burning vision for a people group in the greater Middle East. For over two years he had met, talked, and prayed with potential partner ministries. The two of us had met several times, and he asked if I would act as a kind of advisor in the facilitation process.

Finally, the day came when over fifty individuals came from many countries to pray and explore the potential of working together. The first six hours of the two-and-a-half-day meeting seemed to go well. There was energy, hope, and a sense of value in the discussions. Shortly before the mid-afternoon break, questions were raised about how things might be organized. Differing points of view were raised, with increasing agitation. My friend, deeply committed to the people group, but inexperienced in facilitating a large, diverse group, seemed to be getting more deeply into trouble as the group wandered into a topic that, at this point in the process, was irrelevant. The sense of unity and direction that had built through early afternoon seemed to be rapidly eroding.

From the back of the room I signaled to my friend that I thought it was time to take the afternoon break. On the break we discussed the situation. I said, "You know, these wonderful people have virtually no experience at working together successfully. What you were hearing in the last thirty minutes were their fears, based on the previous failures they've seen. In fact, the group has already agreed on huge, important areas that are vital to partnership. They've forgotten and just need to be reminded of this."

My friend asked if I would come to the front after the break and help facilitate the remainder of the afternoon. I had been introduced a couple of times, so I was no stranger to the group. I started by reviewing, point by point, our discussions of the first four to five hours, and all the key places in which we had agreed. I wrote out the points on a flip chart at the front. I asked the group if they concurred that we had, in fact, achieved consensus or agreed on those points. There was strong affirmation. I suggested, "The points about organization that were being raised are important. But they could probably be addressed more effectively tomorrow, once we've covered some other key, preliminary issues. It may be that we will be able to have a small task force work on issues of organization for us. In the meantime, let's pick up where we left off early this afternoon—those key points on which we've agreed—and move on with our agenda from there." In minutes the mood of the group changed. Hope and forward energy were reignited. The delicate role of prophet and servant had been tested.

The facilitator can only be that. Because of our deep commitment to the vision and the process, it's tempting to cross the line and try to *make sure* the outcomes occur the way we've hoped and prayed for. But crossing the line can easily take us from facilitation to manipulation. It's a dangerous place to be—with a short-term life and dubious future. In the case above, the key thing was not forcing the people to do anything. It was not "regaining control" of the meeting or process. It was, with prophetic insights, as a servant, helping the group members refocus on the importance of their own vision and the consensus they'd already achieved. It was suggesting how their very good start could be a strong basis for moving forward, rather than getting sidetracked on premature issues that could not possibly be answered at that point.

CREDIBILITY AND THE FACILITATOR

One additional thought on the servant's role. My days in journalism remind me of the importance of personal credibility. You may have brains, contacts, knowledge and experience, but unless you are *personally credible*, you won't be able to serve well.

Dictionaries often characterize *credibility* as being trustworthy, believable, or reliable. How do you become credible in the eyes of those in your partnership?

You can possess *ascribed* credibility—that is, folks hear from other sources what you have done in some other situation and believe it, even though they haven't worked with you. They trust others who trust you. They apply or ascribe those qualities to you because of what others have said.

Then there's *earned* credibility. If you are going to work with a partnership over a period of time, even the most generous amount of ascribed credibility has to become earned credibility. People need to get to know you and watch your life and performance day in and day out, week in and week out. They establish their own perception of your credibility.

These factors strengthen your credibility as a facilitator:

- You demonstrate you have a heart and spirit of maturity, clearly committed to Christ and his Kingdom.

- You demonstrate a sense of urgency about the vision on your heart—whether it is a neighborhood, a special sector of people in your city, or an unreached people group in a distant location.

- You demonstrate knowledge about what's involved in successful collaboration.

- Your organization, if you are attached to one, has a good reputation.

- You remain neutral and committed to everyone's success, together, rather than to a private, one-person or one-organization agenda.

- You show genuine interest in other ministry leaders and their vision.

- You are consistent in what you say and how you act.

- You handle confidential or sensitive information responsibly—both what you say and don't say about other ministries and their leaders is important.

- You keep your promises. You do what you say you'll do, when you say you'll do it. If you find you can't keep the promises, you're honest and indicate realistically what you are going to do.

YOUR PERSONAL STYLE

How you work is as important as *what you do*. As you think about the qualities of an effective facilitator, never confuse a strong personality with a loud, dominant, or aggressive personality. Facilitating Kingdom collaboration calls for strong vision, commitment, and willingness to keep going even in the face of daunting challenges. Those challenges may be in communicating the overall vision or in a one-on-one meeting with someone who just doesn't seem to "get it." It may mean playing any of the prophet or servant roles we've discussed. But strength and effectiveness start with who you are—deep inside. Eventually, if not very soon, *who you are* will always come out in *what you do*.

For most of us, it's natural to wonder what others think of us. But to intentionally evaluate your communication and relational effectiveness isn't so natural. Taking time to reflect on how you "come off" to people, *why* they think of you as they do, requires intentionality.

One way to think about your style and, therefore, your effectiveness in partnership development is to ask: "What kind of impression do I make as I meet and work with others? What do folks think or say about my style following our meetings together? Would they recommend that a friend, colleague, or head of another organization meet with me?"

Many times, of course, we can pick up how effective our leadership is by the way things go or the anecdotal things people say. But there's no substitute to simply asking people how they think you're doing.

When you do your partnership evaluation, whether it's at the end of a particular meeting or on an annual basis, always include evaluation of your facilitation team. If the responses are anonymous, you will likely get good feedback. Even more important is to ask those you trust to be honest, not necessarily your friends who will just say complimentary things. It's often hard to ask others for this personal feedback. Sometimes people feel awkward because they want to be pleasant and affirming and avoid issues that seem negative. But here are some approaches you can take:

- "How did you think things went—what did you think was effective and what could have been done better?"

- "What could I (or we, if you're working with a facilitation team) have done differently to get a stronger outcome?"

- "What suggestions would you make about the way I facilitate these meetings (the work) in the future? What would make things work better?"

Experience over the years suggests that the most effective style is one that brings together sincerity, vision, and conviction, combined with a low-key or calm approach to the process. A sense of humor is always valuable, even if you're discussing serious matters. There's always something on the lighter side that can bring smiles and help lower the intensity of the discussions. Take your vision and topic of collaboration seriously. But don't take *yourself* too seriously!

Most of us have a way of communicating or relating to people that we have developed over the years, often almost unconsciously. It is helpful to, first, become aware of the style or communication approach of your audience. Then, while being true to yourself, try to communicate or relate in a way that is consistent with your audience's style. Whether you audience is an individual or a group, the *way* they communicate is important to them and affects how you will be received. Imagine sitting in the other person's chair while looking at and listening to yourself. What's the impression you get? Is it the impression you want to communicate? What, if anything, would help you communicate more effectively? Keep in mind that you're speaking *with* people, not *to* them.

Partnership Suggestion:

✱ With regard to personal style, think of the qualities of a good servant. Take a minute with a piece of paper and brainstorm: What are the qualities of a real servant? Again, think of Jesus as the model.

What kind of a list did you come up with? Here are some thoughts. Good servants demonstrate respect, listen well, and speak with a reasonable voice. They seek the best interests of the ones they serve. They are reliable and can be counted on. They don't try to upstage other people, and they actively work to help the other people's dreams or purposes come true. They have a clear vision of their role(s) and responsibilities. Are good servants weak or passive? Of course not. They have to *know* their role, *believe in it*, and play their part *with appropriate vigor*.

What About Listening?

What do you think is the single most important factor in good, interpersonal communications? Since infancy we've been exchanging information with others. In human relationships our communication goes on at many levels—tone of voice, posture, facial expressions, vocabulary. In the appropriate setting, the gift of touch is a powerful communication tool. Intentional, thoughtful silence can also be an important element. A variety of wonderful books and articles have been written on human communication. Some of the best are listed in the appendix.

But in the partnership facilitator's role, effective listening is so vital it merits specific discussion here. While this may seem obvious, we can all improve as listeners. The problem is that we've been listening for so long we think it's "natural." Almost like the rhythm of our heartbeat, controlled by our autonomic nervous system, we assume we don't have to think about it! Typically, it's only when we're challenged, things aren't clear, or other interpersonal difficulties arise that we even give passing thought to our communications. Even then, our effectiveness as listeners is often last to come to mind.

Here is a place to start. Be quiet. A key element of good listening is *not* speaking. Effective communication is not necessarily eloquence—using words or vocal intonation well. Your effectiveness is often in what you don't say and when you don't speak. But don't think of being quiet as being passive. Being quiet is a vital part of thoughtful, active listening.

Effective listening is also closely linked to being able and willing to ask good questions. An old parable suggests, "The person who knows he's right never has to ask questions." Think of some of the people you know or have lived or worked with. They're absolutely certain of what they know and believe and aren't interested in listening to others—much less asking any real questions. The more certain we are of our position, the less we are likely to be genuinely curious—wanting to ask questions and know even more. Active listening is far from a sign of weakness; it's a sign of maturity and effectiveness.

In this context, think about Jesus. How much does he know? He is the second person of the Trinity. He spoke and the world was created. As we read the Gospels we see that he knew men and women's hearts before they spoke. Yet despite his all-encompassing understanding and knowledge, he was the master questioner.

The Old Testament, from the first chapters of Genesis, points us in the God direction. In short, a closer look reveals that the nature of God's relationship with us is one in which God talks *with* us not *to* us.

Think about it. How did God deal with Adam and Eve after their fateful decision? Did he immediately declare them guilty? Did he immediately pronounce judgment? Go back and read the first half of Genesis 3. At this most critical, watershed moment of the human saga, how did he communicate? God knew what had happened; he knew the hearts of Adam and Eve. He knew what the fateful consequences were going to be. Still, he did not make statements. *God asked questions!* And as he asked, *Adam and Eve discovered their own tragic dilemma.*

All through the Old Testament and the Gospels and the chronicle of Jesus' life, we find account after wonderful account of God in *two-way* communication with men and women.

As a partnership facilitator you need to be deeply committed to the issues you're working on; the basic challenge or vision God has put on your heart, plus the idea that, to realize that vision, his people need to work together. But never think that your commitment to a vision and the need to listen are mutually exclusive.

Unlike God, we don't know everything. Nevertheless, I am sometimes amazed at the way I have acted. I recall standing in the hallway of our family home years ago with one of my young daughters during one fairly tense exchange. I was certain I understood what was going on, why my daughter was saying what she was. But I thought, "Well, I'd better not be too dogmatic here. I need to think of my old professional journalist's approach and ask a question or two."

You can imagine the surprise and chagrin I experienced after asking the question for which I was certain I already knew the answer, when my daughter replied, "No, Dad, that's not what I'm talking about at all." She went on to explain what was on her mind from a perspective I had never even considered!

Here are a few questions that, in almost any situation, can strengthen your communication, raise the effectiveness of your listening, increase your understanding, and strengthen the relationship.

- "I believe I hear what you're saying, but would you mind restating it another way?" (Remember, this is not a game! You're not just playing dumb. If you listen carefully, the answers to these questions will flesh out your understanding and often provide another perspective or information you didn't have.)

- "May I try to restate what I think I've heard you say, to make sure I understand?"

- "Would you mind elaborating a bit more on this?"

- "What other aspects of this issue would be helpful for me to know?"

Asking good questions and listening carefully does several things.

- It reflects humility. We acknowledge we really don't know everything. It's a great place to start.

- It allows us to actually learn—about people, facts, circumstances, history, relationships and a host of other things vital to achieving our vision.

- It communicates respect to the person we're interacting with. It says, "You're valuable—your history and experience. You're worth listening to."

As an effective partnership facilitator, you have to listen to many voices. There's the Holy Spirit, the group you're trying to reach or serve, and the people that make up your partnership (speaking for themselves or their organization). You also need to be listening to your advisors—the facilitation team or steering committee that's behind you and the vision.

Effective, active listening strengthens your credibility, provides access to a rich tapestry of information, and yields fresh ideas about needs, opportunities, or ways the partnership can work more effectively.

Encourage active listening throughout your partnership. Participants who know they will be listened to and taken seriously will listen to others. Relationships will be strengthened, and the partnership will become more effective. What goes around comes around!

So Much To Do, So Little Time!

Check out the appendix, where you'll find a special section outlining the typical objectives, activities, and outcomes you and your facilitation team will be looking for. The list can be overwhelming. "How can I possibly do all that?!" you may say.

A Key Partnership Principle:

It's just as important for the facilitator as it is for the overall partnership or network to set limited, achievable objectives with a realistic timetable. While keeping the big vision always in mind, establish your personal, valuable, near-term goals in a way that allows you to focus and be encouraged as, step-by-step, you see progress.

Building the Team and Widening the Ownership

Early in the process you need to be identifying those who share the vision and can share the workload. If you take a team approach to facilitation, make sure the communication roles and responsibilities are clear. The wider partnership or network needs to know whom they will hear *from* and whom they can go *to* with questions or issues.

Once a partnership gets underway, it will need to have its own steering committee, facilitation team, or coordinating group. (The term you choose for this team has to communicate to the wider group that these individuals are *serving* the partnership, not *telling* members what to do!)

Particularly if you have been instrumental in stating the vision and giving early leadership to the partnership's formation, it will be easy to communicate an exaggerated sense of your "ownership," even though you really do want others to be involved. At times that can lead people to say, "OK, we'll leave it to you."

Or worse, "I don't think you really want others helping in the leadership of this initiative."

I recommend getting others involved "up front" as early in the process as possible so the wider group can clearly see that it isn't a one-person vision. But don't just leave this process to chance or good intentions. You need to work with these people to agree on what role they will play, how the process (meetings, discussions, etc.) will work, and the outcomes you all want.

One of the most important things for the partnership facilitator to do is to give away the vision. That's not giving it up! Give it to others, so they understand, personally own, and are willing to take with you the steps necessary to turn dream into reality.

More on this wider team in chapter 16, "Effective Partnership Structures: Form Follows Function."

SIGNPOSTS OF SUCCESS

Each stage in the development of a partnership or network has its own challenges. Some of the issues, as we've already seen, are ongoing. Check the concluding sections of each of the chapters on Exploration, Formation, and Operation. You'll find practical signposts of success that will help provide you with objectives, encouragement, and course correction, when they are needed.

SERVING EVERYONE BUT SERVING NO ONE

The truth is, serving as a facilitator can be a lonely task. You're helping the partnership ministries and team members realize their individual and collective dreams. But while working for all of them, you don't actually work for any of them.

Personal accountability for a facilitator is vital. We all need to be responsible to someone. In a company, the CEO is responsible to the board. And that accountability goes right on down through the ranks. In the case of a partnership facilitator, it's very important that you define as clearly and early as possible whom you are accountable to. Partnership participants need to know this! Asking for this kind of relationship with the group will enhance your credibility and give you a greater sense of security in knowing what's expected of you. It will also allow you to report on your work with much more confidence. Usually the facilitator is responsible to the steering committee or leadership team. These individuals are often selected by the partnership to represent the group's interests on a day-to-day basis.

Partnership Suggestion:

✱ Based on the expectations for your role (which you have clarified with your steering committee or leadership team), you need to draft a job description or assignment profile. This should define the role, the specific outcomes expected, whom you're responsible *to,* and what you're responsible *for.* Since facilitators are often "loaned" by their parent organization for this role, there can easily be confusion as to whom you work for and what expenditures of time and energy are expected of you. That is one reason why this description of your role is so important.

Then, with your team, agree on a reporting schedule—even a single page with a few standard headings based on your job description, produced regularly (weekly or, at a minimum, monthly) for that team. It is a great discipline for you, and it's a core communications element as you serve the wider group. If nothing else, those reports become wonderful tools for review as you look back over your work of previous months or years. They become a kind of "log" of your journey.

Even in the best of cases, being responsible to a team of people who volunteer (as most do) their time on a partnership or network steering committee—no matter how deep their commitment—just isn't the same as working for one person or organization.

You will read more observations on the facilitator and your relationship to the partnership in chapter 16, "Effective Partnership Structures: Form Follows Function." Just remember—you can't do it alone. After all, this *is* partnership we're talking about! You need prayers, encouragers, and a cheering section.

How Are You Doing with Jesus?

Joe South's song, *Rose Garden,*[1] immortalized by Lynn Anderson, says,

> "I beg your pardon
> I never promised you a rose garden
> Along with the sunshine
> There's gotta be a little rain sometime."

Helping God's people work together isn't easy. Satan's after you. Well-intentioned folks don't want to break from "tradition." Those who, early on, indicated interest with a ready, "Oh sure, that's wonderful. I'd love to help," now don't return your phone calls. Things may have gotten complicated. Relationships may seem difficult. In the middle of it all, remember:

- The idea for God's people to work together was his, not yours. We just need to make sure that what we're doing and how we're doing it is guided by him and affirmed by trustworthy people who love him, listen to him, and are committed to his church.

- The vision is important—what you're trying to accomplish can make a real difference.

- Ultimately, only the love and power of Jesus will carry you through. Unless he's in it, providing wisdom, vision, and hourly and daily encouragement, you won't get far.

The Psalmist said it well:

> If the Lord does not build the house, the work of the builders
> is useless. (Psalm 127:1 GNT)

But, the good news is that he's been there before you. Looking straight at you, he says,

> Come to me, all of you who are tired from carrying heavy
> loads, and I will give you rest. Take my yoke and put it on you
> and learn from me, because I am gentle and humble in spirit;
> and you will find rest. For the yoke I will give you is easy, and
> the load I will put on you is light. (Matthew 11:28–30 GNT)

Because Jesus is alive and loves you and his people, he wants to communicate with you just as he did when he walked around Palestine—healing, encouraging, and bringing hope. Stick *actively* with him. Ask him, listen to him, and reflect on what he says—in your private devotions, through his word, and through the godly people around you. He is the vision. He is the source for anything of lasting value that you will do.

Having been on the Jesus journey for a long time, facing tough, challenging circumstances, the apostle Paul made final comments to the young church at Thessalonica that ring with the certainty. On the facilitator's journey, they should be an encouragement to us:

> He who calls you will do it, because he is faithful.
> (1 Thessalonians 5:24 GNT)

Share your ideas and response to this chapter, tell your own story, or get connected with more partnership resources at the book's website
www.connectedbook.net

15
BUILDING HOPE
MEETING EXPECTATIONS AND SHARING CREDIT

Core Idea

Every partnership has at least four different constituencies or "publics" to keep in mind. Each of
these constituencies has hopes, expectations, and
unique communications needs. Acknowledging and being responsive to these constituencies and their expectations builds hope and strengthens your partnership's
success potential.

This chapter helps you avoid disaster by engaging and
meeting the needs of each of these groups—helping
them understand their role and share in the success of
the partnership.

Hope keeps us alive—whether as individuals or working together in partnership.
The Viennese psychologist, Viktor Frankl, in his book *Man's Search for Meaning*[1]
tells how hope kept him and his fellow prisoners alive during the darkest days of
the prison camps of the holocaust. He credits his ability to survive the death and
despair all around him to the fact that hope kept him looking forward, clinging to
what might be in the future.

One of the most remarkable and satisfying benefits of an effective partnership is that working together brings hope. By helping people work together, you help them develop hope for what can be—dreams that never could be realized if they continued to work alone.

But eventually, hope has to be realized. In chapter 11 we discussed the importance of setting objectives that have high value but that are also achievable. When expectations are raised and not fulfilled, hope dies and often turns to disillusionment. Throughout the book, I've also stressed the critical importance of good communications within a partnership. When positive expectations are realized and people know about it, you have fuel for even greater hope.

We see examples of this in every aspect of our lives—marriage, work, friendships, politics, sports teams and our local church. The energy and vision that empowers a partnership to accomplish the seemingly impossible dream is hope. But if hope isn't buoyed by expectations fulfilled, your partnership can succumb to discouragement, if not despair!

Of course, the people and/or ministries active in your partnership develop expectations of each other and the partnership. But, there are other vital "publics" to keep in mind. While the partnership isn't necessarily responsible for communicating directly with all of these publics, you need to be keenly aware of them and their expectations and to help those who *do* need to communicate with these groups do so.

Who Needs Hope?

Most partnerships have at least four constituencies—four groups that have some vested interest in what the partnership does and its effectiveness. Depending on the partnership's goal and working context, there may be even more groups who feel they have an interest in your partnership and its outcomes. Your ability to actively serve these constituencies and their expectations is a key success factor for your partnership.

Here's a quick overview of the typical groups you are serving. Each of them needs hope to keep them actively engaged.

- The primary audience—the people you're seeking to reach and serve.

- The partnership itself—its active, working participants.

- The senior staff in the administrative offices of the partner ministries that make up the partnership. They can bless or resist their colleagues' participation and access to resources.

- The people who give, advocate, pray, or invest their finances to provide the partnership's resources.

Each of these groups has expectations, and to keep their interest active, *they need hope that will carry them forward.* Working your way through the chapter you'll find four partnership stories. Each one illustrates issues you may face with these constituencies.

Before we look at each of the constituencies in more detail, let's remember a Key Partnership Principle we discussed in chapter 11:

A KEY PARTNERSHIP PRINCIPLE:

Particularly in the early stages, you increase the participants' sense of ownership, heighten awareness of added value to partner ministries, and increase the likelihood of success by setting goals that:

- Are limited and achievable, with a clear, agreed-upon basis for evaluation.
- All participants acknowledge as having real Kingdom value, beyond what any individual ministry can accomplish alone.
- Help each participating ministry achieve its own mission and vision.

With those ideas in mind, let's take a closer look at each of the four major constituencies.

Constituency #1: The Primary Audience

These are the people we want to reach and serve through the partnership. They may be:

- Members of an immigrant community in your city
- Street people and the homeless
- The leadership and teaching staff of schools in your area
- International students at local community colleges and universities
- The whole city—thinking big and looking at the whole picture
- A language group overseas that your church has adopted but not engaged

You can probably name many more needs and opportunities that call for partnership.

Every effective partnership responds to the perceived needs in its audience.

So many Christian initiatives fail because their message and approach to communications is based on what *they, the partnership members,* think is a high priority, not necessarily what the audience thinks is important!

It seems so obvious, but think about it. When was the last time your church actually went into the community within, say, a one- or two-mile radius of the church and asked questions and *really listened* to the responses? I have often been amazed at missionary initiatives that seek to reach an "unreached" people group but can't, with any degree of certainty, identify what members of the *people group* feel are their three to four most critical needs.

In the last chapter we discussed the fact that, when we're convinced of our position, there's a tendency to feel we don't have to ask questions. Unfortunately, often the more evangelical the background or purpose of the group, the more certain people are of both their message and their means of communicating it!

Does this mean that we don't have clear convictions, a clear understanding of the good news, the nature of God and man, and a clear calling to see individuals reached for Christ? Of course not!

As we think about the group we are trying to reach or serve, consider Jesus. The Gospels record twenty-three to twenty-four individuals with whom Jesus met in one-on-one conversation. (There were probably hundreds of others, but only this small group of case histories was recorded for us.) Note that with all these individuals Jesus followed his typical pattern of asking questions. It was central to his approach to communications and often frustrated those who wanted to put him in a spiritual box.

Also note that Jesus, without exception, always started at the individual's stated point of need. No problem, no issue was out of bounds. Did this mean Jesus didn't have a clear message to communicate? Hardly. He declared the good news from every possible preaching point. He debated it in the temples, markets, and synagogues. But his willingness to listen to the needs of the people was a key part of his message—God is prepared to meet us at our point of greatest need, intellectual, spiritual, physical, psychological, or otherwise.

In chapter 6, I cited three of these cases: Nicodemus, the leper in Mark, chapter 1, and Jairus, a leader in Capernaum's synagogue. But consider some of the others.

- The hopeless woman with a hemorrhage—Mark 5:25

- The beseeching, blind Bartemaeus—Mark 10:46

- The brokenhearted widow of Nain—Luke 7:11

- The repentant tax collector, Zaccheus—Luke 19:2

- Mary, Martha, and their brother, Lazarus—John 11:1

- The inquisitive, notorious Samaritan woman—John 4:7

- The man born blind, who created an uproar in the Sanhedrin—John 9:1

In meeting people at their point of greatest perceived need, Jesus not only powerfully affected their lives but also gained credibility that no other approach could have earned him.

Consider the story found in Mark 1:23 of the demon-possessed man in the Capernaum synagogue. A couple of things emerge from this brief account:

- The man himself was probably a local, someone the people in the synagogue had seen and known for a long time. His behavior was familiar to the people in Capernaum. They may have known his family and his history.

- The people's response showed they understood the seriousness of the problem. They knew the man would already have tried any available cure. They may have been aware of similar seemingly impossible cases.

- The people were astonished that Jesus could cure the man, despite the seriousness of his problem. Mark summarizes their response: "The people were all so amazed . . . and so the news about Jesus spread quickly everywhere in the province of Galilee." (Mark 1:27–28)

Jesus' credibility and remarkable power were dramatically fixed in people's minds. Without a marketing or PR firm or the mass media, his reputation and credibility spread like wildfire. He successfully met, addressed, and solved problems ordinary people knew were huge—and real. No one—no one they knew—had ever done that before!

What is the need, problem, or issue that will establish credibility for your partnership as it effectively, successfully responds to the needs of the people you're trying to reach or serve?

PARTNERSHIP IN PRACTICE: Boxon was a small town, even for a mountain state. Nevertheless, it had five Christian churches. For three years the pastors of the churches had met once a month to share experiences and concerns and to pray for each other. The fellowship was rich and the prayer provided real support. But eventually, they agreed, the group would grow stale if it didn't take this same inter-church experience into the community.

Two lay representatives from each church were selected. Along with the pastors, they prayed and decided to survey the town, asking citizens, community leaders, service agencies, and schools what they felt were Boxon's greatest needs.

After compiling a long list, the team from the churches selected one problem that had emerged again and again. They felt that they could be a witness and serve the community in the name of Christ by meeting the critical need of tutoring for students needing special help. Today, hundreds of students are being personally tutored by volunteers of all ages from the Boxon church partnership. Instead of dropping out of school and becoming a community liability, they're finishing school and getting jobs. In the process, families have been strengthened, and the churches have new connections and credibility in the community. In addition, many parents as well as students have come to know Christ because of the program.

Consider this: actively listening to the primary audience and really understanding their needs will impact

- the way you value them.
- the richness and focus of your partnership's vision.
- the partnership's goals.
- the way the partnership communicates the good news.
- how you evaluate your partnership's effectiveness.

Keep in mind that, just as in any other relationship, needs, concerns, and priorities change. We need to *continue* asking questions, making sure we're in touch with the people we're committed to reaching and serving with Jesus' love and power. That's the whole point of the partnership.

Constituency # 2: The Partnership Itself

I learned early that simply sitting down with a person and sharing the dream of partnership between ministries can raise expectations. As we discussed in chapter 10 on Exploration, the facilitator may have to visit leaders of many organizations—often more than once, especially in the early Exploration stage. In this intensive, personal, relational work, our communication often affects others by raising their expectations.

In some cases, people we talk with will talk with each other. They will compare notes on their own sense of how viable the partnership might be. And when people start making those connections, expectations are sure to rise. Some may expect failure; others may just look for you to keep your word. Others may actually have a spark of hope born in their hearts.

Expectations rise even more when you bring these individuals *together* in a meeting. Achieving consensus on priorities, action steps, timetables, and assignment of responsibility significantly builds expectations among your partners.

When you get this far, even though a partnership is still in its early, start-up stages, the group begins to develop expectations at several levels:

- Effectiveness. At least the majority of the participants are hoping and praying for good outcomes. Many will be committed to working toward the positive outcomes all have agreed on. But even among the most enthusiastic advocates, many will be wondering, "Will it really work?" We have seen so many well-intentioned cooperative efforts never get anywhere. Hopes may be high, but quiet (and maybe some not so quiet!) skepticism will still be prevalent.

- Leadership. As participants agree on action steps and partnership responsibilities, they will form expectations of the facilitator or facilitation team and others who have assumed roles in implementing the action points.

- Outcomes. Let's assume your participants have successfully agreed on priority action points. Let's also assume that you and those who agreed to work on specific assignments are all diligent, responsible, and focused on the priorities identified by the wider group.

This is probably a good point at which to review chapter 12, "Effective Partnership Meetings." Trust *inside* the partnership is absolutely critical to its health and long-term effectiveness! Meeting expectations is vital to trust.

KEEP IN MIND THE KEY PARTNERSHIP PRINCIPLE IDENTIFIED IN CHAPTER 4:

Participants in durable, effective partnerships are always looking for two levels of trust:

- Trust in the people—the facilitators, working group leaders, and others who have made a commitment to work together.

- Trust in the process—the way the partnership is formed, the way it's operated, and its effectiveness, whether or not identified objectives are actually met.

PARTNERSHIP IN PRACTICE: The youth outreach partnership, made up of about twenty-five organizations, had come together to help coordinate work in a sprawling urban landscape. The effort involved ministries dealing with homeless and street kids, people running tutorial programs for youngsters from disadvantaged backgrounds, outreach through sports programs, groups working on addiction and substance abuse issues, traditional school evangelistic outreach initiatives, many area churches, and local camping and outward bound programs.

Early on, the group had identified three priority projects: ministry to single parents and their children, outreach to street kids, and student leadership development. Each of these projects developed its own working group. Each working group involved five to fifteen of the participating ministries, based on their interest and expertise. Beyond those specific projects, they agreed on three key overall indicators. Having done some basic research when the partnership was launched, the group wanted to monitor:

- The total number of non-Christian kids involved in the various outreach programs.

- How many were making decisions to follow Christ.

- How many were active in student discipleship programs.

They believed that by coordinating their efforts they could build on each other's strengths, extend their influence, and see much greater impact.

While the project working groups met frequently to deal with operational details, the leadership of the twenty-five member organizations met quarterly to: 1) Get an update on the three priority projects, 2) Hear reports from each group on the three common indicators they had agreed to monitor, and 3) Pray for each other, for school administrative and teaching staff, and for kids and families with special needs.

Fifteen months into the life of the partnership, at the quarterly review meeting, the group got badly sidetracked talking about specific policies in one of the three priority projects. The whole group was involved in the discussion that had gone on for three hours! People were beginning to say they had to leave (early), spirits were clearly on edge, and frustration was high. Wilson, one agency's outspoken leader, said quite bluntly, "I really don't have time for this. I got involved with the partnership because I wanted to see the big picture and to have a chance to work with like-minded people who really want to make a difference. Frankly, this whole discussion has been very de-motivating for me."

Peter, who was heading the facilitation team, immediately sensed the crisis. The spirit of the group was plummeting and the partnership's value was being seriously challenged—just as good things were beginning to happen. Peter did several key things:

- He acknowledged that Wilson's remarks were on target and probably represented the view of many others.

- He asked everyone to give the process at least one more hour (the group had agreed they would give six hours, 9:00-3:00, to these quarterly meetings, and it was now 1:30).

- He asked the project group whose policies had been discussed to death by the whole partnership to take a break, work on the issues, and report back.

- He reminded the overall group of the three primary indicators everyone had agreed were a priority to monitor and suggested the group move into reporting on those indicators.

Within fifteen minutes the mood of the group had changed, as they began to hear encouraging news about the expanded number of kids in outreach programs, those coming to Christ, and the totals involved in discipleship. The prayer time that followed contained as much praise as petition.

Good people with good intent had temporarily lost focus. The group's key expectations had been lost in a fog of aimless discussion. Fortunately, the motivation was there all along.

Participants in a partnership need the constant encouragement that their joint vision is worth the effort and making a difference. If expectations are not being met, that needs to be honestly addressed to find out why (wrong expectations, wrong strategies, or problem relationships?). Then the group needs to agree on an action plan to get back on course.

Expectations. As a partnership matures, expectations involve more people and more complex objectives. Here are some things you can do to help realistically define and then meet the participants' expectations:

- Work hard to keep initial objectives limited and achievable.

- Make sure everyone understands what the objectives are, how you'll know if you've met the objectives (basis for evaluation/measuring), and what the timetable is for meeting them.

- As a partnership matures, it may develop multiple objectives for working toward its overall vision. Identifying multiple "milestones" for a single objective is helpful, allowing those doing the work and those getting news about the progress to deal with realistic, "bite sized" tasks.

- Define communications clearly: Who has responsibility to communicate, by what means (letter, calls, e-mail, personal updates?), with whom, how often, and regarding which aspects of the partnership's efforts?

- Remember, once communications have been promised, those promises must be kept. Nothing destroys credibility (of people and the process) sooner than unmet communications promises.

- Finally, I have found that while people may have high hopes and expectations, they rarely expect perfection. Aspects of the partnership's plans may not be completely achieved. What participants want to know is, generally, how well are we doing, and are we actually accomplishing anything by working together? Timely, reliable communication is vital—whether you have all the good news you would like to report or not.

Constituency #3: The senior staff in the administrative offices of the partner ministries that make up the partnership.

A step or two back from the "front lines," these people and their support are vital for a partnership's long-term health and effectiveness. These individuals may be across town, housed in a church or an office. They may be 1,000 miles away in a regional or national headquarters. For international ministries, the "next level up" may be at the home office 6,000 miles away!

As we work to form and sustain healthy partnerships, keep in mind that 98 percent of the participants probably already have full-time assignments with their own organizations. Effectively meeting the expectations in *that* assignment is usually the first priority for them—and their supervisors. No matter how attractive the partnership vision, the time and energy invested by these people in the partnership, particularly in the early stages, will almost surely be seen as an add-on to their primary job.

Levels of commitment to the partnership (as a percentage of total working time) will vary significantly. The amount of time given is really only relevant to the responsibilities the individual or ministry has assumed in the partnership. The real issue is their belief in and commitment to the partnership. Of course we frequently equate *time* invested with a person or organization's *level* of commitment.

Participants in your partnership have a wide range of autonomy in their jobs. Some are closely watched and supervised by their superiors and have limited authority over their time or other resources. Others will have wide-ranging autonomy and considerable discretion in time and resource allocation.

The most intense feelings about a problem are almost always felt by those working at the front line. As you move back up the ladder of organization or ministry structure, the day-to-day agony and ecstasy are not felt in the same way. This usually means that those most ready to partner and often the most enthusiastic are those who see the needs and problems and experience the loneliness firsthand.

Up the organizational chart, motivations and daily challenges are different. Your partner in the field and his or her boss probably live in two different worlds. In some ministries, their relationships may be close, communicative, and fully appreciative of each other's circumstances. In others, their relationships may seem like being on opposite sides of the moon!

PARTNERSHIP IN PRACTICE: Jack, a participant in the youth partnership previously discussed, couldn't figure out why his senior manager seemed increasingly reluctant to give him the time needed to attend the partnership meetings. Fulfilling his role on the partnership's "street kids" working group was more and more of a challenge.

When the partnership first formed, Jack's manager was enthusiastic. Along with Jack, he had represented the organization at the partnership formation meetings and personally attended a few of the early operational meetings. Jack thought the partnership was making real progress, and the street kids working group had already put together several joint projects that were showing potential. All were projects none of the youth agencies could ever have undertaken alone.

Frustrated and confused by his boss' attitude, Jack consulted with the partnership facilitator. "I think you'd better talk to your boss about his expectations," the facilitator suggested. "He's got to clearly see the value the partnership is bringing to your organization. Remember, his job is to make sure that staff members are focused and productive within your own organization's mission."

Two days later, Jack's conversation with his manager revealed that Jack simply hadn't been communicating the partnership's significant advances. Even more important, Jack had not been communicating how the partnership was advancing his own organization's mission. Jack's manager and other senior leadership had, without Jack's knowledge, begun to seriously question the investment of Jack's time in the joint effort.

In short, a partnership frequently doesn't have the same priority at the regional or home office that it does in the field. Attitudes toward "going it alone" and strategic alliances are changing. More and more ministries are seeing they can't do it all themselves. That's good news. But the motivation for investing time and other resources and the potential or real benefits in a partnership need to be *very clear* to the ministry's administrative leadership.

One danger is that a person will take a key responsibility in a partnership without the awareness (and possibly approval) of his or her boss. This may damage the relationship between an individual and a superior. I have also seen the devastating impact on a partnership when an individual or ministry is withdrawn from the partnership by a superior due to lack of internal agreement regarding the staff member's role or the partnership's value.

It is vital for the partnership facilitator or facilitation team to maintain close relations with the partnership participants. Facilitators need to try to sensitively monitor how superiors view the involvement of their field in the partnership and what expectations those superiors have.

Here are some suggestions for ensuring alignment between the field person's involvement in the partnership and the expectations of superiors:

- If you're serving as a facilitator or member of a facilitation team, make sure the participants themselves understand clearly:

  - The general and specific mission of their ministries in the geographical area of the partnership's focus.

  - The mission of their ministries in the sector on which the partnership is focused. This may be youth ministry, urban outreach, church planting, campus evangelism, medical/educational service, church planting in an unreached people group, or one of dozens of other possible objectives.

  - How their supervisors define success for the geographical area, the ministry sector, and the team member in the partnership. The supervisor's expectation and the participant's ability to report outcomes from the partnership have to be in alignment.

- Work hard at ensuring that each participant has signed off in some meaningful way on your partnership's objectives and can see clearly how achieving the objectives will help his or her ministry realize its own goals.

- Agree on what kinds of information or communications about the partnership are needed by participants in reporting to their superiors.

  - This may be the highlights of the partnership's work and decisions made in any of your working meetings.

  - It may include reporting on the partnership's progress on key objectives, carried out on agreed-upon timetable.

- Partnership participants may need special help interpreting the partnership's operations, objectives, and outcomes "back up the line" to their superiors. This may be as simple as personalized memoranda they produce to go along with documentation the partnership is already generating. As facilitator, you play a valuable role by asking participants how their colleagues view the partnership and how you can help communicate the partnership's work and vision to those colleagues.

- Consider specifically designing at least one partnership working meeting every six to twelve months to include senior leadership of the partner ministries. Make sure the invitations to the event are clear and issued well in advance. The format of those meetings should take into consideration that these additional participants don't have the same depth of experience with the partnership, its style of meeting, making decisions, setting priorities, or other elements you and others may have come to take for granted. You may need at least a brief orientation session for these meetings to bring occasional or new participants up to speed.

Constituency #4: The people who give, advocate, pray, or invest other resources needed by the front line workers.

By definition, a partnership is composed of diverse individuals and ministries drawn together by a common vision. Behind each of those partners is an administrative structure (constituency #3), and, often, behind the administrative structure are the people who *really* make it possible—the individuals praying, investing, and advocating. Ultimately, they are the ones who resource the front line.

This constituency has its *own motivation* for giving, praying, and advocating. They have their *own expectations* about results. And they have their *own ideas* about the frequency and nature of the communications they get from the front line.

This constituency has many faces. It may be:

- A local church investing in a street kids program.

- An individual financially supporting a missionary 5,000 miles away.

- A prayer group supporting a local urban evangelism initiative.

- A foundation committed to funding a special aspect of a Christian health initiative.

- A layperson advocating on behalf of an innovative, Kingdom-value educational/tutorial program.

PARTNERSHIP IN PRACTICE: More than thirty years earlier, churches in Sweden had commissioned and sent missionaries to a challenging Asian country. The churches prayed for and financially supported the missionaries with one objective in mind: seeing individuals in that country come to Christ and a local church established.

In the early years the Swedish missionaries often had to work alone against formidable odds. Over the years, however, more ministries came into the country. In the last few years, missionaries from different ministries had begun to meet, pray, and plan together. The leadership of the small but growing national church joined these planning meetings.

It wasn't long before the individual missionaries and national leaders acknowledged, "The job's just too big and complex for any one ministry." After much prayer and work, with help from a neutral facilitator, a partnership was formed. The Swedish missionaries enthusiastically got involved. But now they were no longer on their own, reporting just on what they did. Suddenly they were working with individuals and ministries from around the world. How would they report back to their supporting churches? The Swedish missionaries' contribution to the partnerships objectives was vital but modest in proportion to the total effort. When advances were made, they could no longer claim sole credit.

As the partnership refined its objectives, agreed on how success was to be defined, and developed its own internal communications process, the churches 6,000 miles away in Sweden needed information, too.

Keep in mind the churches' basic expectations:

- Their missionaries would be preaching the gospel.

- Despite what they understood to be great opposition, individuals would be turning to Christ.

- Local fellowships would be formed by these new believers.

- Emerging leaders in these local churches would be identified, trained, and encouraged to take the vision into the next generation.

The churches in Sweden needed:

- Information from the field using terms they understood.

- Outcomes that clearly aligned with their motivation and expectations in supporting the missionaries.

- From all this, a sense that God was giving them at home a part in the positive outcomes at the front lines.

It was that kind of information flow that encouraged them, fueled their prayers, sustained their motivation, and provided the spiritual fulfillment they needed.

To help all the partner agencies communicate with their supporting constituencies, the partnership did several things:

- Made sure that the partnership's objectives were clear and that the means for measuring progress were agreed on by everyone.

- Made sure the expectations of the various participants were clear.

- Worked hard to report in a timely manner on progress toward the agreed-upon outcomes, thus helping to meet expectations.

- Made sure that the form of reporting included human interest stories about changing lives, not just cold statistics or "partnership talk."

- The facilitation team informally checked with key personnel from each partner agency on the health of their communications up the line. Sometimes that required the facilitators to help find special information or document special stories that were needed by a specific partner ministry.

Was the partnership itself responsible for effective communication with those churches? Of course not. But to keep the wholehearted involvement of the Swedish missionaries, the partnership and its facilitation team needed to:

- Help participant ministries see clearly how realizing the partnership's objectives would help them meet their own ministry objectives. It's a good exercise in a group session to ask each ministry, "Could you summarize in one to two minutes how you see this (these) partnership objective(s) helping your ministry meet its own vision and mission?"

- Make sure they understood the objectives and the communication needs of all the ministries in the partnership.

- Help each partner ministry interpret the partnership's outcomes in terms that supporting constituencies can understand and will value.

Keep in mind: Frequently those faithfully supporting ministries in the partnership know little about how widely different groups can effectively work together at the front line because they haven't seen good examples. Many fear that their organization's distinctives will be diluted or completely lost. They tend to know only the traditional experience most of us have had: that churches and Christian organizations effectively working together, respecting each other's unique contribution, is the exception, not the rule!

PARTNERSHIP IN PRACTICE: A partnership of nearly a dozen ministries was working on a bilingual evangelism project in a very hostile social and spiritual environment. The ministries were both national and expatriate and varied enormously in size. Their financial contributions to the partnership's efforts varied greatly—from the significant resources offered by a major international ministry to the "widow's mite" from an impoverished national ministry. Culture, size, ecclesiastical traditions, and perceived influence of the participants could hardly have been more different. How would they share success if God really blessed their joint effort? Joint prayer eventually produced a remarkably simple solution: "Everyone can claim success for all that God does." Only one caveat remained: "When a ministry refers to the project and God's work through the effort, it must indicate, 'We are seeing these results as we work together with other ministries in a strategic partnership.'"

The existence of four constituencies means four sets of expectations that, at times, may overlap or converge. Frequently the expectations of these constituencies can be unique, requiring active attention and communications. Be aware of the four groups and talk within your partnership about them and their expectations. Meeting those expectations has a powerful effect on hope and the long-term effectiveness of the partnership. Being able to *share successes*, with everyone seeing how God is using the joint efforts of the group, can strengthen the sense of community. It will also build trust and a sense of the richness of God's grace and wisdom, as we see how our different roles are part of his bigger picture.

 Share your ideas and response to this chapter, tell your own story, or get connected with more partnership resources at the book's website
www.connectedbook.net

16

FORM FOLLOWS FUNCTION

EFFECTIVE PARTNERSHIP STRUCTURES

Core Idea

Are you building a hot dog stand or a skyscraper? Trying to gather neighbors to reach the kids in your neighborhood or twenty ministries to reach a major people group? Do you need a constitution, memo of agreement, or simple consensus? Do you need dues or membership fees, or can you realize the dream on voluntary contributions? This chapter helps you take the simplest and most direct route—which is usually the most effective.

I once sat with a leader of a large denominational missions program as we talked about ministry structures. I'll never forget his comments, "You know, in thirty years I've never had anything but frustration when folks want to start by *first* talking about money or about how they're going to organize themselves! It's even worse if they want to start by writing a theological statement that they want everybody to sign! Unless there's a *compelling reason* for folks to come together," he added, "there's really nothing to talk about."

Here was someone who had worked his whole life inside one large organization with a fairly uniform corporate culture and theological views—an organization blessed with major resources. It was striking to me that he should have made the same observations I had in working with organizations of all sizes and backgrounds in collaborative efforts of very different kinds all over the world.

It was a classic, real-world affirmation that to be effective, form must follow function. First, there has to be agreement on the vision and what success will look like. Only then do the other questions follow. In short, *what* you do should always precede *how* you to do it.

PARTNERSHIP IN PRACTICE: The group of more than thirty leaders from over twenty ministries had been working for two days on their new partnership's priorities and action steps. One of the ministries had already agreed to loan a person full time to facilitate the partnership's vision. Even though he was going to take off his own organization's "hat," his support would be provided. His ministry saw him as their contribution to the partnership. Working with the new partnership's steering committee, a modest budget was developed for expected administrative and out-of-pocket costs. The budget was modest compared to the size of the task they were undertaking, but it still totaled nearly $15,000. Now, within a couple of hours of winding up the meeting and heading home, the group was talking and praying about how to generate the $15,000. After a few minutes, one of the leaders said, "I know this may sound crazy, but how about this approach? Each of us knows our ministry's capacity. Let's each take a piece of paper and then take some time to pray silently, asking God to guide each of our ministries as to how much of this $15,000 budget we think our organization could contribute. Keep it strictly confidential. We'll fold up the papers once we've written down what we think God's said to us. Then Jack, our facilitator, can total up the numbers and let us all know where we are."

The group agreed. When the prayers were finished, the folded papers were handed in with a sense of anticipation. When the total was announced, $14,777 had been committed—just $223.00 short of the $15,000! Some had committed significant amounts, others very modest ones. But together, they sang a song of praise as they concluded. For the next five years, that partnership met all its central administrative costs exactly the same way. Even though partner ministries changed and their budget grew, every year the outcomes were almost exactly the same as that first time.

You may think that was a pretty strange approach! But the story illustrates several things about the issues we will face in partnerships. A steering committee reflected the makeup of the wider group. They provided a reference point and counsel for Jack, the recently identified facilitator. They didn't have a president or chairman but made decisions by consensus, not based on some voting formula. They had leadership, to be sure. Clearly they had started with their vision and what they wanted to do. And in the context of that vision, they had worked out an informal administrative structure that everyone felt comfortable with. *It was enough structure to do what they wanted to do.* While it was obvious they needed to cover the costs of the partnership's operations, they had not sorted out where that money would come from. Far from starting with organizational structure and money issues, they had focused on their vision. They were fired by that vision and their potential *together*, and the other elements began to fall into place.

Money—Empowering or Disabling?

The money question can energize the group and help participants see they can do things together they could never do separately or it can be a roadblock—another opportunity to raise the "I don't see how this is going to work" mantra. How you approach the topic can make all the difference.

A Key Partnership Principle:

Working together in effective partnership creates a world where you learn new ways of doing things, imagining outcomes beyond your own capacity. By sharing the load with other ministries instead of just doing what you can do alone, you will make decisions involving people who may share your vision but not your history or organizational culture. Together, you will have to deal creatively with the funding the joint effort requires. Seeing each of these elements as opportunities rather than roadblocks can transform your collective spirit and the success of your outcomes.

Let's unpack the money question. What are the main costs involved in an ongoing partnership or network? Here are the typical main categories:

Facilitation Costs. Someone has to serve the whole group. This may be a single individual or a small, dedicated team that plays various roles. If the initiative has an individual who plays that "prophet/servant" role we discussed in chapter 14, he or she has to be supported financially. How does that work? Here are some of the typical models:

- A partnership that is smaller and/or more localized can be facilitated very well by a volunteer. This is the ultimate low-cost approach.

- In larger efforts, the facilitator can be loaned to the partnership by an agency or ministry that is committed to both the vision and the process of partnership. The organization understands the critical nature of having this sort of person serve as the glue, helping the group stay on focus and in effective relationship. This may be an open-ended commitment or for a specific term. Sometimes at the outset it is a trial arrangement for a year or two.

Note: As we have observed more than once, *continuity* of leadership is vital, both in facilitation and in the general oversight of the partnership's vision and their practical work together. Continuity can be provided by a steering committee, facilitation team, or individual facilitator. The wider the ownership, of course, the greater the likelihood of achieving continuity. When leadership is heavily dependent on a single individual, the effort is on shaky ground!

- In some cases an outside third party, committed to the vision of collaboration, funds the facilitator's role. The funding party knows that the investment is likely to be multiplied many times over, as the partnership or network reduces duplication, increases effectiveness, and encourages new, creative initiatives.

- The partnership grows to such size and complexity that the need for full-time facilitation is recognized by everyone, and the members are prepared to fund that role, along with its associated administrative costs. They develop a budget to cover these costs and share them—equally or by some other appropriate formula.

- Members of the partnership can make non-cash, "in-kind" contributions, such as office space, secretarial or administrative support staff, or book-keeping, mailing, or computer services.

Administrative Costs. Out-of-pocket costs are needed to cover a wide range of issues in a partnership initiative: travel for the facilitator, communications costs, office space and equipment, supplies, and so on. For a proactive facilitator giving serious, regular attention to the participants and the overall partnership, these costs add up. How does a partnership or network meet these costs? Partnerships can choose from several options or select a combination of these approaches:

- Occasionally a facilitator is able to fund his or her own out-of-pocket or general expenses. These may be provided by the facilitator's home agency or built into some type of personal support system. It's rare, but it does happen.

- As a partnership emerges, as in the story cited previously, the group members see the need for the services that help them work together effectively. Through voluntary commitments, participants' assessments, or some other agreed-upon means, the group funds those essential costs. This means, of course, that a team such as a steering committee or a finance working group needs, with the facilitator or facilitation team, to develop an appropriate budget to recommend to the wider partnership. The recommendations need to include not only details of the costs, but ideas for how to share them.

- More formally structured coalitions frequently have well-defined dues or membership fees, often based on the budget of the member agency or some other mutually accepted formula.

Meeting and Conference Costs. Asking questions about partnership finances or organization is much like asking, "How long is a piece of string?" You have to know specifically what kind of string, for what purpose. The same is true in partnerships and networks.

- Early developmental meeting costs are usually covered by each ministry's or participant's own budget—the people or ministries most interested. Occasionally there will be a third party—a foundation, church, individual donor, or other institution for whom the idea of collaboration is a priority. When the vision is appropriately presented, they are prepared to help provide start-up funding. Frequently, funding is very decentralized and ad hoc right through the Exploration and Formation phases. Facilities costs for these meetings are typically shared on some kind of equitable basis, with participants paying for lodging or food costs.

- Once a partnership is underway, the facilitation team (facilitator[s] and the steering committee or other leadership team) needs to develop an approach to funding the group's ongoing work that suits the group. Costs for small committee or working meetings are usually covered by the participants. Administrative costs of larger meetings—particularly those that require advance work, printed materials, larger-scale communications, and on-site costs—are usually covered by a registration fee. Many partnerships and networks have participants who can't afford the meeting expenses, so an amount is built into the general registration costs that can be used as a subsidy for those who can't afford to attend otherwise.

PARTNERSHIP IN PRACTICE: For several months the exploration team had worked to identify Christian agencies that seemed to be key in dealing with homeless people and unemployment in the city. Out of the dozen or so agencies they identified, four were running valuable programs but had virtually no funds. It was agreed that everyone needed to meet, pray, and talk about the city's situation and how these agencies and the local churches might respond to the challenge. The problem was, they felt they needed about thirty-six hours for their meeting, starting at noon the first day and working to late afternoon the following one. They knew that they needed to focus and get away from distractions like office phones, appointments, etc. So a decision was made to use a retreat facility about twenty-five miles from town. However, the four small-budget agencies couldn't afford to send a couple of their team members, even though the cost of the retreat was modest. When the other ministries heard this, they agreed to chip in a little extra and underwrite the participation of the less affluent ministries.

Project Costs. A classic pattern for partnerships is that they develop ideas that are *only* possible *because* they're working together. These projects frequently require new or specially allocated resources—time, personnel, facilities, and money. One of the great experiences in Kingdom collaboration is getting an idea that is "bigger than any of us," then finding a way, *together*, to resource it and make it happen.

What are the typical approaches to this challenge?

- Often projects can be widely owned, with partner ministries contributing different key elements from their own resources. In other words, the project can be resourced from within the partnership.

- Some projects are of such a scale that participating agencies agree to go back to their respective organizations and request that this collaborative project become a fund raising priority for their agency. Each agency actively works with its contacts to fund the joint project. A helpful variation on this approach is for the participating ministries to develop a common set of materials or write a proposal they can all use in their fund raising. It keeps the story consistent and makes it easier for individual ministries to present the project.

- Another approach is for the ministries in the partnership or network to agree on a project purpose and plan, then develop a joint project proposal or presentation. On behalf of the whole group, they present the project for funding to an outside source—a church, denomination, foundation, or other funding resource.

PARTNERSHIP IN PRACTICE: A partnership of about ten ministries was working in a non-Western country with a small but growing church. The lay leaders of the emerging local church asked the partnership for training in developing small, appropriate businesses that could help support the families and, in turn, the life and health of the new churches. The partnership connected with a ministry outside the country that had a good track record in helping national believers develop small businesses and that had expressed an interest in this project. After considerable work and planning between the local church leaders, the specialized resource agency, and the partnership, a plan was agreed on. It would spread over several months and involve at least four trips to the capital by local leaders, and at least three trips by a training resource group to five regional districts.

The total projected cost for the first year came to nearly $16,000. While praying and talking together about how to cover this cost, a couple of the agencies identified large churches they knew that had an interest in the region. The group broke the budget down into average costs for each of the nationals that was to be trained. With nearly twenty potential national participants, that was $800.00 each. It was agreed that the nationals should contribute something to increase their sense of ownership and commitment to the training. However, working together, the partnership developed a proposal for $800 scholarships and asked each of the two major churches to prayerfully consider ten of these scholarships. Eventually, three churches got involved, two of which even sent small teams from their churches to meet the nationals, sit in on the training programs, and report back to their churches. Again, pulling together made something possible that, separately, would have been unattainable.

OK. So money is a core issue. People seem to get nervous and edgy when money comes up. It's caused far more trouble than many other elements that, in the end, are probably a lot more important. But money issues will not go away. Better that you and your team actively work to make dealing with money a good experience rather than the bad experience that everyone expects. Thinking creatively, trusting God to do good things in people's hearts, and putting the money issues in their proper perspective will go a long way toward stabilizing your partnership and making it effective.

We all tend to value those things that are vital to our lives and ministries. The greater the value, the higher its priority for us. This is a basic principle, but it's the engine that drives partnerships and networks. Nowhere is that seen more clearly than in funding. If the partnership is a priority, there will be a way to make it work financially.

A final thought on money. Does God want his people to work together? If we are in God's will, do we believe he will meet our needs—particularly when the initiative we're working on is pointing people to Jesus? The budget for your partnership is a great opportunity to see him confirming what he's put in your heart to do!

CONTINUITY AND PREDICTABILITY

Familiarity and predictability are necessary in a partnership or network to give people a sense of security and a sense of consistency in approach. Predictability and familiarity are important because we come to depend on certain things—certain people, certain routines, certain places we eat or shop.

The style of worship in our church is an important part of why we choose to identify with the group.

At the same time, there must always be renewal of vision, initiatives being undertaken, and encouragement from outcomes achieved. Your partnership needs both reliability and freshness. No matter what your structure, how you handle money, or how you approach decisions, the individuals and ministries in your partnership need to know what to expect. But never let it become boring or business as usual!

In addition, no matter how your partnership approaches structure, money, and so on, *continuity is critical*. Continuity is different from mere predictability, though they're related. Your partnership needs continuity in five key areas: vision, memory, leadership, process, and structure. All of these five, save memory, are covered elsewhere.

As the relationships, information, decisions, priorities, action steps, and good times and bad come and go, they become a kind of partnership memory bank. It's like life. We constantly return to our database of past experiences to make decisions in the present for the future. Imagine what it would be like if you couldn't call on your previous experience. Direction and effectiveness would be virtually impossible. So it is with partnerships. Continuity brings stability and effectiveness as we build on our collective experience. Discontinuity can bring great unease, unwise alterations in course, and reinvention of things we have already been through. It is always expensive and often brings serious problems.

In short, people need to get to know and be comfortable with the way the partnership works.

An ancient philosopher is reported to have said, "The decline of a great nation is marked by the passage of many laws." As the core vision and values erode, the citizens believe they can hold onto predictable or preferred lifestyles by tightening the rules. But it all ends in failure. The heart of the community—its vision and the values by which it lived out that vision—has been lost. Rules can never provide an adequate substitute.

INCLUSIVE OR EXCLUSIVE?

Unless there is a specific reason for limiting who participates in your partnership, I encourage you to structure your efforts to foster a spirit of *inclusiveness*. We need just about everyone who shares our concerns and vision. Of course, practical considerations of communications, budget, complexity, required experience, or a host of other factors may limit who can or should be part of your partnership. The software industry speaks regularly of "open architecture," meaning any programmer can take a look at the inside of a program and possibly even change or enhance the program. Down through history, formal and informal clubs have been established to include *and exclude*.

In our specialized worlds, yes, even in ministry, it is often "us" and "them." The spirit of partnership is to include all who share the vision.

These are days of exclusion, when the world is breaking down into smaller and smaller factions. The results are often horrific. Political, racial, religious, and economic exclusivity almost always mean that a few are in and many are out. A critical element of our Christian witness is the grace we extend and the openness we display. Remember, Jesus was crucified not because of his *exclusivity* but his *inclusivity*. It was his walking, talking, and eating with the sinners and disenfranchised that bothered the establishment so much. While clear alignment on purpose and commitment to core scriptural truth is essential, do everything possible to structure your partnership as an *open* environment rather than a *closed* one. New participants should not only be welcome but also *feel* welcome. The last thing you want to communicate is that you have established an exclusive club.

So then, how do we organize ourselves?

ORGANIZATION AND STRUCTURES —WHAT'S REALLY NEEDED?

If form follows function—that is, *how* we organize partnerships or networks depends on *what* they seek to do—there are likely to be as many *forms* of organizational structures as there are *objectives*. It's obvious, isn't it? Collaborative efforts will range from simple projects undertaken by a few people over a short period of time to complex, long-term initiatives involving dozens of people and organizations. To be successful, these diverse initiatives will need very different organizational structures. In partnerships and networks, one size doesn't fit all! And there is no one right way.

Let's take a look at some of the structures that, over the years, have emerged and met essential needs of people and ministries working together.

Awareness. Simple *awareness* of each other is a real step forward for God's people. Who else is doing what I'm doing or interested in the things I'm interested in? So much duplication of effort, waste of money, hard feelings, turf wars, and dissipation of energy could have been avoided over the years if individuals had simply asked, "Am I the only one with this idea? Is anyone already doing this or something like it? Has anyone already tried this? If so, what happened?"

We tend to imagine that we are the first ones to have thought of a particular idea. Submitting our ideas to the diligent research and checking with other people is a vital first step. In chapter 10, on partnership Exploration, we discussed in detail this phase of partnership or network development and how to do it effectively.

Awareness *may* be enough. It may allow you to move ahead with something truly distinctive or complementary to what others are doing—to avoid duplication of effort and waste of resources. But before you decide to stay at the awareness stage, you may want to ask the "what and where" questions:

- Is what I'm thinking of doing so unique in purpose and character that there's no potential or possibility for collaborating with others?

- Is the geographic area I want to serve one in which no one else is working and other people have no interest in?

Honestly, it's rare that the answer to both of these questions is "yes." It does happen, of course. But if that's your experience, the next question might be, "Who has a similar vision but in a different geographic or functional area and might want to team up with me?"

If a number of people or ministries are working in your area of interest, whether it's a type of work or geographical location—or both—it's hard for everyone to stay in touch. Staying up to date on what the others are doing calls for active ongoing communications. Once you value that kind of communication, you are into the early stages of a network.

Covenant. Often the number of people involved is small, the project is simple, or the geographical distance between the interested parties is great. Making a step beyond awareness is to *acknowledge* each other, commit to each other's best interests, and to acknowledge the common vision you share. The pact may be for a short-term but intensive effort together. It may be to prayer, occasional communication, and possibly occasional face-to-face meetings. A covenant, though less formal than some other approaches to collaboration, can be a powerful means to help you focus resources, reduce duplication, and enhance effectiveness.

Networks. Awareness or a covenant between people or ministries often leads to informal working meetings that, in turn, lead to a network in which participants share information, resource ideas, best practices, and encouragement.

Let's revisit the definitions from early in the book.

Network: *Any group of individuals or organizations, sharing a common interest, communicating regularly with each other to enhance their individual purposes.*

The key words here are *common interest* and *individual purposes*. While the participants in a network may share interest in a particular issue, they are *not* trying to do a joint project. Just raising awareness and strengthening communications usually reduces duplication and helps each ministry increase the effectiveness of its own work.

A KEY PARTNERSHIP PRINCIPLE:

Even the simplest form of collaboration needs active facilitation. Someone must take *initiative*. This is a person equally committed to effective connections within the group and to achievement of the group's objectives. Whether it is an informal covenant group of a few people or a complex, constitutionally based partnership of many agencies, servant leadership committed to both the process and purpose is vital.

As specific issues or opportunities arise, often networks become the "mother ship" for initiatives or partnerships within the network's overall vision and structure.

PARTNERSHIP IN PRACTICE: A city-wide network of more than fifty specialized ministries and local churches concerned about reaching and serving high school kids had formed. One of the specific issues they identified was drug abuse among teenagers. Nine of the ministries and local churches formed a task force that actually became a mini partnership to address the issue. They linked with schools, parents, community agencies, law enforcement agencies, counselors, and other key programs related to kids and drugs. They reported back regularly to the whole network. Because of these links with the wider network, more agencies got involved. The task force was able to connect its efforts to other initiatives within the network dealing with camping, single parent services, and tutoring.

In this illustration, the network had a *general* focus—sharing the love and power of Christ with high school kids. But it was an *incubator and encourager for a variety of specific initiatives* that were important to the network's core purpose.

As we have already seen, the lines between various types of Kingdom collaboration often blur. At the outset of this section on organization and structures we observed that what is usually best is what is *absolutely needed* to get the job done effectively. Awareness can morph into a covenant relationship. Covenants can give way to more active networks. And networks can spawn partnerships of many types.

A KEY PARTNERSHIP PRINCIPLE:

Start with the minimum structure you need. It is easy to add elements to the way you work together. But it is much harder to dismantle structures once expectations and ways of doing things are put in place.

Remember: simple is good. The less structure you need to accomplish the vision, the less maintenance you need and the more resources can be focused on your primary outcomes. An old proverb says: *"Sad is the man who builds a tower to protect his land and in becoming a caretaker of the tower, loses his land."*

Human nature gravitates to safety and predictability. It is the exception, especially for *groups of people*, to take risks. That's another reason working together is not the Christian community's default mode of operation. Whether as individuals or Christian groups, we gravitate toward doing our own thing, where we at least *think* we can maintain control. Taking the time to work with others appears to increase both risk and unpredictability. When we finally do come together around some vision, to reduce ambiguity and unpredictability, the tendency often is to establish the "rules" of the game so tightly that keeping the rules can be more important than accomplishing the mission.

A brief look at the following diagram shows some of the key elements that may help you determine how your collaborative effort should be organized.

- How complex is the vision you have in mind?

- How many people and/or ministries will be involved?

- What is the geographic focus (distance always makes communication and coordination much more challenging)?

- What kind of organizational structure will best help you meet your objectives?

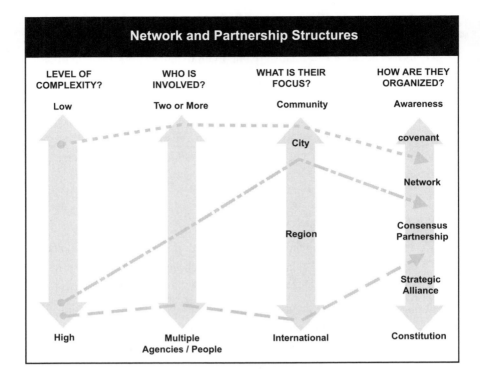

Network and Partnership Structures

LEVEL OF COMPLEXITY?	WHO IS INVOLVED?	WHAT IS THEIR FOCUS?	HOW ARE THEY ORGANIZED?
Low	Two or More	Community	Awareness
		City	covenant
			Network
		Region	Consensus Partnership
			Strategic Alliance
High	Multiple Agencies / People	International	Constitution

Let's briefly unpack the diagram.

1. In the top line we see that the project is fairly simple. Only a couple of people are involved; they have made a covenant to pray and work together; and the project is taking place in their own neighborhood or community.

2. The middle line is a group working on a highly complex challenge. About a dozen ministries and people are involved. Because of the many facets of the vision, they feel that, at least in the beginning, functioning as a network makes sense, and the complex challenge they are seeking to address is their own city.

3. In the bottom or third line we see that the group's vision of reaching an unreached people group internationally is complex. It involves over thirty different ministries, and they have decided to work, at least initially, in a partnership in which they make decisions by consensus.

These questions will help your group think further about what kind of structure or organization will be most appropriate:

- Are we very clear about what we are trying to accomplish?

- How will we measure success?

- Assuming we are successful, how will we share credit?

- How many people or ministries are going to be involved and over what period of time?

- Will each agency work on its own, or will coordination of effort be needed between all of the partners?

- To accomplish our vision, what will be needed in the way of money, people, and other resources?

- If money is needed for joint projects, how will it be raised and managed?

- How critical is ongoing communication and/or reporting between the participants?

As a general rule, the more the group has to do *together*—deal with money, coordinate projects, hold each other accountable, and insure regular communications/reporting with the four constituencies discussed in chapter 15—the more structure it will need.

PARTNERSHIP IN PRACTICE: The group was committed to working together to reach a major unreached people group. On the ground, witness, media, translation, and other specialized ministries were involved. For several years, one of the agencies had been developing a fund of money to be focused on evangelism of this people group but had never felt the circumstances were right for them to go out on their own. This agency happened to have a denominational background of commitment to evangelism in the region but very specific definitions of what kinds of alliances they could and could not belong to. Even if the alliance's theological stance and purpose aligned with the agency's, for historical reasons, they still could not enter agreements that might "dilute" the individual organization's decision-making rights. So a "constitutional" partnership was out of the question. But the representatives of the denominational group made it clear they wanted to be part of the effort and to make the funds available.

Participants spent time praying about their options. They finally agreed that the bare essentials needed were 1) Some agency to provide administrative support to help with logistics and provide regular summaries of their meetings and joint decisions. 2) A facilitator loaned by an agency to insure that communications were kept up and that projects were moving forward. 3) Another agency to handle all the group's joint financial matters, providing monthly reports to everyone in the group. To tie it all together, they simply wrote a memo of understanding among themselves agreeing to these structural elements. The partnership was a model of simplicity, but it was all that was needed. Small agencies and large alike were happy. And the denominational group had what it needed: regular reports that could go to headquarters along with good financial accounting and reporting on how their funds were invested. Interestingly, this fairly informal structure was adequate to serve what became a highly fruitful collaboration, lasting over ten years and carrying out joint projects with budgets at times over $600,000 annually.

American humorist, writer, and folk philosopher Will Rogers spoke to the dangers of complexity when he said, *"Ancient Rome declined because it had a Senate; now what's going to happen to us with both a House and a Senate?"*[1]

TALKING ABOUT IT VS. DOING IT

As we have already seen, working together can take many forms. My experience is that words frequently get in the way and sometimes create confusion and roadblocks to effective communication. That is particularly true in the early stages of developing collaboration. All of us have pre-conceived ideas of what certain words or phrases mean. Usually these are based on our experiences, not on dictionary definitions. Working together is real life, and people have a lot of skepticism about working together, for reasons we've already discussed. So rather than spending a lot of time in advance trying to name the kind of collaboration you have in mind, focus on the *vision* and good communication with others *about* that vision.

This is why, throughout the book, I have said that participants in any collaborative effort must not only believe in the vision but must trust both the people and the process. How do you come to trust these two key elements fully? Only by actually working together.

A KEY PARTNERSHIP PRINCIPLE:

Count on the fact that the more you talk about the structure and use specific words to define it *before* your group has met, talked, prayed, and worked together, the more problems you will have and the more explaining you will have to do—often unsuccessfully. At that point, you and the people you are talking with probably have little mutual experience of working together and, therefore, little in common to draw on. This is why structure should always *follow* and be defined by the purpose—the compelling vision that has brought you together. More often than not, *words need to be defined by action and experience.*

Here's an example:

A friend recommended that I call on a businessman who, he felt, not only had a heart for Kingdom work but placed a real value on strategic vision and effectiveness. When I had my first meeting with this man and gave him a brief description of what we were doing, he responded, "Partnership? Why in the world would you use a word like that? What does that mean? There are so many kinds of partnership. I've heard the word used for so long and not really mean anything."

Well, as you can imagine, I was taken aback. I had assumed that when he heard words that *to me* represented concepts like meaningful collaboration, reduction of duplication, he'd be delighted. Instead, my words only raised further questions. Why? Because the words meant something quite different to him!

Over time, I got to know this man well. We talked for hours about not only *what* our ministry was doing but also *how* we did it. We became friends, and he became a valued advocate for us and a faithful and generous supporter of the work. He had become familiar and comfortable with what we meant by our use of words. But that only happened as the *words were defined by action.*

Imagine if Jesus had come into the world only to talk! It was the complete integration of his words and works that made Jesus' credibility so high and caused the people to say, "He wasn't like the teachers of the Law; instead, he taught with authority." (Matthew 7:29 GNT)

No matter how good your intentions, how much you believe in the vision, how comfortable you are with the words you're using, remember that you are talking about a sector of life and work that calls for *demonstration,* not just talk.

CONSENSUS, STRATEGIC ALLIANCE, AND CONSTITUTIONAL STRUCTURES

These terms speak about the decision-making process, financial obligations, and so on. All three can be equally relevant to either network or partnership development. As a result, I'll comment only briefly on them because every group needs to define exactly what these words mean in its situation. In the end, the structure must suit your purpose and the nature of your group. Keep in mind that, as I said before, collaborative relationships evolve. Your work together isn't necessarily "chiseled in marble." A vision that starts as mutual awareness may move to a network and, eventually, move on to more focused, highly structured alliance. A healthy partnership or network is one that regularly looks at its structure and asks, "How is this working for us and do we need to make any changes to be more effective?" (Double-check the section on Evaluation in chapter 13 and the examples given in the appendix.)

Consensus: A simple definition of consensus is: "An opinion or position reached by a group as a whole."[2] This can be how a partnership or network makes decisions. It may also reflect the culture of a collaborative effort—a culture that is committed to working together but wants to do so informally. It can also mean that a group wants a higher sense of unity than in a constitutional voting process in which "yes" on a decision can be achieved by a numerical count of heads or hands but does not ensure unity. Consensus does not generally mean unanimity. But it does mean that the group affirms an action or decision in spirit. I have often found that partnerships or networks that work by consensus frequently resort to group prayer and reflection to hear God and each other. In some cases, a final decision may follow multiple rounds of prayer and discussion. (Check the sections in both chapters 11 and 13 on decision making.)

Strategic Alliance: "An agreement between two or more individuals or entities stating that the involved parties will act in a certain way in order to achieve a common goal."[3] The agreement here is usually some kind of written document—a memo of understanding, a contract, or a simple letter in which parties state their goals and procedures for working together—that all members sign. Naturally, as is true with many forms of collaboration, strategic alliances usually make sense when the parties involved have complementary strengths.

Constitutional Structures: "The system of fundamental laws and principles that prescribes the nature, functions, and limits of a government or another institution."[4] This definition from *The American Heritage® Dictionary of the English Language, Fourth Edition,* in our case, of course, relates to how ministries work together in collaboration. Constitutions usually define the common purpose, who will be involved, requirements for membership or involvement, how decisions will be made, and how the structure can be changed. For partnerships this usually means definition of the vision, who is part of the partnership or network and who isn't (some have full, associate, or candidate status for members or potential members), how leadership is defined and selected, how decisions are made, how common costs and any special projects are covered, and procedures for making changes in the structure.

To recap, some general observations:

1. There is not necessarily *any* correlation between the strategic value or scale of the vision and the nature of the structure you need to realize the vision.

2. Partnerships need familiarity, predictability, and freshness to give people a sense of security and encouragement.

3. *Continuity is critical,* no matter what the structure. Continuity contributes heavily to your partnership or network's familiarity in five key areas: vision, memory, leadership, process, and structure.

4. The funding and organization of a collaborative effort can involve any combination of the approaches discussed in this chapter—or variations on them. Do what is right for your group. Just make sure that the whole group understands *and buys into* not only *what* you're doing but also *how* you're doing it.

5. Communication is critical. A friend of mine, a president of a bank, once said, "When you can't make your loan payment, the most important thing is not to make promises but to visit the banker in person and explain why and, realistically, what you plan to do about it."

Final thoughts:

Issues related to money and structure will never go away, no matter how burning your vision or compelling your story. The initiative has to be paid for, and to accomplish your goals you have to organize in some reasonably effective way. These twin elements are *essentials,* not afterthoughts! Once you've got agreement on the vision and how you might accomplish it, deal with questions of money and structure promptly, don't procrastinate.

Share your ideas and response to this chapter, tell your own story, or get connected with more partnership resources at the book's website
www.connectedbook.net

17

NETWORKS

INTERNATIONAL, FUNCTIONAL, AND GEOGRAPHIC

Core Idea

! We live in an increasingly global, interconnected
● world. Communications are being revolutionized;
teams connect around the world to complete a
single task. These developments coincide with the
globalization of the church. Linking Christians who are
spread over vast distances but are bound by a common
vision is not only possible but essential. What are the
trends, special opportunities, and unique challenges of
this new world order?

African leaders from every country meet once a year to challenge each other, learn, share case histories, and talk about their mutual and unique priorities. In each country this network of leaders is mirrored by national clusters of pastors and leaders of Christian organizations. Throughout the year these leaders are linked by email and through functional, regional, or national working meetings on topics of critical concern. The vision and practical outcomes of the network called MANI (Movement for African National Initiatives)[1] would have been impossible twenty years ago. Today, transportation is less expensive and electronic communications are cheap. Together, they empower people from diverse circumstances to work together in ways never before thought possible. In a network like MANI, the shared vision, concerns, and experiences of individuals become a resource to a community of people spread over great distance, brought together by common vision and challenges, and connected through new communications technologies.

Each region of the world faces its own set of formidable spiritual, social, and economic issues that must be addressed. The church, locally and globally, wanting to share the power and love of Christ, must be aware of *and engaged in* these issues. The diversity of circumstances yet similarity of challenges gives rise to people not only *wanting* to connect but now *being able* to connect—often on a sustainable, ongoing basis. Hence, the growing opportunity and challenge of forming and sustaining networks that span extraordinarily great distances.

But the same issues pertain at the local or regional level. In my city of Seattle, Washington, dozens of networks link people with common interests: sports, dating, economic development, employment opportunities, the arts, medical research, education, and the environment. Each of these sectors has hundreds if not thousands who share interest in some aspect of the subject. Networks, heavily facilitated by the Internet and the World Wide Web, make it possible for diverse people to connect and group around special interests. Through the network they're able to share information, resources, and, in many cases, develop action groups or partnerships to undertake specific projects.

The number and diversity of these networks in virtually every city of the world continue to grow. It's due partly to changing sociology—we want or need to connect with a more diverse group than just family or close friends—and due partly to rapidly changing technology. Electronic communications (EMS, paging, cell phone, Internet, satellite) enable us to always be connected, never out of reach.

DO WE HAVE TO CHOOSE—NETWORK OR PARTNERSHIP?

Early in the book we defined the difference between networks and partnerships. Let's briefly revisit that definition:

Network: *Any group of individuals or organizations, sharing a common interest, who regularly communicate with each other to enhance their individual purposes.*

Partnership: *Any group of individuals or organizations, sharing a common interest, who regularly communicate, plan, and work together to achieve a common vision beyond the capacity of any one of the individual partners.*

Notice that networks share information and possibly resources so that the individuals and/or ministries can do their work more effectively. On the other hand, partnerships bring people together around a common project or specific vision and, pooling their efforts and resources, they do something they could not do individually.

So, when addressing issues either in a complex setting like a city or over vast distances as in an international network, it is more realistic and sustainable to first identify common concerns and resources. Then develop a network to share those resources, empowering participating individuals or ministries to greater effectiveness in their *own spheres of influence.*

We have also noted that frequently networks are incubators for partnerships. A smaller group of ministries that are part of the network develops an initiative that focuses on specific issues. Many times the network becomes a "mother ship" that fosters two levels of sharing and encouragement: 1) At the macro level, the network links people from diverse circumstances or across large geographical areas around specific but very large topics, such as cities, refugees, sports, or Bible publishing and distribution. 2) At the project level, the network encourages working partnerships composed of its participants to deal with very specific issues. These two elements of collaboration are highly complementary and should never be confused or seen as competitive.

NETWORKS IN PRACTICE: The International Sports Coalition has transformed cooperation for international evangelism through sports. From summer and winter Olympics to World Cup soccer and Formula One car racing, the ISC has helped individuals and ministries work together in hundreds of ways. The ISC links over one hundred sports ministries worldwide.

While the network can link people at the macro level, it's the project or area-specific partnerships that really implement the vision on the ground, in a wide range of practical ways. ISC-related partnerships deal with a variety of initiatives like personal witness to and encouragement of athletes, production of materials for use with athletes, coordination of witness and service at major international sports events, sports-based initiatives for local churches, and outreach through sports to children and students.

Examples of Interlinking Networks and Partnerships

Good news: New networks are constantly emerging! More people are seeing the value of working together, and they are making it a reality! Don't be confused by what may seem to be a bewildering array of options. Each of these types of networks or partnerships developed to meet specific needs. Later in the chapter, a diagram will illustrate how individuals and ministries might link to and through these networks and partnerships.

In the meantime, just think of the medical field. There is a wide range of *individual* doctors, from general practitioners to very specialized physicians. There are specialist *groups* of physicians. There are *clinics*—some specialized, some more general in their services. There are *hospitals*—some small, some large, some focused heavily on research. Each plays a valuable role. Each is a gathering point for patients, specialists, researchers, or technicians. But they are all more or less interconnected. Patient records can pass from one to another. Depending on specific needs, referrals can be made between these people and institutions. Over time you learn which are relevant to your medical needs. It's the same in the growing world of ministry networks and partnerships.

To get a sense of the diversity, check the Networks page on the "Power of Connecting" website, www.powerofconnecting.net. Links on that page will connect you directly with ministry networks worldwide. Here are some of the broad categories of ministry networks operating today and a few examples for each case.

National / International Resource Networks

In South Africa, Singapore, Hong Kong, Canada, Britain, and the U.S., not to mention other countries, dozens of networks are made up of churches, individuals, and ministries that are *based in a "home" or "resource" country* but exist to serve evangelism of a *specific country or language group overseas*. As of this writing, more than a hundred such "resource networks" typically link directly with field partnerships or other kinds of coalitions at the grassroots level. Usually these networks are made up of people, ministries, and churches from inside that one country but focused overseas. They usually have annual working meetings, some have websites, others sponsor trips to the field, and many are a valuable "connecting point" for field personnel to share information.

A variation on that theme are the networks that are *based in a resource country* but are truly international, drawing resource people and ministries from much a larger geographic area overseas. Often they address vast and complex countries like Indonesia or China, or a region that may be made up of several countries that face similar issues, like the Arabian Peninsula. These networks provide a global meeting point for people from the field and those from multiple resource countries. Many of those from the resource countries will never get to the field personally, but these international networks provide an ideal place to meet, share, connect, develop alliances, and explore creative ministry options.

Examples of these international networks:

- Impact Indonesia
- China Challenge
- The Arabian Peninsula Consultation

Typically the networks have at least one working meeting each year both in the region they serve and in a key resource country. Many also have websites and ongoing working groups that provide continuous connection.

National / International / Functional Networks

Specialists concerned with a particular topic find that meeting and working with people who are struggling with the same issues is highly valuable. These networks can function primarily within a single country, or they may be truly international. Almost always they seek to help connect resources in their specialized field with grassroots initiatives.

Here are some examples:[1]

- International Sports Coalition (ISC): Links nearly two hundred ministries around the world committed to sharing Christ through sports-related opportunities.

- Refugee Highway: Though it calls itself a partnership, this network links dozens of Christian ministries in specific initiatives to reach and serve refugees in their "country of origin," in "transit" countries, and in the "destination" countries.

- International Forum of Bible Agencies: Agencies doing translation, publishing, and distribution are linked for greater effectiveness in this global network.

- World by Radio: Facilitates ministries involved in radio broadcasting—both transmission and program production—in coordination of their efforts.

- cityreaching.com: A national network in the United States of ministries, individuals, denominations, and local churches committed to reaching their cities. Training, resources, and local/regional working conferences are features of the network to encourage and strengthen like-minded people.

- Christian Camping International: Provides communication links, working meetings, and access to resources for a wide range of camping ministries around the globe.

- International Orality Network: Over two-thirds of the world population is classed as "oral communicators," and over seventy percent of those cannot read or write. The ION links over 75 global ministries committed to more effective evangelism and discipleship of this vast group largely passed over by Western materials and strategies.

- VIVA Network: Based in the U.K. and linking local and regional "children at risk" ministries around the globe, VIVA encourages high-touch partnerships among its members to train, serve, and strengthen others who are working in this critical field.

National / Regional Field Networks

Some networks link operational people and ministries within regions or countries. Here are some examples.

- LINK: A national network in Indonesia connecting specialized ministries, churches, and denominations that are focused on unreached people groups in that vast and complex country.

- India Missions Association: Based in India, it is the largest national missions network in the world, with 182 member organizations representing over 30,000 workers. The network helps with training, publishing, sharing "best practices," doing research, and connecting its members around current, relevant issues.

- CRAF: Across French-speaking (trade language) sub-Saharan Africa, CRAF links ministries committed to evangelism and church planting. Language-specific partnership initiatives in several countries are integrated as part of CRAF.

- NAC: Linking ministries from Libya in the east to Mauritania in the west, the NAC provides a meeting point for regional task forces working on evangelism-related issues, national leaders who find this a neutral communication venue, and partnership facilitators focused on specific North African language/ethnic groups.

- MANI: Movement for African National Initiatives links national leaders all across Africa sharing a common vision for evangelism of their countries and the unreached people of the region.

There are now more than twenty annual *regional network* meetings focused on facilitating ministry linkage—many with a focus in and around the 10/40 Window.

STRATEGIC FIELD PARTNERSHIPS

These partnerships are typically focused on a specific language group, large city, or some other geographical, ethnic, or linguistic group. Growing rapidly in numbers since 1985, there are now known to be more than one hundred of these grassroots-level partnerships focused on unreached people around the world. Typically they bring together everyone committed to reaching or serving the language or people group, from translators to media personnel, those working in women's or youth ministry, others who are doing health or educational services, and still others who are involved in discipleship and leadership training. By communicating and coordinating their efforts, they reduce duplication, increase effectiveness, and help people come to know Christ and grow in him.

NETWORKS IN PRACTICE: I had lunch with a Swedish colleague and a Danish businessman and his doctor son in Copenhagen a few years ago. During the lunch, the two Danes they said they had been heavily involved in providing a range of medical services to Christians in a very difficult South-Central European country. As my colleague and I listened we were impressed with their knowledge, the innovation of what they were doing, and the tenacity they had shown over several years. As we talked, the two men mentioned that they were praying about visiting a nearby Central Asian country where they felt there was the potential of providing similar services in support of an emerging church. They indicated that sometime in the next two to three months they were planning a visit to the country to explore possibilities and meet national and expatriate leaders.

As we heard of their plans, I said, "Are you aware that there is a working partnership of ministries inside that country—diverse Christian ministries helping grow and support the emerging church? Once a year, leaders of that field partnership meet outside the country with an international network of churches and ministries committed to the country." They were surprised and asked for details.

My colleague continued: "That international meeting is scheduled just two weeks from now, but I'm sure an invitation could be arranged, even now at the last minute. Would you be interested?" To greatly condense the story, the two Danes indicated their interest, my colleague arranged for their invitation (security issues in this country were critical), and, amazingly, the doctor and one of his colleagues were able to visit the working meetings. Several weeks later we got an enthusiastic communication that said, "We are so thankful we could participate in this international network/partnership meeting! In three days we met more people, learned more, and made more connections than we could have by spending weeks in the country just on our own."

The growing potential is extraordinary, as these networks facilitate links between individuals and organizations—either on a regular basis or as needed.

You may be saying, "How does one figure all this out?" The diagram below gives illustrations of how people and ministries can, and in many cases, already are connecting through the growing number of networks and partnerships.

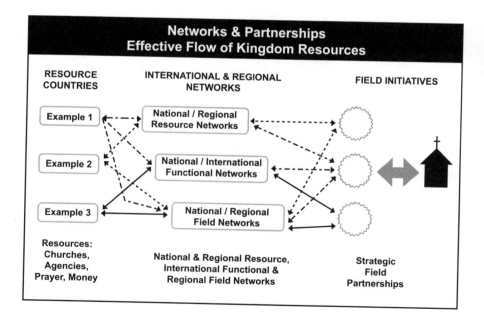

Since all the main categories in this diagram were described earlier in the chapter, let's examine the three examples shown here.

Example 1: This is an international evangelical development agency specializing in health services in Southeast Asia. They have had major programs addressing HIV/AIDS, primary health care, and child immunization. Their network connections are as follows:

- They participate in a Western resource network in order to meet with other Western resource agencies, learning what they are doing in the region and exploring possible collaboration.

- They are part of an international functional network that draws Christian relief and development ministries together and includes a task force on HIV/AIDS services.

- In the region, they regularly participate in a regional field network that brings both national and international ministry agencies and their leadership together. This Southeast Asia network has had several joint initiatives among its participants.

- At the grassroots level, one of the countries in which they work has a strategic field partnership. This partnership gives the agency a broad overview of what is happening day to day inside the country and has produced a number of productive joint ventures that have advanced the witness and service of the participants.

Example 2: This agency is involved in ground-level evangelism and church planting in a specific unreached people group. They have connections with:

- The Western resource network that allows them to meet like-minded people, agencies, churches, and others from the West who are committed to this strategic language group overseas.

- The regional network, which not only includes people working in the same people group but others who are nearby and share similar challenges and opportunities to learn from each other.

- The strategic field partnership related to the specific language group. Working with this group allows them to keep apprised of what's going on in the country, talk and pray with like-minded ministries, plan together and coordinate efforts when common vision emerges.

Example 3: This is a local church that is proactive in its missions ministry and has felt a call to try to speed the good news to the 2.5 billion "oral communicators" in the world—those who can't read Scripture in their own language and are often called illiterate. Geographically they've had greatest interest in North

Africa and India. The network linkages that have been most valuable to them have included:

- Participation in the International Orality Network, a functional network, in which they have been able to meet, learn, share their experiences and link with others to expand the scope of their outreach.

- They participate in two annual regional field networks—one each for North Africa and India. These working sessions have allowed them to meet people with in-depth experience in the region who are wrestling with issues unique to the region.

- Finally, an ongoing strategic field partnership exists for a country for which they are helping fund training and materials. It has allowed them to connect both with resource people and with others who can be part of the ground-level ministry network.

How Did All This Happen?

The sovereign God of history has been at work. As the rush of global change accelerated in the eighties and nineties, the stage was set for God's people to connect in new ways. Comparatively cheap transportation, the ascendancy of the Internet and e-mail, the breakup of totalitarian empires, new options for hundreds of millions of people to meet in previously impossible ways, and the growing globalization of the church all contributed. Many were proactively working to encourage a partnership approach to ministry. But it was the intersection of those efforts with God's hand at work in world affairs that really made this remarkable, continuously growing and evolving Kingdom communication and collaboration infrastructure possible.

Who Knows What—and Why?

You may say, "I've never heard of any of this stuff! If all of this has really been happening and is actually working, why haven't I heard more about it? And if this is happening so much on the international scene, why don't we see more here at home?" Or you may say, "OK, sounds good, but I'm still not sure how to connect with or fit into all this!"

The great heritage of divisions in the human race—ethnicity, language, cultures, tribalism in all its forms, theology, and egos—produces natural barriers that have often risen high and, over time, become almost impossible to bridge. In addition, we are creatures of habit—habits that provide familiarity and security.

Same stores, same friends, same activities. To "break out" and change the routine takes a conscious effort—the intentionality to go looking for new information or experience. You might call it taking risks, small or large.

Added to this is the natural inclination of local churches, denominations, or other Christian organizations to do their own thing, not to connect with what other believers are doing. Unless we specifically go looking for the information or happen to be in a place where a collaborative effort emerges so we can't miss it, it's not surprising that we don't find each other or have a natural way of knowing about these developments.

The appendix is full of websites, bibliographies, and other resources that you'll find useful in helping you connect and stay connected with what God is doing around the world, through people just like you! For a most up-to-date connection list, check the international network and partnership website: www. powerofconnecting.net.

PARTNERSHIP AND NETWORKS IN PRACTICE: It's the mid 1920s and two missionaries meet on the dock in Bombay, both bound for home leave after eight to ten years on the field. Though both are originally from Britain, they were associated with different mission agencies. They had heard of each other but had never met face-to-face, one working in Northwest India and the other in the South. As the days on the steamer trip back home unfold, they meet from time to time, sharing stories, experiences, and questions. Their shared experiences range from wonderful and exhilarating moments of seeing God at work to abject discouragement and despair. The missionaries agree that the areas of the country they worked in were so different, that, except for the national political and colonial structures, they might as well have been in completely different countries. They each face different languages, local customs, and unique challenges.

But as they talk, they find that, beyond their mutual interest in evangelism and encouragement of the national church, many circumstances they face are actually similar. As they listen to each other share stories and what they have learned, they both say rather wistfully, "How great it would have been if we could have connected, not only with each other, but with others facing similar situations—to have been able to learn from and encourage one another." On arrival back in London, they part company.

These people are fictitious, but one only has to read missionary history and talk with those in the field to know that the circumstances the story outlines are all too real. The stories and experiences of seasoned workers were not documented or consciously circulated in the wider missions community. The opportunity for sharing with future missionaries and contributing to the effectiveness and encouragement of current missionaries was largely lost. It was a scenario played out thousands of times from the mid-1700s forward.

This missionary scene was not unique to India. The problem has been an ongoing, worldwide issue. There *were* people valiantly trying to document this kind of information and experience and circulate it—to help make the connections. Publishing houses in Europe, Australia, Britain, and North America churned out magazines and books with information on missionary activity. But there was no means to "connect the dots." The fundamental problem of isolation and individualism has persisted for centuries.

The recent growth of ministry networks and partnerships, combined with technology that facilitates our connections, doesn't automatically solve the problem. *Isolation, individualism, and our sin-based proclivity for doing our own thing still require us to take initiative and consciously work to connect with God's people.*

INTERNATIONAL NETWORKS:
SPECIAL ROLES, SPECIAL CHALLENGES

The good news? International networks help connect you with a highly diverse group of people from across great distances—*with whom you share circumstances and/or concerns.* The bad news? International networks link very diverse people across great distances! Diversity and distance: the two great challenges of international networks. Even among people living together under the same roof, understanding and sharing the responsibilities of life and the goals you've agreed on can be challenging. Add other communications challenges such as vast distances and different languages, and you immediately see what we are up against! Is it impossible? Of course not. Some of the great computer software systems that many of us use regularly were developed cooperatively by global "virtual teams" working 24/7: Europeans doing their part then passing on the work to a team in North America who, after their shift, passed it on to a team in Asia. This is highly complex work that requires great discipline, clarity, and means for evaluating progress. We can't deceive ourselves into believing that such enterprises succeed just because they are dealing with technical or scientific issues. The need for encouragement, camaraderie, and a sense of accomplishment is present in these projects, just as in other human enterprises.

Wide-ranging networks, whether international, regional, or functional, essentially face the same issues as all other networks and partnerships. But in these more complex situations, if you are facilitating or otherwise helping shepherd the initiatives there's a need to:

- Strengthen clarity and commitment to goals and objectives. Remember the classic story about a group of blind men, each one of whom feels a different part of the elephant and then seeks to describe the whole? Make sure at the outset that everyone who is working together knows what the group is trying to do and that they are all committed to that goal. Check the vision by asking the various players to restate to the group their understanding of (a) the group vision and (b) their role in achieving that vision.

- Strengthen the road map. On their way to the destination, how does your network know what progress they're making on the journey? Have you, together, defined the markers or signposts (events, outcomes, dates) that will allow you to mark your progress—or lack of it? If you have, good. Keep coming back to that road map, rehearsing, together, what you are doing, where you are in the process, how this relates to your agreed-upon plan, and what changes, if any, need to be made. Figure out ways to celebrate and affirm your progress and successes—even if you're separated by distance.

- Strengthen "human" communications. In between face-to-face meetings, do everything possible to encourage person-to-person connection among the main players. Exchanging emails, no matter the frequency or volume, is rarely enough. You may find the inexpensive, Internet-based audio (telephone) conferencing valuable. You may be able to use comparatively simple technology to add video to the computer connections. These technologies, even in dozens of non-Western countries, are inexpensive and actually work quite well. But it takes an intentional, committed effort.

- Strengthen the capacity of your participants. While almost weekly change is underway and progress being made, some members of your network may not have the resources others do. It may not be a problem of money. It may be that their computer/Internet connections have low bandwidth, slow connection speed that makes dealing with attachments, pictures, interactive materials, larger files, and audio/video streaming very difficult. Keep two things in mind: First, structure your communications so that everyone can readily access all core materials and can interact on roughly the same basis. Then consider a proactive program to help those with weaker facilities move to more adequate ones. That may mean funding, hardware, or training. Don't assume everyone has the same opportunities!

- Strengthen facilitation and coordination. The greater the distance and diversity, the more the "coach" or, in this case, the network facilitator or facilitation team needs to be proactive with key people in the network. Active rather than passive communications are essential. Set up regular times to communicate. Keep those commitments. Long silent periods are deadly. Encourage key members of the network team to take the initiative to be in touch if they sense problems emerging or have fears that they won't reach the goals the group has agreed to on the road map. Active communication provides encouragement, builds a sense of participation and community, and should be the natural point for affirmation or correction of the group's course.

From local community partnerships to international networks, the Christian community is connecting at many levels. Be part of those connections! The potential for sharing the good news effectively is always higher when we are aware of and effectively coordinate our efforts with others.

 Share your ideas and response to this chapter, tell your own story, or get connected with more partnership resources at the book's website
www.connectedbook.net

18

PARTNERSHIP

THE SPECIAL CHALLENGE OF CITIES

Core Idea

! The migration of world population into the cities is creating unprecedented challenges for planners, governments, educators, sociologists, and businesses—not to mention the impact on individual lives, families, and communities of all sorts. Cities are the most complex of human organizational and social structures. They present unique, extraordinary challenges to those wanting to serve, reach, or see their cities transformed through the power of Christ. Simply put, no single ministry or individual can ever hope to "reach a city." Only by working together could the dream ever come true. This chapter helps you explore the key issues you will face in forming networks, partnerships, or other coalitions to reach and/or serve your city. It will give you ideas and suggest practical steps to "get your arms around" one of the truly great modern ministry challenges.

Over the centuries, cities have served as trading centers, communications crossroads, centers of political and financial power, and safe havens where minorities could disappear and carve out a life for themselves. Because of their diversity and dynamic environment, cities have always been home to the best and the worst: hotbeds for innovation, crime, development of the arts and culture, clustering of technology, and political and financial power. As cities have grown more diverse, they have become a breeding ground for ethnic ghettos and conflict, as well as microcosms of the world's haves and have-nots.

We Live in a New World

Melbourne, Australia, is now the second largest Greek city in the world. Toronto, Amsterdam, and Fremont, California, are centers for Diaspora Afghans. Chicago has more Poles than San Francisco has people. Vancouver, British Columbia, with a large, growing Chinese community is now dubbed HongCouver by many. Los Angeles, called by some, Tehrangeles, is the second largest Persian-speaking city in the world. It's a city in which over 175 languages are spoken every day, and 82 languages are used in formal education. Washington State, fifteenth in population among American states, is third in linguistic diversity, with over 180 languages spoken by its population!

Fifty million Chinese live outside of China. By 2010 there will be more Muslims than Jews in the U.S. And in Brussels, the center of the new "unified Europe," one in every four babies is Arabic.

Powerful Forces Pushing and Pulling People into Cities

Consider—if the whole world were a village of just 100 people:

- 57 would be Asians, 21 Europeans, 14 would be from North and South America, and 8 would be African.
- 70 would be non-white; 30 white.
- 70 would be non-Christian; 30 Christian.
- 50% of the wealth would be in the hands of 6 people, all of whom would be Americans.
- 70 would be non-literate or functionally illiterate.
- 50 would suffer from malnutrition.
- 80 would live in substandard housing.
- 1 would have a full college education.

Then imagine a city ten thousand times that size. Certainly, no city is a perfect representation of global circumstances, but all the brutal realities are ever present—in some cases, in even more extreme measure.

Every year Delhi, India, the capital of the world's largest democracy, grows by the size of the city of Richmond, Virginia—approximately 200,000 people! When I first started visiting Karachi, Pakistan, in the mid-1970s, it was a comparatively quiet trading center on the Indian Ocean with a population of about 3.5 million. Today its size has increased by over 400 percent. The population is more than 14 million, made up of dozens of ethnic groups, most of whom have migrated to the city over the last 30 years. Public services have broken down, violence is rampant, and only the presence of the Pakistani Army provides a modicum of stability.

KINGDOM COLLABORATION: A WAY OF SEEING YOUR CITY

1. See your city in its diversity. Try to break the city down into strategic parts of a size or complexity that can be known and understood. With research, love, and work, you can see your city as an organic whole that has at least four dimensions (and hundreds of smaller, yet vitally important subdivisions):

- Geographic segments: Where do people live or work? What are their natural groupings?
- Demographic groups: What is their age, gender, socio-political association, economic situation, level of education?
- Ethnicity/language: With whom do they identify? What language binds them together?
- Function: What are the natural sectors of interest/activity such as media, labor, youth, business, education, churches, political structures, sports?

These are the natural groupings by which we organize our lives and our relationships. They are the categories to think and pray about when you consider how to reach and serve your city—or parts of it. Each of these four groups is likely to include subgroups. Other groupings may cut across several of the categories.

Some examples:

Ethnic and language background. Possibly the oldest and most predictable clustering of people in cities. Language and culture are the heart and soul of our human experience. With migration so significant—people on the move all over the world—is it any wonder that, in an environment of change and uncertainty, we naturally gravitate to those who think and talk like we do? We want to hear our own language, eat our own food, and know what to expect and how to act when we meet with others. That's why ghettos of all kinds have always been so pervasive in cities. Today those ghettos may not necessarily mean economic hardship but, rather, a simple desire to be with "people like us."

Geographic location. This element of cities and communities has usually been aligned with economic circumstances. How wealthy you are or *are not* was frequently a predictor of *where* you lived in the city. In a high percentage of cases that paradigm continues today. Money provides choice. While this can be a helpful way to look at a city, times are changing. In cities with a growing number of people who possess more evident economic options (usually the middle and upper income brackets), choice is creating very mixed neighborhoods, particularly in the center of great cities. Many people choose to be near the center of the action, where there is a sense of life and diversity. With choice comes independence, and with independence frequently comes new structuring of communities. The old notion of being able to connect with people personally because they are part of a neighborhood or community is, in many cases, a lost dream. High-rise apartments, security systems, and soundproof construction, mean you can live alongside individuals for years and hardly know them. "Don't bother me. I won't bother you." For those wanting to connect with, reach, and serve people like this with the love of Christ, these changes create new challenges for communication.

Function. What do you do or what are your special interests? Union members from the factory may bowl together. Musicians or actors may frequent the same restaurants. Business people may belong to the same clubs. In the Middle Ages it was the guilds that brought specialized trades or workmen together. Today it may be the Rotary Club, women's organizations, educational associations, or other special interest groups.

Cutting across the Lines. Community initiatives like United Way, the symphony orchestra, 4-H Clubs, or youth sports programs frequently bring very different people together. While these activities often reflect influences of economics, the geography of your city, or the education of the participants, increasingly there are groupings that cut across the lines and provide a meeting point for diverse members of the community.

Sadly, or naturally, some might argue, our local churches usually reflect these same realities. The average suburban church has few ethnic minorities. The immigrants—particularly first generation—quite naturally want to hear the music and message in their own language and to be able to interact with others who think like they do! Further, churches frequently reflect an economic and/or educational bias, with higher concentrations of wealthy and influential people in certain churches. While shining exceptions exist, the churches that reflect racial, economic, educational, and vocational diversity are rare. In most cases, those exceptions have been because of great effort, sustained vision, determined commitment, and intentional structuring of the content and style of the church's ministry.

So what does all of this mean? Simply that no single partnership can ever hope to reach or serve these widely varying special needs. This suggests that *any* effort at a citywide initiative will probably be best structured as a network, not a partnership. Networks exist to help individual ministries with a *common vision* do their own individual work better. (They often have specific partnerships associated with them that undertake specific projects.) In partnerships, all members are focused on a *single outcome,* with each partner playing a role in that commonly agreed-upon goal. If you're doing something with a highly specific focus and very specific outcomes, a partnership may be fine.

This diagram may help demonstrate how the various pieces might fit together.

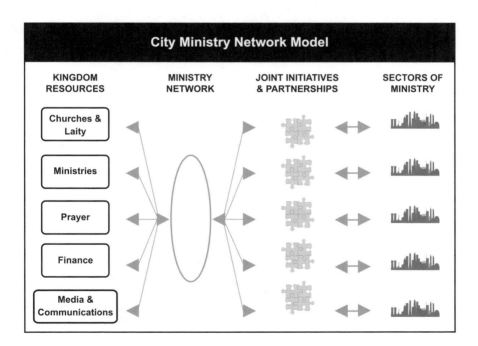

The items on the far left represent the wide range of Kingdom resources in the city.

On the far right is a range of specific points of need that God's people might seek to address by working together. These could include:

- The homeless
- Street kids
- Single parents
- Sports outreach programs
- Camping programs
- Immigrant groups
- Employment/work programs
- Tutoring programs
- Support of public services (police, fire, etc.)
- Support of educational services
- Ethnic services

The puzzle pieces on the right demonstrate that each of these initiatives (and many more I'm sure you can imagine!) needs some kind of partnership or alliance of people or ministries to respond to the challenge.

The oval second from the left represents the fact that, to maximize Kingdom assets, the wide range of people and resources working on the specific or specialized projects on the right need a forum or network where they can connect and:

- Encourage each other.
- Share information on resources.
- Report on challenges and progress.
- Coordinate efforts, where appropriate.

Even in a town of modest size, the challenges are complex and call for specific responses to specific needs. While it may be called different things, a network *combined* with partnerships or alliances addressing specific needs and opportunities is needed.

2. *See your city through the scriptural model of evangelism and transformation.* We discussed some of these ideas in chapter 5. Everyone comes to Christ because of a process. Jesus repeatedly talks about planting, watering, and reaping (John 4:35–38). The missionary, Saint Paul, confirms this vision of individual transformation (1 Corinthians 3:1–9). Being faithful and consistent in our life and witness and realizing that *it takes all of us to do God's work* paves the way for fresh

appreciation of the need to work together. Cities are big, complex places. At any one time, thousands of people are at these various stages of coming into the Kingdom and growing in Christ. Our city's transformation network and partnerships can help link the elements consistently, effectively influencing these lives through a progression from antagonism or indifference to becoming a follower of Jesus.

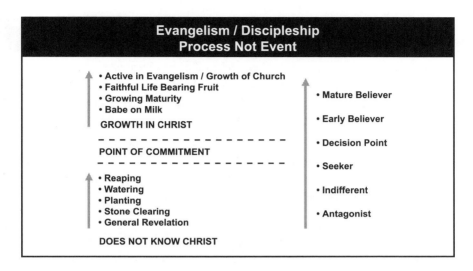

3. *See your city as a collection of individuals in a decision-making process.* Change, spiritual and otherwise, does not happen overnight. We need people who are committed for the long haul, coming alongside and working with individuals

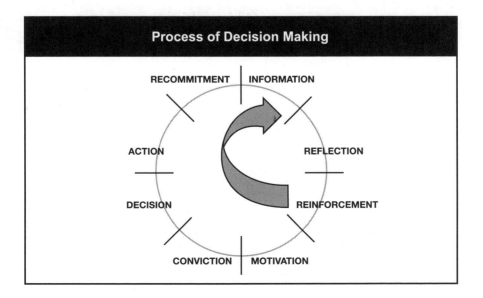

and communities as they move through the process of change. Working together, these different, often distinct, but important roles, can bring about transformation in cities. Check chapter 6 for a more detailed discussion of this decision-making process and its significance to evangelism and development of the church. That chapter has several wonderful case histories from Scripture that illustrate the points.

4. *See your city through the perspective of its many communications channels.* All forms of communication are important—private prayer, one-on-one conversation over coffee, the mass media. Research makes clear that each of these forms of communication plays different roles as people move from stages of resistance or antagonism through indifference to becoming seekers and, eventually, believers. When we value, respect, and link these roles, the potential for transforming our cities becomes much greater! In linking these roles in effective networks or partnerships, we will not only coordinate more effectively, we will be able to see the work of God more clearly, as our conscious effort to communicate with each other will monitor more clearly how God is using our work.

In this chart we see that the influence of the mass media, for instance, can be effective in the earlier stages of the process. But its influence declines as people approach the critical decision-making point, at which interpersonal communication becomes increasingly important. In reaching our cities, all forms of communication need to be coordinated to see the greatest possible influence for Christ.

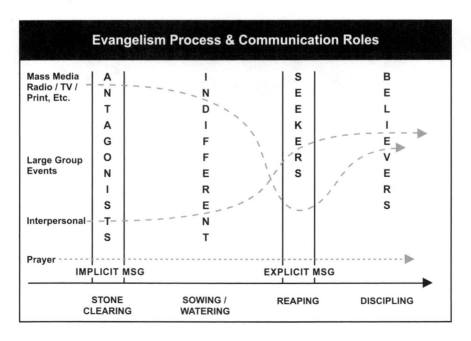

5. *See your city through the perspective of its many collaborative possibilities.* As we discussed earlier, cities usually can be broken down into many segments, some highly visible, others less so. It is of tremendous value for people working in these various segments to have a place to meet, learn from each other, share progress and problems, and be able to pray for and celebrate with each other. In short, partnership is critical. A partnership dealing with ethnic groups in your city, for example, may involve prayer networks, Christian media, local churches, youth or sports, social service ministries, business and marketplace ministries, and those experienced in developing local fellowships of new believers. The diagram below suggests the "warp and woof" of how these opportunities and Kingdom resources can intersect in a city transformation network.

City Transformation Network					
	Ethnic Groups	Street / Homeless	Youth Sector	Urban Initiatives	Suburban Initiatives
Church Planting					
Marketplace Ministries					
Social Service Ministries					
Youth / Sports Ministries					
Local Churches					
Media Communication					
Prayer Networks					

The vital thing is that all of these initiatives have a common point to meet as suggested in the City Ministry Network Model diagram as shown on page 277.

THE CHALLENGE OF CHOICE

Any initiative that will have any real impact has to make difficult choices. As in every aspect of life, you can't do everything equally well. Even when you have made your choice, you must crawl before you can walk, then walk before you can run.

Every city presents a huge diversity of ministry opportunities concentrated in a comparatively small area. That's why seeing with the perspective suggested in the diagrams above is so important. The complex nature of cities means that our earlier discussions about setting limited but high-value, achievable objectives is *so important* in this setting.

A KEY PARTNERSHIP PRINCIPLE:

There is no "right way" for a city initiative to begin or to be organized. However, the key elements discussed earlier in the book, such as strong vision, deeply committed leadership, clear, high-value limited objectives, strong ownership of the process by all the players, prayer support, and practical, short-term outcomes are vital.

THE CHALLENGE OF HOW AND WHERE YOU START

So, if you have a heart for your city, where do you start?

Do you and some of your colleagues call a meeting of "influentials," and try, from the outset, to look at the big picture of the city's need? Does an existing, effective network of specialized ministries working in the city see the potential of wider influence and invite others to help realize the vision? Do pastors who are meeting and praying together try to turn their fellowship into tangible action? Any of those approaches may be effective, depending on the circumstances in your city or community.

You face at least two key questions: Who needs to be involved? Later in the chapter we explore possible answers to this question in a section called *The Challenge of Power and Ownership*. Then, what should the partnership try to accomplish? Let's start with the second question.

You and your friends who are concerned about your city may want to ask yourselves: "If Jesus' power was let loose, top to bottom in our city or community, how would it look different in five years?"

This question poses a tremendous challenge for modern believers because the church, for so many years, has been substantially disconnected from the city around it. Many individual Christians are active in the community's businesses, schools, medical services, and other institutions. But the church, local or as a group of churches in a community, has rarely looked at the whole community and asked, "What is our responsibility and role in the community to demonstrate the power and love of Jesus?"

Such a question raises fundamental issues of how God's grace and power affect everyday life. *It really comes down to this: What do we mean when we talk about the transformation of a city?* When we look at the individuals in Scripture who were touched by direct contact with Jesus, we see him addressing a wide range of human needs. Notice he never demanded that they first talk about religious issues or use religious terms. Wholeness in people's lives *was* his business. While his ministry, of course, was ultimately focused on redeeming our eternal destiny, day to day he lived out God's vision: "I have come that you might have life—life in all its fullness." (John 10:10 GNT) So we ask, "What does that mean in *our* community or city?"

Partnership Suggestion:

Try this with your partnership facilitation team or the leadership of your local church. Next time you have a retreat or some space to think, talk, and pray together, meet where you have a white board, flip chart, or other means for recording your thoughts. Then ask, "If Jesus' power and love were let loose in our community, top to bottom, how do we think it might look different?" It's another way of asking, "What are the elements of daily life in which we think Jesus wants to make a difference?" Start by brainstorming some of those categories. Each community is unique but, across communities, there are many similar needs. What are the signs of brokenness in your community? What circumstances seem to be out of sync with what you know to be God's character? Remember that often the brokenness can be well disguised! It is not only individuals who are good at "faking it." Communities do it, too.

Once you've identified some of the categories in which you think Jesus wants to make a difference, ask, "Which one or two of these issues would seem to be a priority for attention?" Once you've worked through that prioritization, ask, "What do we think it would take for God's people in our area to see a breakthrough in this (these) issue(s)?" I strongly urge you and your group to take time to pray and listen to God's Spirit at each step along the way. As you do that, I believe you will hear his voice and, as a result, will have greater conviction and clarity in any action you are led to take.

Frequently citywide spiritual initiatives were the last thing on an individual's mind when they helped launch a ministry. Here's an example.

PARTNERSHIP IN PRACTICE: Small Beginnings Birth Big Vision

Naomi's vision was to minister to single mothers by demonstrating Christ's love. She had started by getting women volunteers together to provide a variety of support services to single mothers whose children were in day care or early school years. At first it involved just people from her church and mothers of children in a couple of local schools. Within a couple of years women in other local churches had heard about the program, and by the beginning of the third year over fifty women from five churches were touching the lives of dozens of single mothers with children in about ten area schools.

In the third year the members of Naomi's leadership team asked themselves, "Why couldn't women from churches all across the city do this?" Within months, they had identified individuals leading women's ministries in more than forty local churches. Some were volunteers, others members of church staff.

When a larger working meeting was called, Naomi's group indicated they just wanted to share what had been happening in their initiative and explore whether others might like to be part of extending the vision to touch other single mothers in need. They told stories of the challenges and blessings. When it was over, representatives from twenty-five other churches said they would like to explore doing the same thing in their areas of the city.

The next year, the expanded group began to talk about all of the other needs and opportunities they were finding in the local schools; things local churches and volunteers could do. They came up with a list of potential points of service and ministry—key roles that volunteers could play. When they called a working meeting this time, their church list had expanded to more than fifty, and they invited both men and women to the discussions.

Within another twelve months, what had started as a small, local initiative from one church had expanded to involve committed believers from more than forty churches volunteering to provide services to parents and children in more than twenty schools.

Naomi's small beginnings eventually became a network of God's people who were committed to the young people across the city. Working together, they were able to look at the big picture of children and young people from a Kingdom perspective and seek to implement initiatives that would impact a wide range of the next generation.

THE CHALLENGE OF POWER AND OWNERSHIP

Often in city initiatives, particularly if we think of a vision for citywide transformation and who needs to be involved, it's natural to think of the senior pastors of the larger, influential churches. The local fellowships of believers are the heartbeat of God's community, whether these are small house churches or high-visibility, large congregations with substantial facilities. Ultimately, local church involvement in virtually any collaborative Kingdom city initiative is essential. However, that may or may not be the place to start.

As far as we know, not one of Jesus' disciples had formal theological training. In short, they were ordinary men whose lives were touched, challenged, and changed by the power of Christ. They were ordinary people doing extraordinary things through God's power. The story of Naomi above illustrates the point.

Consider the true scope of Kingdom human resources in your community. Think of the hundreds of influential and highly competent, Kingdom-minded laymen and laywomen in business, education, government, law enforcement, social services, and the legal system. These are people who, day after day, routinely set objectives, make plans, and successfully execute those plans. They have to be able to ask the big picture questions like, "What's going on in our specific sector of responsibility and our surrounding environment that guides us regarding *what* to do and *how* to do it?" They have learned how to engage other resources and work together for common goals. These are the often invisible and overlooked core of God's army in your city.

Then there are the countless parachurch ministries serving various elements of the city's needs—youth and student ministries, ministries for homeless and street people, Christian media organizations, ministries specializing in urban service and outreach, and organizations dealing with specific ethnic groups. These ministries are populated by highly committed, often very experienced leadership and staff. And at the heart of their programs are volunteers from that vast group of laypeople mentioned above—God's "invisible army" in the community.

In your city partnership or network you need the widest ranging ownership possible. The effort must be *in*clusive. If it's *ex*clusive, it will never get to first base. But often, the apparent power and Christian influence in a community is held by a few senior pastors of large, influential churches. You will be challenged to have these influentials as part of the partnership's guiding team, while engaging the parachurch ministries, and the large number of highly competent, spiritually mature laypeople. In an effective city partnership or network, you cannot afford to have power and/or ownership in the hands of a few.

THE SPECIAL CHALLENGE AND ROLE
OF THE LOCAL CHURCHES

Because of the role local churches do play, the perceived authority ascribed to them, and the vast human and other resources concentrated in them, they *must be* part of any plan for spiritual initiatives in your community. At the same time, pastors, particularly senior pastors of the larger churches, are frequently intensely busy, with dozens of voices demanding access to their time and energy.

The senior pastors of the more influential churches in your area need to be aware of what your initiative is doing. Their reaction and vision for the issue you're trying to address needs to be heard and seriously considered. You will need the affirmation of at least a representative group of these pastors. But, typically, they will not be able to give you much time. Their blessing and the involvement of people in their church are likely to be vital to your partnership dreams. Remember that not only do pastors have multiple demands on their time, they have had dozens of well-intentioned individuals bring ideas for outreach or ministry initiatives to them. If your vision gains "traction" and, with that, credibility, you will find the pastors and the churches much more ready to talk.

In some city partnership initiatives the leadership has not felt they could move forward without a high percentage of the senior pastors' blessing *and involvement*. For the reasons already outlined, my recommendation is that while churches, particularly the influential ones in your community, need to be aware and involved at some level, you should not be intimidated by their perceived power or influence.

Once pastors are aware of and committed, at least in principle, to the partnership or network initiative, often a way to engage them without placing undue expectations on their time is to establish an advisory board or committee to provide input for your effort. Just make sure that those on such a group are genuine advisors—sought out and listened to, not just window dressing!

This might be a good time to go back and reread chapter 10 on "Partnership Exploration," which focuses on these issues in much more detail. As you consider whom you *really need* in the early stages of your initiative, prayerfully consider the *whole range* of God's people in the city. Remember those that I outlined in the last section on Power and Ownership. Many of your city's less well-known Christians may, in fact, be huge assets to your partnership. Remember: *in*clusive not *ex*clusive. Keep in mind this principle from chapter 10:

A KEY PARTNERSHIP PRINCIPLE:

You don't need to have all the players ready to talk about possible cooperation. But you do need people with a vision for the outcomes, commitment to the idea of God's people working together, and some of the agencies, ministries, and their leaders that are already recognized as credible and competent in the field you want to reach or serve.

THE CHALLENGE OF SUSTAINING COMMITMENT

Life is a process, not an event. That is true with individuals, families, and communities. That process of living is, of course, made up of countless events—some large, some small. Events can be a source of inspiration and anticipation; they can be fulfilling or a source of great disappointment. They provide the fodder for our memories—good, bittersweet, or filled with regret. Linked together, they often demonstrate a lifestyle pattern, productive or destructive, whether for an individual or a community.

Much Christian collaboration, just like that in the wider community, has been focused on events. The classic illustration is a crusade by Billy Graham or some other well known individual or group. Despite best intentions, as we discussed earlier in the book, the partnerships or coalitions that are forged for such initiatives rarely last beyond the event itself. For these events to be successful, these coalitions require tremendous focus and commitment. Ask anyone who has been active on the organizing committee or part of the working team for such an event.

Countless cities have talked and prayed together about the desire to sustain the work of the coalition beyond the event—to further deepen spiritual impact in the community. While the event may have long-term impact in individuals, sustained impact across the city rarely happens. Why is this? Here are some common reasons:

Fatigue. Frequently events require people to make an intensive effort over what seems to be a comparatively long period of time. That may be weeks or months. When the event is over, everyone says, "I've got to get back to my life!"

Scale of the goals. Events usually are associated with special goals for special reasons. Major goals are often established that are only possible because of a highly concentrated effort.

Diversity of those involved or touched by the objective. Partnerships, networks, or other alliances are usually most successful when they have well-defined, limited objectives. It's something we have said again and again in different ways in this book. A Billy Graham crusade, for instance, calls on volunteers across a huge range of age, denominational backgrounds, and vocational and educational differences. Often hundreds of churches that would never work together under other circumstances are linked to support this event, and the audience the event seeks to influence, hopefully, reflects the city's diversity.

Developing the vast array of people, prayer, money, and other resources necessary for such an event is a huge, intensive task—usually supported by a professional staff. Structuring some kind of ongoing alliance that addresses the tremendous diversity of resources involved and lives touched is almost impossible. Particularly since, once the event is over, the professional support team that served as a catalytic force behind the scenes, guiding and holding the collaborative effort together, is usually gone—quickly. In a sense, the very strength of the event is its weakness for long-term sustainability; its goals are too large, and the group it seeks to serve is too diverse.

Again, we see that the more specific the focus of your partnership, the more you can break down the long-term goals into attainable yet clearly valuable elements, the greater the potential for sustainability.

It may be that your partnership or network is coming together specifically to stage an event more effectively by working together. That's fine, just as long as you are aware of the difference between an event and objectives that take long-term commitment.

Transformation is a process, not an event. Individuals may have exceptional "Damascus Road" experiences like the Apostle Paul (Acts 9:3–9), in which their lives are turned around in a single experience. But, for even the most deeply committed, our spiritual journey will be a process. As Peter was reminded by Jesus, he would not have to forgive seven times but "seventy times seven" (Matthew 18:22). Likewise, cities may be shaken by exceptional events. *But the fundamental changes that transform and last are rooted in sustainable work, prayer, and commitment over the long haul.* That is why your partnership or network needs to take the long-term view.

Here is a brief checklist you can use to evaluate the sustainability of your partnership or other collaborative initiative in the city:

- ☐ Is the goal or are the objectives clear and compelling?

- ☐ Have you and your team been able to break down the larger goal(s) into achievable, near- and medium-term elements, where you can see success, mark your progress, or correct your course?

- ☐ Have you established a challenging but realistic timetable for action?

- ☐ Do you have a prayer team that understands the challenge of what you're taking on and will stand with you through the process?

- ☐ Do you and your leadership or facilitation team have a long-term commitment to this vision? Is there going to be continuity? Are you ready to stick with it, though it takes time and you are likely to face moments of great discouragement?

- ☐ Is there a growing sense of ownership of the vision among the participants?

Seeing lasting change in cities calls for long-distance runners! Sprinters may be good for short-term projects or events. But to see real transformation, your team has to function like long-distance runners. Clear objectives. Deep commitment. Concentration and discipline. Ready to pace yourselves. Clear markers of progress along the way. As God fuels your vision, your spirit, and your energy—jump into the race! We won't ever change the world standing on the sidelines.

The appendix has books, websites, and other resources specifically for those interested in more help as they seek to reach or serve their city.

If you have ever worked in any aspect of the business world, take a look at the next chapter. These principles have practical implications for business and the marketplace. God's principles of Kingdom collaboration are true and applicable everywhere!

Share your ideas and response to this chapter, tell your own story, or get connected with more partnership resources at the book's website
www.connectedbook.net

19

PARTNERSHIP

IMPLICATIONS FOR BUSINESS
AND THE MARKETPLACE

Core Idea

All truth is God's truth. The central, lasting values of effective partnerships and networks are relevant everywhere: in your business, your service club, law enforcement, social work, science, education, or the arts. See how the Kingdom values and the principles of partnership and networking described in this book are relevant no matter where God has placed you.

It is self-evident that you do not have to believe in God to put an astronaut on the moon. Neither do you have to be a believer to be a successful wheat farmer in the eastern part of Washington State. When I sit down with my cardiologist, I want to know that he is a highly experienced, proven professional. If he happens to know Christ, wonderful. But I go to him because I know he has a track record of integrity, concern for his patients, and success in treating them. Jesus reminds us that God's grace extends to everyone and that truth and blessing are accessible to all.[1] Simply put, this means that an individual can acknowledge the principles and benefit from them without acknowledging the Person.

For the believer, there is no such thing as "secular" and "sacred." All good things are from the hand of God and need to be seen through his eyes. Our great privilege and obligation as Christians is to be part of releasing his nature, power, and love into this wonderful but broken world.

Amongst all the principles that power effective, durable partnerships, the tracks of God's character and presence are evident. Of course, if your eyes, ears, and heart are open, you can see that in just about every sector of life. No surprise, right? So why be surprised that just about everything we have discussed in this book so far also works in business, medical and social services, industry, education, and the sciences? All you have to do is read the growing number of secular books on partnerships and networks and you see the clear parallels.

ISSUES WE ALL FACE IN OUR PERSONAL AND WORK EXPERIENCE

Let's review some of the issues we have covered regarding Christian work and ministry. Then let's identify the issues that appear again and again in different ways in our ordinary lives at work, in our schools, in the community, or maybe even in our families.

Here's a checklist of things experienced every day in business and community life. Do any sound familiar to your work experience?

- ☐ Duplication of effort and waste of resources.

- ☐ Turf wars, ego-based empires—small or large—and isolation of people, departments, or organizations due to lack of effective communication.

- ☐ Critical issues that fall between the cracks due to lack of coordinated assessment and response.

- ☐ Increasing demand for efficiency and productivity and questions about how to achieve them through coordination, focus, and greatest efficiency.

- ☐ People who are forced to do tasks others could do better but who were never included in discussions or planning.

- ☐ The challenge of taking on high-risk projects: how to evaluate the risk, share it, reduce, and finally overcome it by working with others rather than going it alone.

- ☐ The desire to turn complex dreams (computer systems, community schools, new products, etc.) into relevant, practical, working goals that can be achieved and celebrated.

- ☐ Isolation among workers focused on a common goal but having no means to connect and share what they are learning and provide encouragement and motivation for each other.

☐ Departments, organizations, or teams skilled in one area being asked to undertake projects in another area for which they are not equipped. Effective collaboration with others could have put the right team on the right project.

☐ The need to build and sustain trust in the community or workplace to achieve common goals.

☐ Wanting a high sense of ownership of, participation in, and loyalty to projects we're working on—in the community, on the job, or in our families.

☐ The need for resources, people, money, technical skills/experience beyond what any single company or organization has.

☐ The challenge of consistent, creative communication between departments in colleges and universities, hospitals, government, law enforcement, and businesses, in which a lack of real partnership and effective coordination often creates problems, waste, and inefficiency.

☐ Seeing needs that appear to be high priority in your business or the community but knowing that, working alone, the challenge of meeting them is too great.

☐ Wanting to give all those working on a project a sense that their part is valuable—that they are playing an important role in an important effort.

Effective partnerships deal, at one level or another, with every one of these issues. Of course, there's no simple cure, and one size does not fit all. But this book focuses explicitly on Christian ministry and covers principles that are equally relevant in business and the general marketplace. The contents can serve as a resource to help you, your friends, and your colleagues look at the issues around you and explore ways to *consciously work together* and, therefore, be more effective.

PARTNERSHIP IN PRACTICE: Following a workshop I led on partnership development with a mixed group of laymen and pastors in the midwestern part of the U.S., a businessman approached me with the basic Fifteen Key Principles of Effective Partnership in his hand (See chapter 1, "Quickstart" and the appendix for your copy). He said excitedly: "You know, I think nearly every one of these principles can be applied in my business! Is it OK if I take these with me, rewrite and organize them for my business and our relationships both with customers and our suppliers? We need to see what we're doing as a partnership, but that's going to take some real changes."

I asked him the nature of his business. He explained his company was a major regional metal industrial building fabrication and installation business, with suppliers and clients spread over a number of surrounding states. A few weeks later he sent me the version of the key principles he had developed for his company and said his team was already excited to begin doing business with this different perspective.

I recently met with the faculty and administrative leadership of a high-quality liberal arts college for their pre-term annual retreat. The president asked me to focus on the topic, "Working Together: Partnership Inside and Outside the College." A complex agenda: working together inside the college, between departments and key administrative units; working together with the community and its businesses, schools, and churches; and working together with students, parents, and alumni to increase the size and quality of the school's program.

It was a classic case of good people doing good things but so busy and pre-occupied with the challenge of their own programs, they had no time to explore what might be accomplished by linking with others. The retreat produced a number of "aha" moments, many ideas for synergy both inside and outside the school, and decisions on practical steps to put feet to the ideas.

Among the many authors I have found addressing these issues, this comment was among the most compelling:

> What is needed is a vision of a new culture—a collaborative culture—that incorporates the most admirable qualities of [each partner]. Collaborative partnerships within and across organizational settings are flourishing as educational and service institutions cope with increasing complexity and change.[2]

The issues we have discussed in this book and their application to the world of the church, mission agencies, evangelism, and Christian ministry are deeply rooted in the character of everyday life. This is the life God designed us to live—fully, *together*, and in productive working relationships.

APPLYING THE CONTENTS OF THIS BOOK TO DAILY LIFE

This book focuses on partnerships, networks, and other kinds of collaboration in churches, mission agencies, and evangelism. How to transfer these ideas to your personal life and your world of work and community involvement?

If you'd like to try making that application, I suggest you go back and scan:

Part One: The Big Picture (chapters 1–3) includes material that is directly relevant to principles of *what needs to be done* and the *motivation for doing it*—together.

Part Two: The God Design (chapters 4–6). While the specifically Christian perspective of much of this section may not be applicable to your workplace or community projects, the principles embedded in each of these chapters *are* relevant. Check out:

- Chapter 4: Open, trusting relationships are vital, whether in our personal lives, work, sports teams we play with, or the community institutions we depend on. Unpack these principles and you'll have a better handle on working together.

- Chapter 5: Whether it is in the local school system, your company, or the Scout troop you advise, when you are considering groups of people, change can have a powerful effect—and not always good. Understanding how change occurs and preparing for it is vital to working together effectively.

- Chapter 6: Families, companies, and communities are composed of individuals. Individuals make the important decisions in their lives in fairly predictable ways. Understanding more about how people you live and work with make their decisions can go a long way toward developing understanding and effective working relationships.

Part Three: Behind The Scenes (chapters 7–9)

- Chapter 7 focuses on the powerful idea of having a vision that drives us on—in our lives, our families, our work, or the community projects in which we're involved. Working together makes big dreams possible. No great company or community organization has made a consistent profit, returned serious equity value to shareholders, or had a lasting impact on the community without a compelling, consistent vision.

- Chapter 8, on prayer, may not be a topic for discussion in your workplace. But it certainly is a potentially powerful tool for you to employ if you are trying to get people to work together, whether at work or in the community. Not only your prayers but, possibly, getting those of other believers whom you ask to pray with you specifically about your desire to encourage greater cooperation and collaboration. It could be a vital role they could play behind the scenes while you work up front.

- Chapter 9 unpacks the idea that no great idea that has lasting value is an event but involves a process of events, decisions, and ongoing work. In business and the community, a firm grip on this principle can strengthen strategies and provide encouragement as people see incremental but meaningful successes.

Part Four: On The Way (chapters 10–13) has dozens of principles, ideas, illustrations, case histories, and plenty of nuts-and-bolts, how-to ideas. As you think about collaboration or partnership in your workplace or community, you will quickly see the parallels and potential application.

Partnership Suggestion:

 Check the website www.connectedbook.net for questions and ideas you can copy or download that relate to each chapter in the book. These generic questions may be helpful for you to use where you work or in your community.

Part Five: Working It Out (chapters 14–16) addresses three of the most critical elements in any business or community partnership. The text and stories are focused on Christian ministry, but the implications for everyday life are huge.

- Chapter 14 suggests that effective, lasting partnerships or alliances have someone, or a small group of people, specifically charged with carrying the vision for the partnership. Their primary concern when they wake up every day is the partnership—its health, effectiveness, and durability. Every case history in business collaboration affirms this.

- Chapter 15 demonstrates that everyone in the "supply chain" needs to see how relationships make a positive difference. How are the people in our business or community relationships defining success, and how is our alliance with them helping to realize that vision?

- Chapter 16 focuses on the fact that our alliances, whether ministry, business, or community institutions, need to be structured in a way that is appropriate to the task. Bureaucracy may appear to provide security, but your collaboration will function best when your structure closely matches your goals and methods.

Part Six: Special Cases, Special Opportunities (chapters 17–19)

- Chapter 17, on networks, may suggest ways you and your friends who share some interest may be able to link with like-minded people across the state or country, or around the world—to share information, develop common plans, or provide mutual encouragement—within your business sector or in some aspect of community service.

- Chapter 18 can help you and your friends look at your city, whether you have a specifically Christian initiative in mind or not. The principles in that chapter, combined with those in chapters 11–13, can empower almost any collaborative effort you have in mind.

Partnership Suggestion:

Consider picking up copies of the book for your friends and then meeting to talk about the principles that apply to the project or vision you share. You might:

- Read a chapter at a time and discuss the implications of the content for your work. Think together about how to translate the ideas into action.

- Ask yourselves, "Practically speaking, what will it take to actually put these ideas into action on our vision or project?"

- Discuss and prioritize ways to turn the principles and your dreams into action steps that will move the vision forward and give you the experience and encouragement you need.

Share your ideas and response to this chapter, tell your own story, or get connected with more partnership resources at the book's website
www.connectedbook.net

20

THE FUTURE OF PARTNERSHIP

Core Idea

In this world of amazing change, where stability seems elusive and tradition almost gone, what is to be done? In this chapter I outline some challenges that are deeply connected to this vision of God's people working together in partnerships, networks, and other forms of collaboration. Then I briefly suggest, in broad terms, action steps we might take.

Elements of the world we live in today were unthinkable even ten years ago. At the current rates of change, in ten years the world the church seeks to reach with the power and love of Christ may be unrecognizable. The future is in collaboration. Doing it alone won't work any more. God has great blessing ahead for us. But we in God's company will need to face profound changes to experience those blessings. The journey will be marked by wonder, faith, and tears, but, most certainly, with great new experiences. Listening to God's Spirit and other people, you can be part of shaping the future with the power of the good news!

MEGA-CHALLENGES FACING THE CHURCH
AND ITS COMMITMENT TO PARTNERSHIP

Challenge # 1: Individualism has displaced community.

The landscape of relationships has drastically changed over the last four to five decades. The change is having social, economic, spiritual, and political implications of previously unimagined proportions.

There has been a drastic decline in the perception of the value and influence of relationships and community life, which were once seen as essentials or anchor points. The roles of family, social and service clubs, lodges, neighborhoods, and churches have changed.

Denominations are one example. Once a dominant influence on the nature of the church worldwide, denominations are increasingly marginalized. Local churches are exercising new, independent initiatives. They ascribe less value to the denomination for its practical service to the local church and its mission or vision.

A very different example illustrates changes in social life. Bowling alleys in America that were built around groups of people—bowling leagues—have closed by the thousands. If people want to bowl, they now bowl independently, with people of their choice at times of their choice.[1]

As the perceived power (and authority) of the center of old social structures has declined, power and initiative have rapidly migrated to the edges of society. For instance, in 2002 the political leadership of the world's sixth largest economy, the State of California, was overthrown. Not by revolution in the streets or even at the ballot box, but through an initiative launched and sustained through the Internet.

What to do?

We must first recognize that isolation, individualism, and fragmentation of relationships are at epidemic levels. Second, we must understand and reflect on the implications. Finally, particularly in the West, we must recognize and, through repentance and radical renewal, come to grips with God's original design: we were created to live in community. Personal, family, and community health depend on it. Ultimately, the fabric of wider society depends on it. Equally important, the spiritual vitality and credibility of the church depends on it.

Conscious, pro-active commitment to partnerships, networks, and other forms of collaboration must become the *norm*, not the exception. Internally, each church should be working to this end. In communities, churches should be working *together* to this end. And, nationally and internationally, the extent to which initiatives show a healthy component of collaboration should be a significant criterion of evaluation. (A reporting/evaluation tool, *Our Ministry Investments: Are They Partnership Based?*, has been developed to help churches and other sponsoring groups assess the extent to which the people or projects they are sponsoring are committed to collaboration. This tool will help you evaluate whether those involved are actively connecting with other people or agencies or just doing their own thing. See the appendix.)

Challenge # 2: Information is pervasive and influential

Missionaries have faced an increasing challenge upon returning to their home countries, in Holland, the Philippines, Nigeria, the U.S., or Brazil. While they have been away on the field, their friends, leaders of their home churches, and their supporters have been reading newspapers, listening to the radio, and watching the ever-present plethora of news on television. In recent years, they have been receiving increasingly up-to-date information via the Internet, instant messaging on cell phones, or other electronic devices. Right or wrong, more people know more about the world than ever before—often at frighteningly superficial levels and almost always interpreted from their own limited cultural perspective.

This can create a confusing picture, and there are few sources of clear information about what's going on. "Information overload" is a pervasive expression.

With all this information, right or wrong, there is a perception that older sources of information and, therefore, authority, are not as important and possibly not as trustworthy. That means government, the church, and other social structures that once provided the information on which we based our lives seem less significant. In a recent Internet review of the book, *Disaffected Democracies: What's Troubling the Trilateral Countries?*, Princeton University Press attributes the change to "governments' diminished capacity to act in an interdependent world and a decline in institutional performance, in combination with new public expectations and uses of information that have altered the criteria by which people judge their governments."[2] With the proliferation of information sources that bear on our decisions, how does one piece together a coherent, trustworthy picture?

What to do?

As we have seen throughout the book, healthy, strong relationships take active, intentional communications, whether in marriages, families, communities, churches, or nations. The natural tendency for relationships is *disintegration,* not integration.

Independence breeds isolation. Isolation breeds misunderstanding.

To help people "connect the dots," understand, and make sense out of life, we in the church need to intensify our commitment to communication. Proactive collaboration through partnerships and networks, even at the most local, grassroots level, can help renew communications and, with that, a sense of understanding, community, trust, and belonging. But as we have consistently seen, just getting people together in partnerships or networks isn't enough. An ongoing, conscious commitment to communication is vital—both within the partnership and between the partnership and its various constituencies.

Partnership and collaboration can help people turn what often seems to be a dizzying picture of isolated bits and pieces, the individual pixels of life, into a more coherent whole. One by one, the elements in information overload can be analyzed and either understood and seen as part of an overall picture or simply discarded as irrelevant. Making information choices is more important than ever.

On the mission field, active participation in effective partnerships and networks helps international Christian workers (missionaries) understand what is going on and where their contributions fit in and helps them report on the big picture to the folks back home. The story of God's work in their lives becomes more credible and richer. At home, the same commitment needs to be made; a proactive effort to connect the dots and help people see how the various pieces fit together.

Active partnerships and networks rooted in strong communications and relationships will strengthen the effectiveness inside our churches, between our churches, and between our churches and the community, as we join the global church in sharing the good news.

Challenge # 3: Dealing with success—connecting the resources of the proliferating global church

What were we thinking?! Haven't we prayed that there would come a day when God's people would be present in every major language and ethnic group of the world? Though we are still some distance from seeing "every tongue and tribe" acknowledge Jesus Christ as Lord, there are believers in hundreds of language groups in different countries around the world.

What kind of a future did we imagine when we got to this point? That, somehow, everything would be business as usual? That all the new churches around the world would act independently as their Western mentors had modeled, but the churches in the West would continue to act as parents rather than adults in a community of equals?

The rapidly escalating resources of the global church are being frittered away because of individualism, nationalism, arrogance, and, often, ignorance. Turning the success God has given the missionary movement of the last 200 years into a coherent, effectively resourced, continuing witness is the challenge.

If you had traveled to Kazakhstan prior to 1990 you would have found only a handful of expatriate Christian workers. But today you will find believers from more than twenty-five countries sharing Christ's love and power in dozens of ways. Working with each other, working with national believers, and sharing Christ's love in the wider society, they reflect the global church. Did we ever imagine, much less pray for, the day when you would sit in a national working meeting of believers in Kazakhstan and find *Western personnel in the minority*? Do we see it as good news—a sign of success? It is, of course. It's the realization of the vision shared by Jesus in Matthew 28:19–20! Now our brothers and sisters from the global church are taking up major portions of the load. The major problem is an identity crisis—on both sides!

What to do?

Effective partnerships and networks, as we have described throughout this book, are crucial to this new world order—to identifying the assets and effectively allocating them. Committed to Christ and the holistic proclamation of his love and power, these new, inclusive forms of Kingdom collaboration provide options for effective connection that are simply impossible with the old organizational paradigms. Koreans, Senegalese, Egyptians, Guatemalans, Norwegians, Canadians, and Chinese need to be able to sit together, plan, pray, and fashion a way forward as God works through the church in their countries to reach the world.

The big challenge is for the global church to see East, West, North, and South as genuine partners. Too often material and technical resources are perceived as having higher value than, say, vision, spiritual energy, and power in prayer. Members of the global church need to see each other as great deposits of Kingdom resources that, linked effectively together, can have remarkable impact.

Whether the collaboration is focused on witness and service in a major language group, linking ministries and people across a region, or focusing the resources of many groups on a single, high-priority project, each case provides a means for engaging all the vibrant, diverse elements of the global church. It's a scenario critical to the future of our effectiveness, our stewardship, our credibility, and our spiritual power!

Challenge # 4: East-West, North-South relationships in the Church

Cross-cultural communications have always been a challenge. It's an issue as ancient as the Tower of Babel. Wars have been fought, revolutions born, and communities divided because of communication problems between people—sometimes because of bad information that leads to even worse outcomes! The book of Acts and a number of the epistles illustrate the inevitable misunderstandings when believers link across cultural backgrounds.

In late 2004 a group of about sixty-five network and partnership leaders from more than twenty countries met in Thailand for several days. As part of a wider working conference called by the Lausanne Committee for World Evangelization, they explored issues that would help move the Kingdom partnership and networking movement forward. The first ever international survey of leaders had been conducted prior to the conference, exploring what were felt to be the main issues. Amid all the other issues discussed during the meetings, the one that emerged as the most acute challenge to God's people working together was the health of relationships between churches in the West and North and the growing *majority* churches in the East and South.[3]

We may think that "partnership issues" were dealt with during those tumultuous postcolonial years when dozens of non-Western countries received their independence. We may also think that because representatives of these countries appear on our nightly news screens, somehow, communications and relations are better. But with the reality of a truly *global* church and high interconnectedness, we must think again.

With all our *functional* commitment to individualism, why are we surprised that in the postcolonial period and even up to today, great difficulties have persisted in relationships between Western and non-Western churches? The pride and energy of the often rapidly growing younger churches runs head-on into the parental spirit of control held by the established church.

What to do?

Now more than ever, local churches, mission agencies, denominations, specialized ministries, and funding sources in Western countries must examine afresh how they view their partnership relationships with fellow believers from other countries and cultures. This is not a unilateral problem. Work must be done from both sides to develop understanding and new levels of trust and effectiveness. However, a disproportionately *large* part of the world's money and technical resources controlled by a disproportionately *small* part of the world's population represents an inherent problem of major proportion!

Of course, the very same issues pertain to complex church relationships in the great cities, particularly in the West, which are often a microcosm of the world. Lack of trust and understanding between white and black churches and the functional divisions because of ethnicity or language are major barriers to effective ministry and spiritual impact.

Seeing each church as the steward of significant assets, quite different but of real value, will go a long way toward effective communication and collaboration for missions and evangelism. Sitting together in a conscious partnership context, working out the issues of trust, vision, achievable objectives, and the roles each party will play, will go a long way toward turning conflict into community, effective witness, and outcomes we can celebrate *together*.

Unless we address this issue, lasting, effective networks and partnerships in this new global context, often reflected in our local communities, will be beyond our reach.

The bibliography in the appendix identifies a number of books and other valuable resources for churches or ministries wanting to more effectively identify the issues, listen, and build durable relationships across cultures.

CRITICAL COMPONENTS IN MOVING THE VISION FORWARD

If we are committed to the paradigm of Kingdom collaboration, what key things need to happen?

Partnership as the DNA of Church ministry. We have to truly believe God will bless our efforts more if we link with others—this is *absolutely core* to Christian faith and practice. Partnership with others is not an option—it's essential. Pastors, laypeople, and other Christian leaders must believe this and be committed to it. This is not the fad or trend of the month.

Once we are sure our plans are something God wants, questions should always follow, like: "Who else is doing this? What have they learned? Should we be talking with them about possible collaboration?" If there really is no one else doing what you're considering, ask, "Could we do this better by working with others? Who are those people or ministries?" We should never leave the starting gate if we have not asked these questions.

Advocate for partnerships and networks in all centers of influence. Proclaim the partnership message in pulpits of local churches, classrooms of Bible schools, seminaries, and missionary training centers. Then preach the message through Christian communications channels of all kinds. This will require visionary *advocates* of partnership among church and lay leadership and *champions* for partnership in every ministry and Christian initiative.

Like-minded men and women, committed to Kingdom collaboration through partnerships and networks need to be actively linked, to encourage each other, and share what they are learning. The linkage may be face to face, in regional or specialized networks, or through the Internet. The main point is that the advocacy and encouragement has to be between networks and partnerships—not just within the projects or initiatives they are helping. (See the website www.powerofconnecting.net for opportunities to link with like-minded people working on Kingdom partnerships and networks.)

Be proactive in training, modeling, and coaching for leadership. Whether they are professional or lay leaders, the next generation of Kingdom leaders around the world must be *intentionally trained* in the *why* and *how* of effective partnership.

I'm sure you've heard the story about the man who was asked about his hobby and responded, "On the weekends I'm an amateur brain surgeon." When was the last time you flew in a commercial airliner with an amateur pilot in command? Pilots need licenses that demonstrate their skills, and flight examiners are held responsible for certifying that skill. Experienced professional doctors help establish standards of performance. Medical examiners enforce those standards.

In short, in other sectors we assume it is not only possible but also vital to master complex issues calling for specialized knowledge and skill. With the church's history of brokenness and individualism, we need to be similarly committed to teaching how to build Kingdom partnerships and networks. We need vision, training, and ongoing mentoring for the leaders and facilitators of Kingdom collaboration.

This book demonstrates that building and sustaining effective partnerships and networks is not a mystery. *It is possible, has been demonstrated many times, and can be learned.* But effective collaborative initiatives don't happen by chance. The goal of this book has been to distill and share some of what God's people around the world are learning about working together successfully. Its purpose is to help us understand that, like doctors and pilots, we can learn, reproduce, and evaluate how to do this kind of work in professional, reliable ways. Despite the church's long history of division and Satan's success at keeping us apart, not only is it God's design for us to work together, recent history proves it can and *is* being done.

Success in this sector will mean new research, practical curricula for teaching grassroots personnel as well as senior leaders, and ongoing coaching to encourage and help those committed to the vision. Training centers, multilingual materials, websites, and a host of other means need to be employed to share both the vision and the essentials of partnership and network "how tos."

Finally, a few thoughts about where effective Kingdom partnerships and networks should help accelerate spiritual breakthroughs.

STRATEGIC SECTORS WITH EXTRAORDINARY POTENTIAL IMPACT THE CALL FOR COLLABORATION

*1. The 2.5 billion illiterate oral communicators who **only** get information orally.* Along with another 1.5 billion who get over ninety-five percent of their information orally, they are the true "hard core" of the world's unreached. For 200 years Western strategies and materials have been designed by literates for literates. Only a collaborative approach has any hope of addressing this enormous challenge.

2. Nearly 400 cities of more than one million in and around the 10/40 window. By 2025 two-thirds of the world's population will live in cities. It is the loneliest, most bewildering challenge facing the global church. Without communication between workers in these cities to coordinate resources, information, and encouragement, we have no hope of seeing real breakthroughs of God's transforming power and love.

3. The non-English users of the Internet. With 530 million English speakers in the world and 5.8 *billion* non-English speakers, it's not hard to see where the growth in Internet use will occur. While this growth will be uneven, already, non-English users are well past one billion. To reach and serve these people with the good news, we need to be connecting and sharing with each other.

4. Our local communities. Consistently, those who were around Jesus spoke in awe and wonder about his life and power because they saw him touch people at everyday levels of need, doing things others had never done. To restore its credibility, release the power of the Holy Spirit, and energize and encourage its people, the local church must connect with the everyday needs of its local community. Determining the most critical needs and shaping a credible response empowered by the Holy Spirit is only possible as local churches *come together* in our communities. Our churches are filled with millions of gifted, highly motivated people who are waiting to be led to follow God's design and produce outcomes that provide fulfillment and ongoing motivation.

5. The world in crisis. The world's attention is regularly captured by international emergencies: famines, starvation, the plight of refugees, and disasters such as the Asian tsunami of 2004 regularly affect thousands or tens of thousands of people. Other crises such as infant mortality, the HIV/AIDS epidemic, and child slavery and prostitution consistently appear in our headlines. Dozens of international Christian relief and development agencies, local churches, denominations, and other specialized ministries respond in various ways to these needs, often heroically. But the greatest capacity of the Christian relief and development organizations is dwarfed by the demands of such international challenges. Still, consider the technology and financial resources available to the church. There is not a single Christian ministry that cannot communicate with others for pennies, almost instantly.

The U.S. church alone, were it giving just a *tithe*—forget gifts or offerings over and above the tithe—it would now be giving about $190 *billion* dollars per year. As it is, we are giving about $70 billion. The staggering sum of the $120 billion difference is, essentially, money U.S. church members are holding back in their pockets. Of course, it is fantasy to act as if it's *our* money. It really is *God's money.* Imagine what might happen if those funds *were available* for coordinated Christian response to some of these critical and highly visible international crises!

But forget about new or additional money for the moment. Even current budgets of the Christian relief and development ministries—backed by their individual constituencies—*if combined for selected initiatives*, could have a remarkable impact and witness for Christ. Non-Christian religions are daily decrying the Western church and its lack of credibility. For the church to respond to criticism of this kind, Christian organizations need to *come together, in advance*, putting collaborative infrastructure in place so when the needs arise, the church is ready. There is no reason it cannot be done. Only a lack of will and commitment to the priority stand in the way.

Is it possible that the world might say of today's global church, "Others talk, the Christians act. Other groups spew empty words. Christians don't just talk, they actually respond. And they do what they promise." Imagine what a difference we could make!

You are blessed when you can show people how to cooperate instead of how to compete and fight. That is when you will discover who you really are and your place in God's family. (Matthew 5:9, The Message)

Share your ideas and response to this chapter, tell your own story, or get connected with more partnership resources at the book's website

www.connectedbook.net

APPENDIX

INTERNET BASED RESOURCES

1. Check the web site www.connectedbook.net. *It specifically links to the content of this book.*

The web site –

- Has resources you can download, print, and use.

- Gives more and recently identified resources to help your partnership or network efforts.

- Lets you interact with the *Well Connected* book content—sharing what you've found helpful, your experiences that may be different. You can share your alternative views and make suggestions for others to consider.

- Lets you interact with others on the subjects raised in the book.

- Encourages you to share your own partnership or networking story.

- Helps all of us write a "living book" of our real life experience in helping God's people work together.

By helping God's people share their experience through this web site, we hope to publish a follow-on book of partnership and networking experiences from around the world; real people, real lives, and real stories of God's people being well connected. Check it out!

2. Check the website, www.wellconnectedbook.net for information regarding the *Well Connected Workbook* which will soon be available for you to use in your organization, with friends, your church, or with those who are helping in your collaborative effort.

3. Check three web sites specifically dedicated to helping expand and strengthen the partnership and networking movement:

www.powerofconnecting.net – The comprehensive resource site for those in the growing, global partnership/network community.

www.interdev.org – The site operated by Interdev Partnership Associates, a group of experienced men and women committed to supporting and encouraging those wanting to start or strengthen ministry partnerships focused on the unreached.

www.visionsynergy.net – The site for the organization committed to development and strengthening of strategic ministry networks helping the global church speed world evangelization.

4. Partnership eNewsletter – sign up for this free monthly electronic newsletter that provides suggestions, news, new resources, and other current things that will help. Go to the bottom of the front page of the web site, www.powerofconnecting.net.

OTHER RESOURCES FOUND HERE

Our Ministry Investments: Are They Partneship Based?

Visit the resource web site, www.powerofconnecting.net and click on the section "Evalutation Tools." You can copy or download this questionnaire.

Our Ministry: Are We Good Partnership Material?

A tool you and your colleagues can use to assess your organization's "Partnership Readiness Index." Be prepared for tough questions and honest discussion in your group.

Partnership/Network Evaluation

A tool to help you look at your initiative's process, quality of its relationships, communications, outcomes, effectiveness.

Being Well Connected: 15 Critical Principles

If all else fails, work hard to put these principles into practice in your partnership or network. Doing so will greatly increase the likelihood of your success. Ignoring them you run a high risk of disappointment or even failure.

Selected Bibliography: Partnerships and Networks

Want to read more? Here's a good place to start.

Our Ministry:
Are We Good Partnership/Network Material?

Over the years it has become clear that certain organizations or ministries are able to work and contribute in partnerships or networks more effectively than others. There are reasons why that's true. It's not just the "personality" of the leadership. Taken together, the questions here form a kind of picture of how you and your organization or ministry see yourself. And how you see yourself will have a major impact on how effectively you can and will work with others.

Those completing the form should be from different sectors within the organization from leadership to rank and file colleagues. Once the forms are complete and compiled, make sure you meet to discuss the results. You may want to go question by question and compare why you answered the way you did. Then it would be helpful to discuss what these results suggest to you as you consider working more closely with other agencies or ministries. See below for scoring guidelines.

On a scale of 1–10 (1/low, 10/high) rate your ministry by
answering the following questions.

1. My ministry/organization has a clear mission and vision statement. _____

2. My ministry's specialty is in demand. _____

3. My ministry's leadership is clear and confident about our purpose. _____

4. My ministry is inclusive (will work with a wide range of other agencies). _____

5. My ministry is growing (range of services/budget/staff, etc.). _____

6. My ministry is open to significant innovation and change. _____

7. My ministry has a strong desire to expand its impact. _____

8. My ministry is considered by others to be a leader/innovator in our field. _____

9. My ministry is confident about its identity. _____

10. My ministry is willing to share its "trade secrets." _____

Partnership Potential Index — Total _____

Scoring:

- A total above 80 suggests your organization will probably do well in a collaborative effort.

- A total between 60–80 suggests you may need to look at those points where you are rating your organization below a "7." What might be done to strengthen this area?

- A total below 60 suggests that a meeting of your leadership would probably be good to review the evaluation and ask whether the score and evaluation point to areas that need work.

EVALUATING/DIAGNOSING YOUR PARTNERSHIP OR NETWORK'S HEALTH

All collaborative efforts are challenging. As good stewards, we want to know if we are being effective. Additionally, it is vital to be able to identify points of progress for encouragement and points of need for further development.

This generic diagnostic/evaluation tool helps you look at some of your initiative's most important elements. Not every point will necessarily be relevant to what you are doing. You may want to take elements from this tool and make up your own form.

Three suggestions:

1.　Have as many in the partnership or network as possible participate in the evaluation. You may want to put the tool on line so folks can complete it on their computer. (Tools like www.surveymonkey.com are simple, powerful resources to help you do that.) You need a good sampling of what your participants think.

2.　Once you have compiled the information, share it with the whole group—discussing the strengths and weaknesses that may appear. Make sure you celebrate progress, share credit where it is due, and talk honestly about changes that could be made to do better.

3.　If you are in an international setting or some other, specialized context, you may want/need to add categories to this questionnaire. For instance, if your initiative is international, you may want to ask questions about the mix between Western and non-Western partner agencies—or about the role that non-Westerners are playing in the leadership.

Ask the tough questions as you go. You'll be encouraged, be able to fine tune your effort, and keep the negative surprises to a minimum!

Partnership / Network
Diagnostic/Evaluation Tool

Partnership/Network Name: _____

Today's Date: _____

Date Partnership Formed: _____

Date of Last Review: _____

Facilitator or Facilitation Team: _____

1. Please rank all characteristics on a scale of 1–10: (Most ideal/10, Least ideal/1)

2. Note: All characteristics may not be equally applicable or relevant to your Partnership or Network operation. Consider only those you feel applicable.

3. Note: Throughout, the group you are seeking to reach or serve is referred to as GRS (Group Reached/Served.)

1. COLLABORATIVE PROCESS

RATING	COMMENTS	WORK NEEDED

1.1   Spirit in the Group

1.2   Relationships

1.3   Leadership

1.4   Organization/Structure

1.5   Defined Objectives

1.6   Partner Agency Ownership of Objectives

_____   _____   _____

1.7   Objectives Implemented

_____   _____   _____

1.8   Working Groups or Task Forces Active

_____   _____   _____

1.9   Communication Between Partner Agencies

_____   _____   _____

1.10 Conflict/Problem Solving

_____   _____   _____

1.11 Growing Sense of Trust/Interdependence Between Partners

_____   _____   _____

1.12 Partner's Value of the Partnership/Network

_____   _____   _____

1.13 Group's Openness to Change/Development

_____   _____   _____

2.   *COLLABORATIVE ACTIVITY*

RATING   **COMMENTS**   **WORK NEEDED**

2.1   Research Being Done by the Group

_____   _____   _____

2.2   Training in Collaboration Skills

_____   _____   _____

2.3   Quantity of Project's Outcomes

_____   _____   _____

2.4   Quality of Project's Outcomes

_____   _____   _____

2.5   Diversity of Partner Agencies

_____   _____   _____

2.6   Project Resourcing: People, Money, Facilities

<u>   </u>   <u>   </u>   <u>   </u>

2.7   Documentation of the Initiative's Activity

<u>   </u>   <u>   </u>   <u>   </u>

2.8   Evaluation of Your Collaborative Activity

<u>   </u>   <u>   </u>   <u>   </u>

3.   *COLLABORATIVE OUTCOMES*

RATING   **COMMENTS**   **WORK NEEDED**

3.1   # of Contacts w/GRS

<u>   </u>   <u>   </u>   <u>   </u>

3.2   Continuity of Contacts

<u>   </u>   <u>   </u>   <u>   </u>

3.3   Quality of GRS Contacts

<u>   </u>   <u>   </u>   <u>   </u>

3.4   # of GRS Being Served/Impacted by the Program

<u>   </u>   <u>   </u>   <u>   </u>

3.5   Quality of Service/Follow-up of GRS

<u>   </u>   <u>   </u>   <u>   </u>

3.6   # of GRS Emerging As Potential Leaders

<u>   </u>   <u>   </u>   <u>   </u>

3.7   Connection of Program w/Other Relevant Programs For GRS

<u>   </u>   <u>   </u>   <u>   </u>

4.   *PARTNERSHIP STEWARDSHIP*

RATING   **COMMENTS**   **WORK NEEDED**

4.1   Progress on Objectives

<u>   </u>   <u>   </u>   <u>   </u>

4.2   Reduction of Duplication

_____ _____   _____

4.3   Return on Investment of Resources

_____ _____   _____

4.4   Costs

_____ _____   _____

4.5   Value Recognized by Constituencies

_____ _____   _____

TOTALS

_____ _____   _____

Totals on Last Review

_____ _____   _____

Change (+/- %)Since Last Review

_____ _____   _____

Being Well Connected: 15 Critical Principles

For Christian ministries working together in local cities/communities or internationally, success is often elusive. Nearly twenty years of field experience has revealed certain core principles that are common to virtually all really effective, lasting partnerships. Build your ministry partnership with these principles, and the likelihood of success is high. Ignore them, and failure is very likely!

Suggestion: A helpful way to use this list is to consider it a "checklist." Evaluate how you, your colleagues, or the collaborative project you are doing line up with these core principles.

---

1. Effective partnerships are built on trust, openness and mutual concern. Partnerships are more than coordination, planning, strategies and tactics. The heart of the gospel is restored relationships. Spending time on getting to know, understand, and appreciate each other is not an option.

2. Lasting partnerships need a committed facilitator—someone who, by consensus, has been given the role of bringing the partnership to life and keeping the fires burning. This "honest broker," usually loaned or seconded from a church or ministry, committed to the task, must be a person of vision who will keep on despite all discouragement. Prophet, servant, and resource person—this individual has to be trained and nurtured. One person serving everyone in a partnership is a lonely task.

3. Successful partnerships develop in order to accomplish a specific vision or task. Partnership for partnership's sake is a sure recipe for failure. Warm fellowship is not enough. This means lasting partnerships focus primarily on what (objectives) rather than how (structure). Form always follows function—not the other way around. Consensus is usually better than constitution! Focus on purpose. Structure should be only the minimum required to get the job done.

4. Effective partnerships have limited, achievable objectives in the beginning; more expansive as the group experiences success. Though limited, these objectives must have clear:

A. Kingdom significance that captures the imagination and provides motivation for the group.

B. Relevance to each church or partner ministry's vision and objective.

Bigger spiritual 'payoffs' begin to occur as a partnership becomes more mature and gains confidence in its own capacity to realize spiritual change through its efforts.

5.   Effective partnerships start by identifying key felt needs among the people being served. They do not start by trying to write a common theological statement. From these needs, Kingdom priorities, barriers to spiritual breakthroughs, and the resources available or needed, realistic priorities for action must be distilled and agreed.

6.   Effective partnerships have a partnership "champion" inside every church, ministry, or organization in the partnership—a person who sees how his or her group can benefit from such practical cooperation; an individual who will sell the vision to his or her colleagues and keep the partnership focused to realize those benefits.

7.   Partnerships are a process not an event. The start-up, exploration and formation stages of a partnership often take more time than expected. Call a formation or even exploratory meeting too early, and you will likely kill the possibility of a partnership. Ultimately, personal trust is required. Taking time to establish it privately in one-on-one meetings, the facilitator will find that later, in the group, it will pay rich dividends.

8.   Effective partnerships are even more challenging to maintain than to start. To make sure the vision stays alive, the focus clear, communications good, and outcomes fulfilling takes great concentration and long-term commitment by the facilitator or facilitation team.

9.   Effective partnerships are made up of partners with clear identities and vision. The churches and other ministries involved must have their own clear mission statements and live by them. Otherwise they will never understand how they "fit in," contribute to the overall picture, or benefit from the joint effort.

10.   Effective partnerships acknowledge, even celebrate the differences in their partner ministries' histories, vision, and services. But partnerships must ultimately concentrate on what they have in common, like vision, values, and ministry objectives rather than on their differences.

11.   Effective partnerships serve at least four constituencies: the people they are trying to reach/serve; the partner churches/ministries with their own staffs and vision; the partner funding and praying constituencies behind each of these ministries; and, eventually, the partnership itself with its growing expectations. There are many more players around the table than we often acknowledge. We must remember their need for information, participation, and a sense of fulfillment.

12. Effective partnerships have a high sense of participation and ownership. Facilitators need to give special attention to the widest possible participation in objective-setting, planning and the process of meetings, and on-going communications—increasing the likelihood of widest possible ownership and commitment to the common vision. Let people in on the process, not just the dream.

13. Effective partnerships see prayer and communion as uniquely powerful elements to bind partners together in Christ. Effective partnerships are refreshed and empowered by frequently praying in small groups where individuals can express concern for each other's personal needs; and by the group taking communion together—whenever that is possible and appropriate.

14. Effective partnerships do not come free. Just participating in the exploration, planning, launching, and coordination takes time and money. Deeper commitment may take still greater investments. But the return on Kingdom investment through the partnerships should more than offset the contributions a church or other ministry may make.

15. Effective partnerships expect problems and pro-actively deal with them. Make sure a process is built into the partnership for dealing with changes, exceptions, disappointments, unfulfilled commitments, and simply the unexpected. Small problems must be addressed immediately. A wise man knows one thing—the only predictable thing is the unexpected.

Selected Bibliography: Partnerships & Networks

1. Mission oriented "how to" / thematic books on partnership

Addicott, Ernie, *Body Matters,* (Seattle, WA: Interdev Partnership Associates, 2004).

A guide to partnership in Christian mission. Testimony, analysis, and field-guide for Christ-followers who are looking for help in working together.

Bush, Luis and Lorry Lutz, *Partnering in Ministry: The Direction of World Evangelism* (Downers Grove, IL: Intervarsity Press, 1990).

A broad, readable introduction to the field of mission cooperation. It covers topics such as biblical basis, paternalism, accountability, and local church partnerships and includes sample working agreements.

Denison, Jack, *City Reaching: On the Road to Community Transformation* (Pasadena, CA: William Carey Library, 1999).

Valuable for anyone committed to seeing their city reached. Denison revisits "God's vision for the city" and the role of the church. It then moves straight into the necessity of "moving from scattered tactics to a comprehensive strategy."

Rickett, Daniel, *Making Your Partnership Work* (Enumclaw, WA: Winepress Pub., 2002).

A readable, highly practical book filled with insight and tools that can be adapted easily and applied to your context. The book's many checklists help in applying the material to "my" context.

——, *Building Strategic Relationships: A Practical Guide to Partnering with Non-Western Missions* (Pleasant Hill, CA: Klein Graphics, 2000).

Taylor, William D. (Ed.), *Kingdom Partnerships for Synergy in Mission* (Pasadena, CA: William Carey Library, 1994).

In this compendium of essays, the authors deal with the foundations of partnership, then discuss critical issues such as cultural dynamics, control, and accountability.

2. General "how to" books on inter-organizational partnership

Austin, James E., *The Collaboration Challenge: How Non-profits and Businesses Succeed through Strategic Alliances* (San Francisco, CA: Jossey Bass Pub., 2000).

Focuses on the "Seven C's of Collaboration," including Connection with Purpose and People, Clarity of Purpose, Congruency of Mission, Creation of Value, Communication Between Partners, Continual Learning, and Commitment to the Partnership.

Dent, Stephen M., *Partnering Intelligence* (Palo-Alto, CA: Davies-Black Pub., 1999).

Looks at the stages of partnership and "what could possibly go wrong?" in the process. Develops task and relationship and makes a four stage continuum of partnership.

Lipnack, Jessica and J. Stamps, *The Age of the Network: Organizing Principles for the 21 st Century* (Essex Junction, VT: Oliver Wright Pub., 1994).

——, *Virtual Teams: People Working across Boundaries Using Technology* (New York, NY: John Wiley and Sons Inc., 2000).

The Age of the Network is an introduction to how one can prepare their ministry for a collaborative approach. A usable introduction to make your ministry integrate more effectively with others. The second book addresses how to make virtual teams work. Excellent for anyone trying to make widely distributed teams work in ministry.

3. Negotiation skills:

Fisher, Robert and W. Ury, *Getting to Yes: Negotiating Agreement without Giving In* (New York, NY: Penguin Books, 1983).

——, *Getting Together: Building Relationships as We Negotiate* (New York, NY: Penguin Books, 1988).

These books are written with a view to transforming locked battles of the wills into "hard-headed problem solving." The first deals mainly with very practical issues related to conflict transformation. The second focuses on the more human-relational side to negotiation and seeks to mark the way to relational development in the midst of negotiation.

Karrass, Chester L., *"In Business as In Life You Don't Get What You Deserve, You Get What You Negotiate."* (Los Angeles, CA: Stanford Street Press, 1996).

One of the most practical, readable books on negotiation. Not a Christian book. However, once some of these strategies are understood, it will be easier to identify both constructive and negative tendencies within a partnership and to move decision-making toward a more constructive conclusion.

4. Understanding the human side of partnership dynamics

Augsburger, David, *Conflict Mediation Across Cultures* (Louisville, KY: Westminster / John Knox Press, 1992).

Augsburger emphatically calls for "conflict transformation" (as opposed to conflict management of resolution). He acknowledges conflict as a universal, cultural and personal reality, then moves into the basics of conflict as a creative versus destructive process.

5. Developing trust

Lewis, Jordan D., *Trusted Partners.: How Companies Build Trust and Win Together* (New York, NY: The Free Press, 1999).

——, *Partnerships For Profit: Structuring and Managing Strategic Alliances* (New York, NY: The Free Press, A Division of Macmillan, Inc., 1990).

6. Other relevant books

Bell, Chip R. and Heather Shea, *Dance Lessons: Six Steps to Great Partnerships in Business & Life* (San Francisco, CA: Berrett-Koehler Publishers, Inc., 1998).

Bergquist, William, Juli Betwee, and David Meuel, *Building Strategic Relationships* (San Francisco, CA: Jossey-Bass Pub., 1995).

Harbison, John R. and Pekar Jr., Peter, *Smart Alliances: A Practical Guide to Repeatable Success* (San Francisco, CA: Jossey-Bass Pub., 1998).

Kraakevik, James H. and Dotsey Welliver, eds., *Partners in the Gospel: The Strategic Role of Partnership in World Evangelization* (Wheaton, IL: The Billy Graham Center, Wheaton College, n.d.).

Litteral, Robert L., *Community Partnership in Communications for Ministry* (Wheaton, IL: The Billy Graham Center, 1988).

Mattessich, Paul W. and Barbara R. Monsey, *Collaboration: What Makes It Work* (Saint Paul, MN: Amherst H. Wilder Foundation, 1992).

Winer, Michael and Karen Ray, *Collaboration Handbook, Creating, Sustaining, and Enjoying the Journey* (Saint Paul, MN: Amherst H. Wilder Foundation, 1994).

ROLES OF PARTNERSHIP & NETWORK FACILITATOR
OBJECTIVES/ACTIVITIES/OUTCOMES

Stage 1: Exploration

Objectives:
1. Identify resources, leaders, and ministries interested or already involved in the Kingdom issue the network will address.

2. Enlarge data base of knowledge/information about the issue.

3. Identify histories of agencies currently involved in the issue and their perceptions of self, others, the task, priorities, and roadblocks.

4. Identify problems/roadblocks in current activities or relationships in the potential network's sector of interest.

5. Grow the number of relevant contacts/relationships.

6. Evaluate current overall socio/spiritual/economic/organizational context of the issue under consideration.

7. Determine consensus re: interest in exploring development of a network.

Activities:
1. Individual private meetings.

2. Small group meetings.

3. Bibliographic research.

4. Communications: travel, email, telephone, correspondence, fax, etc.

5. Analysis/feedback/confirmation.

6. Report/letter writing.

7. Listening/Prayer!

Outcomes:
1. Preliminary/exploration meetings with leaders/ministries.

2. Current resources identified and available.

3. Readiness of ministries to meet and explore cooperation.

4. Advisory and prayer support groups in place.

Stage 2: Formation (Go/No-Go)

Objectives:
Seek consensus on—

1. Current context: social/political/spiritual/operational.

2. Long-range Kingdom outcomes desired.

3. Priority needs/roadblocks.

4. Limited, high value, achievable near-term objectives with clear relationship to medium to long-term objectives.

5. Plan for evaluation (metrics)/feedback/reporting.

6. Plan for distribution of responsibilities and form of leadership.

7. Timetable/schedule for action.

8. Policy on security/information-sharing issues.

9. Policy on shared reporting of outcomes/success.

10. Means for monitoring problems/dealing with conflicts.

Activities:

1. Individual meetings with leaders/ministries.

2. Encouraging/building vision.

3. Close work with advisory group.

4. Initial exploration/organizational meeting of larger group.

   • Setup/planning

   • Administration

   • Meeting facilitation

   • Follow-up

5. Listening/Prayer!

Outcomes:

1. Vision/long-range Kingdom expectations/impact clarified

2. Relationships strengthened

3. Near to medium-term objectives and timetable agreed

4. Structural/organizational approach agreed

5. Individual, working groups, and leadership roles defined

6. Agreed expectations re specific outcomes, communications, and reporting

7. Participants encouraged/given hope

8. Communications undertaken with partner agencies' leadership and funding/praying constituencies

Stage 3: Operations

Objectives:

1. Near to medium-term objectives being met, communicated to all parties, appropriate "celebration" of progress to date

2. Enlarged objectives, increasing integration of strategy, wider cooperation in/with the network

3. Deeper sense of ownership/vision/commitment by partner agencies

4. Identification/availability of additional priority resources

5. Evaluation/monitoring/reporting-feedback system working effectively

6. Ministries organizing into functional working groups to meet the network's specialized ministry tasks/objectives.

7. Individuals emerging to share partnership/working group leadership roles.

8. Effective inter-agency and inter-personal communications.

9. Growing trust and openness among partner agencies.

10. Effective documentation program operational.

11. Balance of agencies/resources: church, para-church, ethnicity, etc.

Activities:
1. Individual meetings

2. Annual review/planning meetings with leadership

3. Working group meetings

4. Encourage/facilitate:
   - Coordination
   - Communications
   - Evaluation
   - Reporting/feedback
   - Training
   - Sense of success

5. Travel, phone, correspondence, fax, etc.

6. Monitor progress/problems and develop appropriate response

Outcomes:
1. Near to medium-term objectives (metrics) being met and celebrated.

2. A clear connection between these network objectives and the network's spiritual priorities.

3. Setting of 'next level' objectives—building on network's growing maturity.

4. Growing sense by partner agencies of the network's 'added value'—to their individual ministries and impact through their joint effort that would otherwise be impossible.

5. Growing sense of community and strength of relationship between partner agencies and their leadership.

6. Network's self-evaluation indicates growing maturity and realization of agreed objectives.

NOTES

Introduction

1. Brief definitions are provided for new terms introduced throughout the book. Chapter 3 elaborates further. Of course, each chapter addresses the relevant new ideas extensively.

2. Jeanne Curd, my first wife and initial teacher about real partnership, died of cancer six months short of our 25th wedding anniversary. Two years later I married Sybil Stanton. Her journey with me and my two daughters, Shelley and Karin, who were at college when their mother died, brought another level in my understanding of partnership. She has been a rock of love, encouragement, and hope in every dark and light step of the way on this most recent twenty-year chapter of life—specifically exploring God's vision for Kingdom partnership among his people.

3. Robert Banks' book *Paul's Idea of Community* (Hendrickson Publishers) offers rare insight into Paul's true perspective, contrasted with typical Western interpretations.

4. I examine the scriptural roots for these and other partnership-related issues in greater detail Part Two: *The God Design*.

Chapter 2

1. Lewis, Jordan D., *Partnerships For Profit: Structuring and Managing Strategic Alliances* (New York: Free Press, 1990).

2. Speech to 2002 Sabin Institute Vaccine Symposium on global advances in child vaccinations. Dr. Carol Bellamy, Executive Director, UNICEF.

Chapter 3

1. The website, www.powerofconnecting.net, operated for the global partnership/networking community by visionSynergy, provides access to people globally who have wrestled with problems similar to yours. Check the section: "How Do You Do It?"

Chapter 4

1. Genesis 1:26, 3:22, 11:7

2. John 10:30, 17:11, 22, 23

3. The extraordinary good news of redemption, however, is that believers' access to the Tree of Life is restored (Revelation 22:14) because of Jesus' redemptive work on the cross. Three trees mark the great life cycle of God's plan: the Tree of Life in Genesis, the Tree of Calvary in the Gospels, which provided the bridge, the "way back," to the Tree of Life for redeemed man in Revelation.

4. This strikingly simple definition of the basis for salvation raises some interesting, even disturbing, questions about the more complex, often formulaic approaches that have infiltrated the church's evangelistic enterprise over the last few hundred years!

Chapter 5

1. Heraclitus's famous statement, "You never step into the same river twice," acknowledges that countless influences make each day's journey a part of a long and complex process.

2. One of the greatest of all tragedies in the Western church is that, following the Enlightenment and the Renaissance, we've squandered the vision, rights, and responsibilities given to us in Genesis 2 and our natural ability to relate the message of Jesus to everything around us. Slowly but surely, with a few (in some cases glorious) exceptions, we have detached the spiritual life and the truth on which it is based from the created order and all the wondrous elements that flow out of it, such as science, art, the humanities, aesthetics, the bio world we live in, and so on. Each of these glorious things (though often distorted or even perverted by sin) flows out of God's nature and his creation, which we are supposed to know about, treasure, celebrate, be responsible for, and use creatively as wise stewards.

3. Barton, Bruce, *The Man Nobody Knows* (Indianapolis: Bobbs-Merrill Company, 1925), 104–105.

Chapter 6

1. The notes are now so old as to be irretrievable and, though I'm sure considerably modified over the years, I believe I owe my thanks for this approach to the decision-making process to my friend and long-time colleague, Viggo Sogaard. I readily accept responsibility for any changes to the original.

Chapter 7

1. Chapter 11 examines this process in detail and offers practical suggestions on helping a group of people with very different backgrounds but a common vision develop consensus on priorities for action.

2. Chapter 4, "The God Design—Relationships: Wholeness, Unity, and Diversity," has more on the implications of the drama and tragedy played out in the Garden of Eden—particularly the implications for relationships and what that means if you're working on partnerships.

Chapter 8

1. Relevant passages:

   A. Eloquent testimony to God himself living in community, outside of time, can be found in sections of Job (1:6; 2:1; 38:7), Daniel (3:19–25; 4:13–18; 8:15–18; 9:20–23; 12:1; 10:4–11:2), and Ephesians (1:21–23; 3:9–10; 6:12–13).

B. That God created man in his own relationally oriented image is clear in Genesis 1:26, 3:22, and 11:17.

C. Broken relationships at five levels are outlined in Genesis 3:8 (with God), Genesis 3:10 (with man's own "self"), Genesis 3:12 and 4:9 (with others), Genesis 4:16–19 (with the created order), and Genesis 3:22–24 (with eternity).

2. Passages suggesting the impact of relationships on the life of the individual believer, the wider Christian community, and the witness of the church are found in such passages as: Matthew 5:23–24; 18:15–17; John 13:34–35; 15:11–17; 17:20–23, Romans 16:17; 1 Corinthians 1:10; 1 Peter 3:7; 1 John 4:7–11.

3. Passages suggesting Satan's explicit design on dividing the Body of Christ: John 10:10; Romans 12:21; 2 Corinthians 2:10–11; James 4:7.

Chapter 14

1. *Rose Garden:* Joe South, (© ASCAP) From "Rose Garden", © 1970, CBS.

Chapter 15

1. Frankl, Viktor, *Man's Search for Meaning* (Boston, MA: Beacon Press, 1992).

Chapter 16

1. Will Rogers, *www.worldofquotes.com,* 2005

2. *The American Heritage® Dictionary of the English Language,* Fourth Edition. (Houghton Mifflin Company, 2004, 2000).

3. *ibid.*

4. *ibid.*

Chapter 17

1. For further, current information on virtually all the network examples cited in this chapter, consult the network/partnership website, www.powerofconnecting.net. Go to the "Networks" page, where you will find links to these and other similar networks. The "Power of Connecting" website encourages you to share information about existing or emerging networks, to help maintain an up-to-date listing for all to use.

Chapter 19

1. Matthew 5:45

2. Schroeder, Charles C., Vice Chancellor, University of Missouri. *Collaboration and Partnerships,* American College Personnel Association.

Chapter 20

1. See the landmark book, *Bowling Alone: The Collapse and Revival of American Community,* Robert D. Putnam (New York: Simon & Schuster, 2000), for a wide range of trenchant observations on the decline of community and social capital.

2. Pharr, Susan J. and Robert D. Putnam, eds. *Disaffected Democracies: What's Troubling the Trilateral Countries?* (Princeton: Princeton University Press, 2000). Cited on Princeton University Press website: www.pupress.princeton.edu, 31 Jan. 2005.

3. For more information on the outcome of these working meetings, go to www.powerofconnecting.net, where proceedings are summarized.